To my father

Alby Cockrell

Thank you for sharing your life
And your death with me

The Invisible Garment

JODERE

GROUP   SAN DIEGO

The Invisible Garment

30 Spiritual Principles that Weave the Fabric of Human Life

Connie Kaplan

Jodere Group, Inc.
P.O. Box 910147
San Diego, CA 92191-0147
(800) 569-1002
www.jodere.com

Book design by Jenn Ramsey
Editorial supervision by Chad Edwards

The author of this book does not dispense medical advice or prescribe
the use of any techniques as forms of treatment for physical, medical,
emotional, or spiritual problems for you or your child without you
seeking the advice of a physician or mental health professional, either
directly or indirectly. The intent of the author is only to offer information
of a general nature to help you in your quest for emotional and spiritual
well-being. In the event you use any of the information in this book for
yourself, which is your constitutional right, the author and the publisher
assume no responsibility for your actions.

CIP data available from the Library of Congress

ISBN 1-58872-089-6

07 06 05 04   4 3 2 1
First printing, April 2004

Printed in the United States of America

Contents

Prologue

We are all caught in an inescapable
network of mutuality, tied into
a single garment of destiny.

~ MARTIN LUTHER KING, JR.

The title *The Invisible Garment* introduces a metaphor, which flows throughout this book. We each wear an unseen garment, woven in divine threads, which holds us, shrouds us, veils us, protects us, and simultaneously connects us to every other being in the universe. Through the general knowledge of the tenets of quantum physics, most of us now intellectually know that life is a holistic experience—that every being, organic and inorganic, is a unique thread in a galactic interwoven fabric. Each of us is not only a fiber in this tapestry, but we are also embedded (cloaked) in its weave.

But intellectual knowing is not enough. We long to experience our connection. In a tapestry when one thread is either missing, faded, or damaged, a hole exists in the whole. When we feel ourselves unraveling, we want to be reminded of our connection to something greater than our small, separate realities. *The Invisible Garment* outlines a practical way for you to chart the soul's purpose for your lifetime, and therefore to understand your own spiritual wardrobe. It shows you how we each are simultaneously unique and one with The One. Because we are each integral aspects of an awesome cosmic weaving, it is not only to one's personal benefit but also to the benefit of the universe for each person to understand his or her life's purpose.

This book makes the radical (although not original) suggestion that *who you essentially are* is good. It alleges that in other dimensions of consciousness, each of us writes a pre-natal contract with life, which we sign and seal at first breath. These contracts are spiritual (being), not actual (doing). They function as our clothing, our fiber, our safety net, our deep and unfettered connectedness to Creation and Creator throughout our lives. They consist of a configuration of spiritual principles, which articulate what is good about us—what is right about us—what is never broken in us.

These principles remind us of the wonder of life, the awesome nature of each person's uniqueness, the incomparable miracle of humanity. When you learn about your own spiritual principles, you realize the beauty of your beingness, and your behavior spontaneously becomes beautiful. When your goodness is articulated, you begin to experience the all-embracing love, which is the fabric of the universe living itself through you. And as you wear your own invisible garment, whether impeccably or imperfectly, you so contribute to the tapestry of society.

> The fabric of society is not finished....
> It is on the loom, and it is made up
> of constantly changing relationships.
>
> ~ GANDHI

Acknowledgments

~ First praise always goes to my husband, Vic Kaplan, for his never-faltering belief in and support of my work.

~ A deep bow to my children, Ben, Sara and Lauren, who never complain when I sequester myself to write, and who always show their appreciation and affection unashamedly.

~ Thank you to my sister, Marsha Hartos, for her tireless proofreading and perceptive suggestions.

~ To my mother, Nila Cockrell, who passed to me the gift of dreaming, may your dreams always be sweet ones!

~ Nancy Jackson, my sister in waking and in the dream, thank you for holding the kite string at times when I fly too high.

~ To Bonnie Solow, the midwife of my career, may your generosity be rewarded with ever-abundant blessings.

~ Profound appreciation for the special support from my colleagues, Tamar Frankiel and Judith Yost.

~ Immeasurable gratitude to the faculty members at the University of Creation Spirituality who helped mold this work: Matthew Fox, Brian Swimme, Andrew Harvey, and Mary Ford-Grabowsky.

~ My most important thanks go to the people who contributed dreams and insights shared in the body of the book: Penny Andrews, Sara Cooper, Karen Cooper-Martin, Dionna Cordova, Cammie Doty, Marci Fabrici, Wynn Renee Freeman, Judy Greenfeld, Lindy Hopkins, Annette Hulefeld, Bonnie Littman, Daniel MacKenzie, Marion Mayer, Annette McMurrey, Marcie Neville, Adriane Oliver and Wayne Wolf.

~ To my production team at Jodere for your care and compassion in helping deliver this baby into the world, much gratitude.

~ And finally, thanks to the hundreds of clients who have put this information to work in their lives, thereby creating a better world.

Introduction

It may seem ludicrous in this scientific age to put forth the possibility that human life is influenced and guided by intangible spiritual principles. It is perhaps even more outlandish to suggest concrete ways to discern those principles. And most frivolous is the idea that one uses those principles to design the blueprint for one's life before his or her birth. That is tantamount to saying that each person is a divine co-creator of life.

Yet the older I get, the *truer* these outrageous ideas become. It now seems highly plausible to me that we sign a prenatal contract with life. It is sealed the moment we are born. It is readable in the stars for those with eyes to see. It becomes our template, our blueprint, our core patterning. It is the agreement our soul makes with life; it is the invisible garment we wear throughout our lives.

I suspected and simultaneously doubted all this in my earlier years. Then came the day that changed the direction and work and meaning of my life forever.

MEETING THE ANGELS

It was just before dawn, the morning after my 44th birthday. I knelt next to my father's deathbed, praying for his release from the body. My sisters and I had come back to the small West Texas town where my parents grew up to sit vigil with my father during his dying days.

Daddy was a Methodist minister of the old-fashioned sort: He was a sweet man who loved his family and God with equal intensity. In his aging process, his faith faded along with his memory. His last few years were dreamlike—not grounded in the same ordinary existence in which most of us anchor our reality. In short, he was "out of it." However, he pulled himself together one day to tell my mother and the director of the nursing home that he was ready to die and that he would not take any more food, water, or medication. That day, my sisters and I went home.

Several days later, as I prayed beside Daddy's bed in that pre-dawn hour, I heard the door open and close behind me. It was still dark outside, and I doubted that anyone might be coming to visit. I assumed it to be a caretaker wanting to check his vital signs. I quickly ended my prayer and stood to greet our guest.

Two angels stood at the doorway. I call them "angels" for lack of a better word. I had been repulsed by the recent onslaught of tacky angel merchandising in America and had decided, in response, that I did not "believe" in angels. "Angel" is not a word I use lightly.

Here I was, however, standing face-to-face with two very tall, brightly backlit, incredibly benevolent beings. What could they be but angels? I do not know how else to describe them. They had no distinguishing facial characteristics that I could see in the dim light of the room. They had no wings—just a magnificent light behind them. They wore clothes of nondescript color. They were simply the embodiment of love. I have never felt such intense appreciation and acceptance—such profound peace.

I glibly asked, "Why did you use the door?" They laughed. But the one on the right countered, "We're here to open the portals." I knew that I was in the presence of life's most holy experience: death.

They told me they had come to take my father home, but first they wanted to talk to me. This conversation was telepathic. There was technically "nothing" to it. They asked me to work for them. They said that a body of information was ready to be distributed to people and that they wanted me to bring that information into form. They told me to give the information to anyone who had the wisdom to ask for it.

I was skeptical and fearful. I had no idea what they were asking. As they spoke, I experienced an eerie otherworldly reality. On four different occasions during our conversation, I found myself wandering in a grid-like landscape of geometric form, color, and sound. Nothing else was recognizable. I knew I was in the place of knowledge—the place where everything is known.

I walked into this grid amazed at the magnificently brilliant luminescent lines of light. I have since come to understand those grids as matrices—each matrix being more sophisticated and less personal than the one before. It was as if the first grid were the matrix of my own "higher self," the second was the matrix of my ancestors or my lineage, the third felt like the matrix of humanity, and the fourth the matrix of the level called "soul." This last matrix looked like a mandala and was so stunningly beautiful that it brought tears. The information I absorbed from each matrix was pre-verbal and life changing.

I was strangely comfortable in this alien place. I knew that I had been there before although I could not remember when.

After some discussion, I agreed to work for the angels and do the best I could to bring this information into form. Since then, I have spent several years teaching what I learned that day to private clients and small groups. Sometimes, I ask myself why I do this work. I always have the same answer for myself: I have never trusted anyone or anything so completely as I trusted those angel beings.

I watched my daddy's magnificent transformation that sweet December morning. As the sun rose through the east window in the room, the laser-like first morning's light beam stabbed my eyes, my daddy breathed his last sigh, and his spirit left the body. After a few minutes of absolute peace, I came back to regular consciousness in an empty room with Daddy's corpse on the bed, having no real clarity about what had just happened. Later, as my mother and sisters arrived, I considered the possibility that the whole thing had been a figment of my imagination—the result of sleep deprivation.

Over the next several months, however, this promised body of information formulated itself. Mostly, I received it in dreamtime and then woke up to write it down. Often, I would awaken and sit for a long period of time in receptive meditation. Through these meditations, I received the words that described and communicated this amazing set of teachings.

At the time of my angelic encounter, I had not published a book. And the thought of trying to print and widely distribute something that a couple of angels told me was too astonishingly "New Agey" to consider. However, I did consent to writing it down in my personal journal, and I promised I would tell my few closest friends and students about it. They then told their closest friends, and soon, I was giving "soul contract" readings almost daily. In this book, I use the phrases "soul contract," "invisible garment," and "soul pattern" interchangeably. I refer to your being "contracted" with a principle when I explain the principle's impact on you. I refer to your "wearing" the principle to describe how you (as an agent of the principle's influence) impact the world.

This book is the result of the work and research that I have been conducting since then. Skeptic and cynic that I am, it took almost a decade of testing this material on hundreds of clients before I was ready to speak publicly about it. By now, however, I have every confidence that this information is valid, profound, significant—and most importantly, it carries deep truth to the heart of any reader.

This transmission from the angels is a much-needed missing piece in present-day understanding of the meaning of life. It gives one the language to articulate his or her blessing, his or her unique enduring traits, his or her spiritual DNA, his or her invisible garment. I have found in my counseling practice that abstract theory about the soul is not enough for most people. They want to know about themselves—specifically, their soul's intent. They ask, "Why am I here?" This body of information provides a structure in which you can work to understand your own blessings more thoroughly. This book is carefully organized so that you can clearly understand the fibers that weave your life.

PART ONE
REMEMBERING YOUR INVISIBLE GARMENT

Chapter One, "What is the Soul?" provides an overview of the angel's radically unique definition of a human's real relationship to higher consciousness—soul. This information challenges and corrects certain errors in the human belief system about life and death.

Chapter Two, "Constructing Your Personal Weave," describes a simple and specific technique, usable by anyone, for determining what spiritual principles function as fibers in your personal weave. Reading your pattern involves using your astrological chart as a basis. However, this work actually has little to do with traditional astrology.

Even if you do not know your astrological chart, you can use your dreams to remember and reconstruct your weave. This chapter outlines some dream-charting techniques to help you do that.

PART TWO
UNDERSTANDING YOUR INVISIBLE GARMENT

Chapters Three, Four, and Five define the 30 spiritual principles that make up the pattern of a person's invisible garment. These chapters contain information from many sources, which I have indicated by using different fonts. The words that I received and wrote in my journal that are direct quotes from the angelic beings are in *italics*. My own words and interpretations are in normal print.

The angels made it clear that these agreements are about *being* and not *doing*. However, sometimes, by looking at people's "doings," we can better see how their "being" created their life path. Because astrological charts of famous people are readily available on the Internet, I have referenced the principles of people who may serve as helpful examples as you read each of the principles. These references are also in normal print.

In researching the validity of these teachings, I have taught several classes on these principles over the years, and I often use my students' responses and realizations in these chapters. Those quotes are in "quotation marks."

Also, I have drawn extensively from the wisdom of dreamtime. When I use a dream as an example for one of the principles, it is in *handwriting font*.

Words received from angels	*italics*
My own words	normal print
Student responses	"quotation marks"
Dreamtime	*handwriting font*

PART THREE
WEARING YOUR INVISIBLE GARMENT

The last chapter, "Your Spiritual Wardrobe: Wearing it Daily," describes how consciously wearing your invisible garment changes your ways of relating to the world. The subheadings describe the kinds of relationships that are transformed by this new understanding of your life's purpose: "The Relationship to Self"; "The Relationship to One's Family of Origin"; "The Relationship to One's Spouse"; "The Relationship to One's Children"; "The Relationship to One's Clients or Colleagues"; "The Relationship to One's Community"; "The Relationship to the Planet, to Life, to God."

In the Epilogue, I provide a very simple and incredibly powerful meditation you can use to help you remember, live, and wear your unique garment. The "I Am" meditation calls on the holy words, I Am, to remind us of the profound gift of being.

APPENDICES

Finally, I have included lengthy but extremely important appendices. These pages are to be used like a reference book. Here, every position in the astrological chart is placed in each of the spiritual principles. You can look at the paragraphs in this reference section that apply directly to you and get a short, clear "bottom line" of the meaning of each of the threads in your weave.

Appendix B is a simple chart outlining all the principles and their internal and external points of focus. It is a quick reference to use when you are exploring someone's principles.

I recommend that as you read this manuscript, you construct your own pattern and those of your nearest loved ones. You will be able to grasp deep meaning in these pages and in your life by reading it this way.

PART I

Remembering Your Invisible Garment

Chapter One

What Is
the Soul?

Wherever and whenever God finds you ready,
he must act and infuse himself into you.

~ MEISTER ECKHART

WHY DO WE INCARNATE?

Most of us have absorbed from our culture a basic belief about why we are alive. Some indigenous cultures have specific beliefs about carrying on the work of the ancestors. Western cultures are a little more abstract about human life, although many Western practitioners have in recent years adopted a schoolroom mentality about life: We are here because our soul needs to learn lessons. The angels lovingly laughed at this concept. The soul, they explained, exists on a level of consciousness that is beyond school. The incarnation is not about learning or getting—it is about giving.

According to the angels' teachings, a human soul takes an incarnation primarily to send its gifts into the physical, dense, touchable world of form. It is as if the realm of form puts out a radar signal that it is ready for an infusion of a specific energy or spiritual principle. The soul hears the call and prepares to infuse the world by sending human beings onto the planet who can bring the needed energies. It is a call-and-response reality. In meditating on this teaching, I perceived that although there is certainly a reciprocity in an incarnation (the soul receives as much as it gives), the primary reason for incarnating is the "giveaway." The soul is much more interested in bestowing its wisdom and love on the earth than it is in taking anything from the experience.

While this idea directly contradicts the trendy New Age belief that a soul takes an incarnation to "learn lessons" and "work out karma," subsequent research has shown that this idea is not new. The concept that the soul is the aspect of us that resides in the Mind of God is in fact rooted in the mystical lineage of all traditions. Meister Eckhart, the medieval Christian mystic, called the soul the aspect of the human that is made in the image of God (Fox, 1991, p. 77). No lessons are required. The soul knows.

In my book *Dreams are Letters from the Soul*, I discuss in great detail the concept that soul consciousness is not personal or separatist in nature. The term "soul" refers to a vast level of consciousness that includes rather than separates, and that exists before and beyond the separation and isolation that we experience as humans. For this reason, I always refer to "the" soul rather than "your" soul. Soul is not a personal possession. It is a universal consciousness. It is not a separating concept. It is a unifying term. For human beings, the level of the soul is our spiritual interconnection.

Lal Ded, also known as Lalla, was a fourteenth century mystic born in Kashmir. In her early years, she strove to live the life expected of a woman of her position. Eventually, however, she chose to leave her abusive husband to become a disciple of Shiva. She shares her wisdom of the truth of the soul through poetry:

> My teacher told me one thing:
> Live in the soul.
> When that was so,
> I began to go naked
> and dance.

> *Women in Praise of the Sacred:*
> *43 Centuries of Spiritual Poetry by Women*
> Hirshfield, Editor

Hildegard of Bingen explains that the soul's longing is to be fully embodied, and the body's longing is fulfilled when it is fully ensouled. She says, "When the soul overcomes the body in such a way that the body is in agreement with the soul in goodwill and simplicity of heart, and refreshed by good treatment as if by nourishing food, we cry out in our longing for heaven: 'How sweet are the words of justice to my throat—even sweeter than honey to my mouth'" (Fox, 1987, p. 113).

She goes on to describe the relationship between the soul and the body when they are in communion with each other: "Within the body, the soul acts in accord with the requirements that it makes of the body" (p. 114). She is indicating here that indeed, the soul needs the body to deliver its gifts and bring its message into form, and it is the soul's intention to create the right circumstances so that can be done. "In its control of the body, the soul is like the wind. We cannot see it blow; we can only hear it" (p. 118). As incarnating personalities, we can only be subtly aware of the soul—like the sound of the wind. My work with the angels has shown me that our job is to develop sensitivities to the messages and urgings of the soul so that the gift can indeed be delivered.

As mentioned above, these teachings include the idea that an incarnation does give the soul the gift of experiential exploration of the great mystery. In that sense, the soul receives. It becomes purer by expressing itself in form. A journey into form is the soul's repayment for its gifts.

According to the angels, an incarnating personality may need to learn certain basic lessons in order to deliver the soul's gift most efficiently. This vision showed me that each personality is connected to the level of soul by a grid-like matrix, a spiritual fabric, that creates the uniqueness of that particular person. It is the personality of the reincarnating being who participates in the laws of karma. It is the ego that "learns the lessons." The ego (personality) is not to be confused with the soul.

THE 30 PRINCIPLES

This teaching from the angels describes 30 spiritual principles that drive human incarnation. These invisible forces or principles weave themselves together to create our physical experience of the world. While humans can and do "work" with all 30 principles during a lifetime, each person is connected in a unique and personal way with a specific few of them. The interrelationship of those principles gives each person the potential for a profoundly unique expression of life force.

The 30 principles are divided into three sets of ten. Each set will be more thoroughly discussed in subsequent chapters.

The first ten principles, numbered 0–9, are called the "Ascending Principles." They are the most elemental, foundational principles of form. They reach their highest expression through encountering human consciousness. They are natural or belonging to nature. They are fundamentally connected to the natural realm.

0. Placement
1. Innocence
2. Purity
3. Memory
4. Beauty
5. Extension
6. Regeneration
7. Generosity
8. Goodness
9. Awareness

The second ten, numbered 10–19, are called the "Containing Principles." They allow the expression of the soul to extend into the physical world and be expressed in its most efficient way through human consciousness. They create a vessel (container) for form. They are relatively mental, carrying mostly human qualities.

10. Reciprocity	15. Resistance
11. Flowering	16. Unity
12. Creativity	17. Attraction
13. Intelligence	18. Focus
14. Ecstasy	19. Service

The third ten, numbered 20–29, are called the "Descending Principles." These are the very subtle, galactic principles that reach down into human consciousness to achieve contact with form. They are almost undefinable because of their heavenly qualities.

20. Gratitude	25. Desire
21. Harmony	26. Silence
22. Dreaming	27. Peace
23. Randomness	28. Love
24. Humility	29. Movement

The Soul Cluster

As I meditated on these teachings about the human incarnation, I learned about a phenomenon that the angels called the "soul cluster." According to this aspect of the teachings, when a human soul takes an incarnation, he or she engages with all the principles and all the possibilities. However, because human bodies are still primarily carbon-based (very dense) and human consciousness is still relatively limited, not one of us can carry all of the light, all of the gift, all of the love our soul has to offer. Therefore, we incarnate in clusters. There may be 30 or 40 individuations of the soul expressing life on behalf of soul's intent at one time. In other words, we all have soul siblings.

These soul siblings are not "soul mates" in the commonly-held meaning of the word. They are not the perfect marriage partners waiting out there to be discovered. Soul siblings are aspects of *you*. Marrying one of them would be redundant, and in fact could lead to such self-absorption that you would forget to live fully. Soul siblings are individualizations of the same source.

The angels explained that in Western society, we do not necessarily know our soul cluster brothers and sisters. Indigenous societies apparently reincarnate into villages and tribes of their own cluster, and they often recognize each other as aspects of the same soul intention. But in the mobile, industrial world, we are separated from our tribes.

It was explained to me in one of my receptive meditations that we westerners meet up with soul siblings from time to time. They touch us deeply, inspire us to live our potential, and then to move on. One of them may be encountered at a party, on a bus or plane, or in a coffee shop. When such a meeting happens, the siblings are zapped with soul consciousness for a moment, and then it is gone. One may wonder if the whole experience were real—the way I wondered about the angels after they had left. The angels told me that in rare circumstances, soul siblings may be life-long friends who function as touchstones for each other throughout an incarnation. Such a person in your life inspires you to be the best of yourself. Sometimes, this person knows you more authentically than you know yourself. For reasons that we do not understand, this relationship is sometimes part of our contract with life.

As specific incarnating personalities evolve, some become capable of carrying greater levels of the soul's light. For example, by the time Jesus reached the end of his life, he existed on a level of perfect divine clarity. Buddha, at the Bodhi Tree, reached enlightenment, and was thereafter able to carry the full message of his soul into every incarnation. The prophet Mohammed, after his illumination, was able to embody divinity for the rest of his life. Many other enlightened beings have incarnated and brought these profound gifts to our species. You probably know someone who just seems "more whole" than most people. That someone may be carrying a more expansive level of his or her soul's gift than most people do. We are all evolving toward the perfect expression of our Divine Nature.

THE GARMENT'S PATTERN

The garment's pattern (your principles) helps you remember your Divine Nature and your deepest purpose. It reminds you of the energies you came here to live. It gently urges you to become that perfect expression of your soul's intent, and to wear your garment with grace.

According to this teaching, you design your specific garment's pattern before conception. The seams are sewn during the mother's pregnancy. At the infant's first breath, destiny begins to unfold and the child becomes the official bearer of the gift of the soul.

The weave has twelve fibers. Each one contains a specific energy and purpose that will define the way this incarnation is lived.

You come into incarnation as an emissary of your soul's intent. Your primary principle is represented by the Sun's placement in your astrological chart. Each of the other planets (including the moon) represents a principle that helps you achieve your primary purpose (Sun principle).

You can know your principles because their numerology corresponds to the numbers on your astrological chart. In other words, if your sun is at 5 degrees of a sign, you know that you are primarily working with the principle of Extension, because that is principle number five. Each planet has a degree, and each degree tells you what principle that planet represents. In the next chapter, you will find clear instructions as to how to construct and read your own pattern.

The language and vocabulary I received from the angels is highly unusual. On the deepest levels, words separate us from understanding. Words take us into an analytic reality, which is a separation from the truth of experiential reality. When trying to identify the Source, or God, it is paradoxical to use words because the Source of all things is before and beyond words. Yet in order to share these teachings, language is necessary. Each word the angels gave me has a "mundane" meaning, and it also has a "divine" meaning. It takes practice and discipline to unlearn the ordinary, socialized meaning of a word and to hear its deeper melody. The words do not define you, but rather they point you toward your inner self. You have to study your pattern and find its meaning in your core. Otherwise, this is just another ego-building device.

BEING VS. DOING

Your invisible garment is about *being*, not *doing*. Reading your pattern will not tell you what you should *do* with your life. It simply reminds you of what you came here to *be*. The doing presents itself to be done because the being magnetizes certain experiences. The person who impeccably wears his or her garment magnetizes the things he or she needs to do to amplify and deliver the soul's gifts to the planet. In other words, reading your pattern will give you important information about why certain possibilities are placed in front of you. Your energetic clothing pulls those possibilities to you. How you embrace them and dance with them is the doing of life.

No one is living the same pattern as yours, but many may share the same principles. Each person has a unique, absolutely individual garment. And yet each person can see similarities and mirrors in every other person. Knowing your principles liberates you to live the life you came here to live, and it gives you permission and vocabulary with which to encourage every other person to do the same. The experience of realizing your uniqueness on a core level is amazing. Such an experience of self-realization paradoxically also allows you to realize your profound connectedness to the all and the everything.

One of my clients wrote the following words about her experience:

> "This is 'isness' information. It describes what 'is' when I let my life simply be. It is a verbal template of my essential self. Now I am so much more open to see the lofty, and not just the details that have sometimes left me in the pity pot. I will continue to sift through the information in order to understand it on deeper levels. It brings such eloquence and clarity to my life. Understanding my invisible garment gives me an unbelievable sense of being cosmically supported."

THE COMMUNITY OF THE SOUL

After many years of sharing this information with "anyone who had the wisdom to ask for it," I can certainly testify not only to its richness and truth but also to the blessing it brings to one's life. The first reaction from clients is usually a sense of being overwhelmed. The person who asks for this information has no idea what is coming. It is almost too much to have oneself so clearly exposed!

Later, there is an elated joy. When you digest the deep meaning of the principles that guide your incarnation, you suddenly reframe your life—past, present, and future. That which may have seemed victimizing or unfair in your past becomes the experience that clothed you, molded you, amplified your principles, and gave you the strength to experience life fully. That which is "unexplainable" in your present becomes the great mystery of the unseen forces guiding you toward your destiny. That which may seem unreachable in your future is the natural unfolding of your destiny.

Next comes a sense of deep repose. Knowing that you wear a unique spiritual garment (that indeed you are living your contract) and that you have soul siblings out there picking up the slack gives you a deep sense of relief. Your divinity is leading the way. Your personality is in the service of the divine. You are at peace. And that peace extends from deep in your core outward. You are able to see the divinity of others even when they cannot. You are able to grant beingness to the unseen because you actually feel its effects. Your life becomes a metaphor for a story greater than you could write alone.

Then, at long last, your true spiritual community begins to form. The people who can truly see you and who can truly be seen by you—your tribe—begin to show up around you. They are not necessarily whom you expected. They may not be of your same religious belief, your same gender, your same race, or your same social circle. You may not socialize with these people at all. But you will *know* them, and they you. You will support them, and they you.

In his book *The Healing Wisdom of Africa*, African shaman Malidoma Some discusses our need to be known and supported, calling it the "Western world's crisis of identity and purpose." He reminds us that it is not enough to know ourselves. We long to be seen authentically by others, and until we get the fuel we need from external recognition, we will not be inspired to achieve our life's purpose. We will, instead, spend our lives in deep nostalgic depression. He goes on to say that if we do not feel that our personhood is truly endorsed in our family of origin or in our "village," we will spend our lives on a sojourn, looking for our community (p. 27).

Knowing the threads of your weave allows you to see yourself authentically. That experience of inner authority will call others to you who want to validate you and be truly seen by you. Your community will come when you have the ability to remember your own essential pattern.

Chapter Two

Constructing Your Personal Weave

*Then it was as if I suddenly saw the secret beauty of their hearts . . .
the person that each one is in God's eyes. If only they could see
themselves as they really are. If only we could see each other
that way all the time, there would be no more war, no more hatred,
no more cruelty, no more greed. I suppose the big problem
would be that we would all fall down and worship each other.*

~ THOMAS MERTON

Thomas Merton's words sum up my experience. As the information of the invisible garments unfolded before me, I suddenly saw each person as a weaving of spiritual principles, and I knew that if we could see ourselves and each other in this way, human life would be totally transformed. I found myself in deep awe of every person I knew. I did fall down and worship life.

The process of receiving this information was intense. My sleeping patterns changed dramatically. I slept only a few hours at a time and woke often in the middle of the night with an urgency to write down something I had perceived in a dream—a message that was a part of this body of information. Then, during my waking hours, I would sit for long periods of time in a state of receptive meditation, contemplating the cryptic messages I had scribbled in the middle of the night. One by one, over a period of months, each principle revealed itself to me. Although I never again saw the angels who were present in my father's last moments, I intuitively knew that they were the messengers who delivered all the subsequent information.

When the definitions of all 30 principles were roughly in place, I began sharing the information with my friends and clients by giving them "soul contract readings." Each person who received a reading commented on the empowerment they felt from the information. Many of them also discussed the difficulty they had in fully understanding these principles, because the definitions were so unusual.

However, before we investigate each of the principles, let me show you how to construct your own pattern. If you will take time to do this for yourself (or for someone you love and know well), the rest of the information in the book will most likely mean more, create more "aha" moments, and resonate with your personal truth more clearly.

The pattern of your garment is based on your astrological chart. If you are a skeptic about astrology, then let me assure you that this is neither a traditional astrological reading nor does it reflect traditional astrological perspective. The position of the planets at the moment of your birth is the best record available to help us understand your unique spiritual patterning. In other words, the stars do not determine your fate, but their relative positions at the moment of your birth do record your agreement with life.

I suggest you take the steps described on the next page to chart your own pattern. There is an example provided for you on pages 26 and 27 if you get confused. Next, read the rest of this chapter carefully and thoughtfully, because it explains what each aspect of the pattern reflects about your basic blueprint (and your spiritual choices) for this life. When you have absorbed this information, move on to the next chapters to read the definitions of the various principles in order to help you understand (and perhaps remember) your pattern.

CONSTRUCTING THE GARMENT'S PATTERN

You need an accurate astrological natal chart for yourself from a reliable source (either a software system on your computer or through an astrological service). This shows the positions of all the planets at the moment of your birth. Preferably, the chart will be a Tropical, Placidus Chart. If that is not possible, then any chart will do except a Vedic chart—which is a different system.

On your natal chart, which is circular, each planet symbol has a number and an astrological sign followed by a second number next to it. You are interested primarily in the first number. It will be a number between 0 and 29. It will look something like this: ☉ 3° ♒ 43'. You are to copy the 3 (first number) onto your chart. If the second number is larger than 55, round the first number up. For example, if this number had been 3° ♒ 55', you would round the three up to four. I have provided a blank chart in this chapter. Transfer the numbers from your astrological chart into the second column of the blank chart.

Each of the 30 principles also has a numerological correspondent, 0–29. You will also find in this chapter a list of the principles with their numbers. Transfer the name of the corresponding principle into the third column of the chart. In other words, if you have put the number 3 next to the Sun ☉ in the second column, then you will place the principle "Memory" in the third column because Memory corresponds to the number 3.

Do this for each planet and placement listed on the blank chart. You now have your garment's pattern. As a sample, I have provided my own astrological chart and my pattern so that you can refer to it if you like.

The Garment's Pattern

PLANET OR PLACEMENT		NUMBER	PRINCIPLE
Sun	☉		
Moon	☽		
Ascendant	ASC*		
Mercury	☿		
Venus	♀		
Mars	♂		
Jupiter	♃		
Saturn	♄		
Uranus	♅		
Neptune	♆		
Pluto	♇		
Mid-Heaven	MC**		

* The ASC or Ascendant is the line that separates the first house from the twelfth house. It will be the line that points due west on your chart.

** The MC or Mid-Heaven on a Tropical Placidus chart is the line that points due north, separating the ninth from the tenth houses. If you have another type of chart (other than Tropical Placidus), be sure to find the line that is marked "MC" to determine the Mid-Heaven.

The Principles and Their Numerological Correspondents

0: Placement

1: Innocence

2: Purity

3: Memory

4: Beauty

5: Extension

6: Regeneration

7: Generosity

8: Goodness

9: Awareness

10: Reciprocity

11: Flowering

12: Creativity

13: Intelligence

14: Ecstasy

15: Resistance

16: Unity

17: Attraction

18: Focus

19: Service

20: Gratitude

21: Harmony

22: Dreaming

23: Randomness

24: Humility

25: Desire

26: Silence

27: Peace

28: Love

29: Movement

CONNIE KAPLAN

Dec 16 1948   10:45 A.M. CST
Lamesa   Texas
32N44   101W57
Dec 16 1948   16:45:00 GMT
Tropical   Placidus   True Node

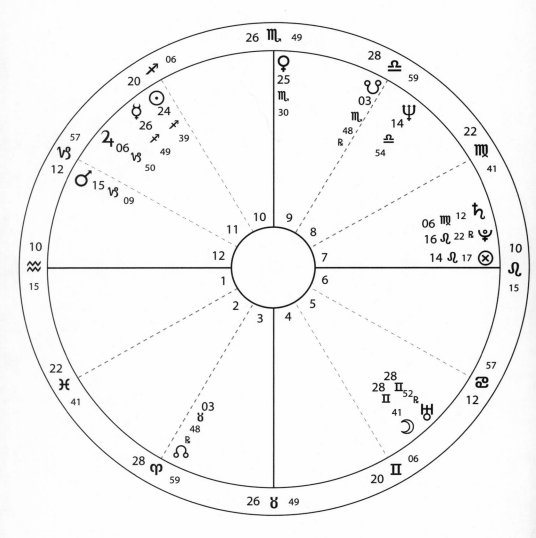

Prepared By:
CONNIE KAPLAN
Santa Monica, CA 90402

The Garment's Pattern
CONNIE KAPLAN

Planet or Placement		Number	Principle
Sun	☉	24°	Humility
Moon	☽	28°	Movement*
Ascendant	ASC	10°	Reciprocity
Mercury	☿	26°	Silence
Venus	♀	25°	Desire
Mars	♂	15°	Reciprocity
Jupiter	♃	6°	Regeneration
Saturn	♄	6°	Regeneration
Uranus	♅	28°	Love
Neptune	♆	14°	Ecstasy
Pluto	♇	16°	Unity
Mid-Heaven	MC	26°	Silence

*Rounded up by author.

The Threads of the Pattern

The following information is part of the original transmission by the angels. It summarizes each of the threads in your pattern. It details a sacred way of seeing yourself. This system is a step beyond a psychological self-understanding. Psychology helps us understand our ego self and our socialized self. This system takes the spiritual practitioner to a level of understanding the relational self or the self that participates in the evolution of all sentience. While this system relies on astrological information, it also varies quite dramatically from traditional astrological definitions.

~ Sun ~

The first thread in your pattern, the Sun, tells us your primary reason for coming into an incarnation. According to the angels' transmission, you are here delivering a specific gift sent into form from the level of human soul. The Sun's spiritual principle points you toward deeply understanding that gift. The Sun principle, in specific, asks the practitioner to contemplate his or her purpose for embodying at this time.

In purely physical terms, every person is a star being. All the minerals that make up this earth—indeed all the minerals that make up your physical body—came to the planet as the result of a supernova's explosion. A star died to extend itself into life. Our star, the Sun, lives in order to send life to us in the form of heat. Our sun is the source of life on this planet, and for that reason, the Sun's placement in the heavens at the moment of birth is one's most significant marker of life. The degree of your Sun tells us the primary reason you came to live a human life.

~ Moon ~

The Moon represents your mastery. The angels explained to me that in some other lifetime or some other dimension of consciousness, each being achieves mastery of certain principles according to his or her own rate of spiritual development. Each of us brings that mastery to a lifetime. The Moon principle serves as your most reliable staff or plumb line in this incarnation. It is part of the great gift you bring to earth.

For many people, the Moon principle is so deeply embedded in their being that they either take it for granted or ignore it completely. Because you have a relative mastery of this principle (relative to the other principles in your chart), you may not be aware of its operation in your life even after you have examined your chart and brought awareness of it to consciousness.

Let us say, for example, that your mastery is in the principle of Humility. According to its spiritual definition, Humility is the principle that implies a close connection to the earth and an authentic knowing of your deepest self. You may simply be so "in touch" with yourself that you never consider that as an extraordinary gift that you bring to the world.

Florence Nightingale had a Moon at 24 degrees—the principle of Humility. Her life was driven by her deep knowing that she was a healer and a caretaker. Her knowledge of herself and her gift motivated her to do incomparable work in developing the field of nursing. Yet at the time, she was simply doing what she did—unaware of the legacy she was creating. It was her mastery of Humility, I am sure, that kept her going against some rough odds.

The Moon principle has an interesting ebb and flow in our lives. While it remains steadily our mastery throughout our lifetimes, it has a rhythm and is more present at some times than others. Hildegard of Bingen saw this in one of her visionary experiences. Her way of describing it is interesting. "If the moon is waxing, the brain and blood of human beings are also increased. If the moon is waning, the substances of the brain and blood in human beings also diminish. If, indeed, the human brain were to remain the same, we should fall into madness. When the moon is full, our brain is also full. We are then in full possession of our senses" (Fox, 1987, p. 47).

Emergency room workers might not agree that we are in full possession of our senses on a full moon! That night is usually the strangest night of the month for them. But being in "balance" with the cosmic forces may look like craziness in ordinary reality, for our societies are no longer in balance with the universal law. Spiritually, the fluctuation of our Moon principle is what keeps us most closely aligned and attuned to our soul purpose.

PERSONAL PILLARS

When we agree to take an incarnation, we agree to create the personal pillars necessary to be fully human. These pillars are the behavioral body, mental body, emotional body, and physical body. In a garment's pattern chart, these bodies are represented by the Ascendant, Mercury, Venus, and Mars respectively.

In a weaving, the horizontal (weft) threads determine the look and feel of the desired fabric. In your invisible garment, the weft threads may be compared to your personal pillars. They comprise the texture, design, and aesthetic of your personality. They give you a unique interfacing with the larger world.

~ BEHAVIORAL BODY ~
ASCENDANT

Your Ascendant or rising defines the first pillar, your behavioral body. The behavioral body is your personal ethic. You have probably observed how one set of parents can give birth to several children, all of whom are raised in the same emotional and socio-economic environment, and yet those children can be completely different in the way they respond to life. That is because each of us has a very specific ethic. Each of us has chosen, prior to birth, the yardstick by which we measure our behavior. Any woman who has ever given birth to more than one baby can tell you that even *in utero,* the personality of each child is determinately unique.

Also, the Ascendant is, by definition, the boundary between the first and the twelfth houses. The first house is the most personal of the houses in the zodiac. The twelfth house is the least personal and the most collective. This means that your behavioral decisions—your personal ethics—are the mediators between your most personal self (first house) and your most philanthropic and collective self (twelfth house).

~ MENTAL BODY ~
MERCURY

Every person processes information in a unique and exciting way. Some people are more adept than others. It is not as simple as measuring an intelligence quotient. The more interesting measurement of information processing is the mental principle under which the incarnation is operating. This principle basically determines how the personal mind interfaces with the Great Mind of the cosmos.

Mercury represents that part of you. Mercury was the messenger god who brought messages back and forth between the upper gods (Great Mind) and people (lower mind).

~ THE EMOTIONAL BODY ~
VENUS

The third personal pillar through which we express is the emotional body. Each of us agrees to build an emotional body, because as human beings, a part of our imperative is to give dimension and meaning to life's experiences. Of course, many plants and animals show significant feeling response and have emotional bodies. But no other species can nuance a feeling into so many fine and subtle expressions as we humans. The emotional life of a human being is surely one of his or her most powerful and interesting aspects.

Venus was the Goddess of Love but certainly not of Unconditional Love. She was evocative, manipulative, and controlling, as are our emotions from time to time. However, she was also inspirational, motivational, and stimulating, as are our emotions most often.

The Venus clause is particularly interesting because most of us do not realize how uniquely each being experiences life's circumstances. When we share an event with another person, each of us colors that event with a unique emotional response. However, what is painful to one may be benign to another—what brings particular joy to me may be silly to you. To learn to see, sense, and honor those differences is the goal of the mature emotional being.

~ THE PHYSICAL BODY ~
MARS

The fourth personal pillar is the physical body. We can see the agreement you made with human physicality by looking at your Mars principle. Of course, to become human, we must condense our vast consciousness, our immense beingness, into the density of a physical body. This is often the hardest part of the pattern. We are beyond physical, and yet we must learn to express through the physical.

Eckhart says, "The body is often too strong for the spirit, and thus a battle constantly goes on between them, an eternal quarrel. The body is bold and strong here below because it is here in its own country. . . . The spirit is in a foreign land here" (Fox, 1991, p. 132).

We forget in our dealings with each other that each person has a unique physical configuration. Our bodies are so similar that we tend to get lost in appearance and think that we all have the same relationship to the body. It is not true at all. Each person's agreement with the body is unique. One of the most important aspects of compassion is to remember that the individual's relationship to his body may not be the same as yours.

~ UNIVERSAL PILLARS ~

The universal pillars are forces in the cosmos that give a larger and less personal level of support to a person's life. They are the aspects of the universe that simply hold the stage on which an individual can act out his or her dream. They are represented by the planets that are farther out in the solar system—the planets that glue the solar system together, so to speak.

When a weaver sets up her loom to create a fabric, she strings the loom with the "warp" threads first. The decisions she makes about how to thread these vertical strands determine the ultimate design, look, and feel of the fabric. Your universal pillars may be compared to the warp of your invisible garment. You uniquely interface and interweave with the cosmic laws , and that uniqueness in turn helps articulate the great web of life.

~ UNIVERSAL SUPPORT ~
JUPITER

There are times in every person's life when everything falls into place and that person feels that he or she is totally supported and safe in the right place at the right time. In those moments, Jupiter, the god of good fortune, has aspected the person's life. In space, Jupiter is the big planet with a huge gravitational pull that has gobbled up most of the meteors that have entered our solar system. In that sense, most scientists believe that Jupiter is highly responsible for the Earth's being able to develop into such an Eden of life. Jupiter protects us from cosmic harm. In your invisible garment, the Jupiter principle is your personal safety net.

The Jupiter experiences come just often enough to keep you going in life. They come when you need them the most. They come when you least expect them. They come to remind you of who you really are and why you are a human.

In a sense, you could look at Jupiter as a higher octave or a collective version of your Ascendant. Your personal behavioral ethic gives you a template from which you make all your "doingness" decisions. When those decisions are made in integrity with your pattern, Jupiter steps in and says, "Job well done." In those Jupiter moments, you are pulled up out of your personality, above your egoic view of life, and into a galactic overview! You realize that your life is much bigger than thought—that it is not just you struggling and bumbling along, but that it is you dancing with the universe in a divine choreography!

These Jupiter experiences simultaneously bring you to humility (because you realize the holy nature of your connection with the Earth), and they expand your consciousness (without inflating it) so that you recognize your greater connection with the big dance.

~ LIMITATION SUPPORT ~
SATURN

The Saturn thread in your pattern determines the way you perceive the realm of form. We live in a consensus reality, meaning that on some level of consciousness, we all agree to certain "laws." Trees do not jump out in front of us in the forest because we agree that their configuration of energy stays rooted in the ground. Chairs hold us when we sit on them because we agree that their configuration of atoms is weight bearing.

However, within that consensus, each of us has a unique perspective. We see form and experience concrete reality according to our own bias. This is why two people standing next to each other can witness an accident and see completely different events.

The Saturn principle is one of the most important aspects of our incarnation. We must limit our consciousness in order to focus and give attention to whatever we are seeing. Exactly HOW we limit our consciousness determines our point of view throughout a lifetime.

~ THE SUPPORT OF YOUR AUTHENTIC SELF ~
URANUS

Uranus is an electrical jolt-like energy that reminds us from time to time of our authentic self. Through Uranus's shocking reminders, we wake up and remember why we are here.

Uranus is often experienced as if it were an interruption in the normal programming of your daily life to bring a news update. It is live and in the moment.

The Uranus experience is paradoxical. It simultaneously reminds you (personally) of who you are on the most essential levels, and it takes you out of your ego and puts your life in a much bigger arena. Brian Swimme, in *The Universe Story*, talks about a concept that he calls the idea "worth risking everything for." It is this idea that makes the horse gallop wildly, makes the birds soar and dive daringly, and makes people defy death to save another person from disaster. Uranus is the planet that holds deep memory of Who You Are on that level—it holds the idea for which you will risk everything. It brings you up out of your littleness and shows you the grand design of your unique blueprint.

Authenticity means that your actions, beliefs, and words are all perfectly consistent. We are rarely authentic. Very, very few people live authentically. But all of us, from time to time are struck, like a lightening bolt, with an authentic moment, and with those moments (Uranian moments) come deep memory of who we truly are.

~ THE BIRTH GROUP SUPPORT ~
NEPTUNE

Neptune is the god of the sea. Therefore, his turf is the collective consciousness of the great cosmic waters. As a planet, Neptune lives at the edge of the solar system. He moves slowly, backs up often, and starts again. It takes months for Neptune to move out of one degree of one sign in the zodiac. During those months, thousands of babies are born on planet Earth. All the babies who are born with Neptune in the same degree of the same sign are called a "birth group." Members of a birth group support each other in consciousness for all of their lives. It is also important to note that Neptune takes about 360 years to move around the sun. That means that your birth group is bringing a principle to consciousness that has not been delivered in 360 years. A lot has changed since last time Neptune sent this idea forth.

On a personal level, Neptune is your emotional connection to your birth group. Venus is your personal emotional body, but Neptune holds the greater picture of who you are (emotionally) in relationship to the whole species. The house in which you place your Neptune is the personal aspect of this planet, and it tells us something about the way you have agreed to be an emotional anchor for the greater birth group with which you have incarnated.

~ ULTIMATE VICTORY OVER LIFE ~
PLUTO

Pluto is the god of the underworld. As you well know, each of us has underworld journeys from time to time. They range from mild depression to outright dark nights of the soul. The experience and results of those journeys, however, vary from one person to another depending on the Pluto thread in their garment.

Briefly, I will remind you of the Persephone myth in which Zeus (her father) sold her to Pluto without Demeter's (her mother) knowledge. Pluto opened the ground and kidnapped her one day as she innocently picked flowers. He took her into the underworld, raped her, and held her against her will. Demeter had to go through all sorts of antics to secure her release.

Interestingly, there is also a pre-patriarchal telling of the myth that states that Persephone went into the underworld voluntarily because she was fascinated with the roots of the wheat. Since Demeter was the goddess of grain and harvest, she had taught Persephone of the need for the grasses to grow as deeply underground as they did above ground. While Persephone was under there, she discovered some lost souls and showed them the way back to the light. Pluto found out about this, summoned her, and told her it was against the laws for her to perform acts of power in his realm. Persephone's solution was that they should marry—making her queen of the underworld so that she could perform acts of power there and giving him the heaven's most beautiful virgin for a wife.

One story is a lose-lose. One is a win-win. The point is this: We all go into the underworld. We can go kicking and screaming, or we can go as an act of power. But whichever way we go, we end up (at least partially) victorious. The Pluto thread in our garment defines and determines our ultimate victory over life and death. The more adept we are at our underworld journeys, the more victorious we are over the upper world path. The Pluto principle marks our ultimate victory over life—and death.

Pluto is a planet that also helps us with species memory. Pluto is a "higher octave" of Mars, the physical pillar. Pluto holds the part of your blueprint that is connected to the entire development and evolution of the species. For that reason, we use myth to talk about Pluto—because it is an archetypal energy.

I have used the Persephone myth, which is the women's archetypal journey through which we remember the rape and violence of the feminine, as well as the power and divinity of the feminine. Perhaps the story of the Holy Grail—the search for the holy container—would be the masculine counterpart to the Pluto energy.

Pluto helps us remember that if we see life as an act of power and if we act in absolute integrity and alignment with the intention of our souls, every experience—no matter how it looks externally—is an experience of victory!

~ MID-HEAVEN ~

This part of the pattern is less precise than the others. These principles are really just words that are encoded with sounds that remind you of your deep contract with life. The Mid-Heaven principle, more than any other, reminds you of your essential self. You may come back over and over as a man, as a woman, as an Asian, as a Caucasian—but the essential core stays the same. The Mid-Heaven points you to the essence that stays the same. The Mid-Heaven points you toward your unique soul energy. This is not a reference to how "evolved" a person is. It is, instead, a reference to the position this person plays in the greater body of which we are all a part: where you sit in the godhead, so to speak.

The numerology of your Mid-Heaven degree gives us the information about who you are as a being. The sign of your Mid-Heaven tells us how you as an individual have pledged to live your essence in this lifetime.

~ DREAMING YOUR GARMENT'S PATTERN ~

Even if you cannot acquire a correct copy of your astrological chart, with a little detective work, there is another way to learn about your pattern. Your dreams will help you. You simply need to track your dreams in a certain way, and pay attention to the messages they give you. After becoming familiar with the basic definitions of the 30 spiritual principles, you can look for specific information in the dreams that will point you toward your own principles.

Location of the Moon

A lunar calendar (which you can acquire at almost any bookstore) tells you the location of the moon at any given point in the month. The moon moves through all 12 signs of the zodiac every month, staying in each sign about two days. Start paying attention to the location of the moon during your dreaming. Even if you do not know all of your natal astrological information, you most likely know what "sign" you are, meaning where the sun was when you were born. You can always look at the dreams that you have each month when the moon is in your Sun's sign for information about your primary spiritual purpose in life. The same would be true if you know your natal Moon sign and rising (which are the three things most of us casually know about our charts).

Aspects of the Moon

Your lunar calendar will also tell you what planets the moon may be aspecting during a night. A lunar aspect occurs when the moon and a planet form an imaginary angle in the sky. In astrology, the sky is seen as a 360° circle with the Earth at its center. A lunar aspect is considered significant when the angle between the position of the moon and the position of another planet is at 90° (square), 180° (opposition) or 45° or 120° (sextile). Also, when the moon is conjunct (there is no angle because they are in the same astrological space), the moon's influence is particularly powerful. When you awaken from a dream, look at your lunar calendar. If the moon was aspecting a specific planet during the night when you had the dream, you may want to examine the dream story from the point of view of that planet's role in your pattern.

For example, if you have a dream on a night when the moon is aspecting Mercury (no matter what sign it is in), you can know with considerable certainty that the dream that night is telling you something about your own mental body. In other words, simply look at the dream and ask the question: "What is this dream saying about how my personal mind processes information?"

Numerology in the Dream

When your dream contains numbers, those numbers may very well correspond to the principles of your pattern. If you have a dream, for example, which contains the number five, there is a high possibility that this dream is teaching you something about the principle of Extension (the fifth principle).

Parts of the Body in the Dream

Each of the spiritual principles corresponds to a part of the human body. As you study the principles, you may realize that you often dream of your eyes, for example. Eyes correspond to the principle of Desire in this system, so it could be important for you to look indications of how Desire is expressing itself through your dream.

~ KNOWING YOUR PATTERN ~

Whether you learn about your pattern through your astrological chart, or you learn it by becoming a dream detective and watching the principles that appear in your dreaming, there are enormous personal and spiritual benefits to knowing your own weave.

First, it is extremely important to know the basics of your unique garment. Your Sun principle is your primary gift to life. That is the principle you came into this incarnation to live. Your Moon principle is the primary, most fundamental support you have for living your Sun/purpose. The personal pillars are the four quadrants of your personality that help you express your purpose. The universal pillars are the five cosmic aspects of your life that continually hold you together, no matter what the *world of doing* brings your way. And your Mid-Heaven is the connection to soul—your direct path to remembering who you are on a level beyond human—your inspiration for taking a human incarnation at this time.

You might use a set of statements like this to sum up your pattern: My main purpose is to live (**Sun principle**). (**Moon principle**) is my primary support in this project called "life." (**Ascendant principle, Mercury principle,**

Venus principle, and Mars principle) create the personality through which I can best express (**Sun principle**). (**Jupiter, Saturn, Uranus, Neptune, and Pluto principles**) are my cosmic silent partners in this venture. And it is in behalf of (**Mid-Heaven principle**) that I deliver my blessing into form.

Another important benefit of knowing your pattern is the freedom that knowing gives you. The first time I looked up my own principles, I experienced enormous relief just to realize that I do not have to be all things. I can be the "me" things, and that is not only enough, but it is beautiful and important.

Knowing your pattern allows for enormous efficiency in your life, because if you know who you came here to be, what you came here to do takes a back seat in importance. The more you trust your beingness, the more you will allow your doingness to just reflect who you are naturally. Too often, we willfully make the decisions about what we are to do in life without first considering the much more important aspect of ourselves—what we are here to BE. Because they are not rooted in "being," those "doing" decisions often create problems for us that make life difficult, frustrating, and confusing.

Most importantly, knowing your principles broadens your perspective, liberating you from the incessant competition and comparison games most of us play in the external world. If you know who you are as a spiritual being, then you are more able to look at the behavior of others not as aberrant, not as enviable, not as "better than"—but as an attempt to express another configuration of spiritual principles. By looking at the world through the lens of these principles, you achieve a new level of compassion toward and cooperation with other humans.

As you read these next pages, if you know your astrological chart, pay special attention to the principles that you have agreed to wear as your invisible garment. Give yourself "extra credit" for all the ways in which you live those principles impeccably. And enjoy looking at the ways that all the principles are mirrored to you in your dreams. If you do not know your specific chart, use your dreams to help you determine which principles you most ardently live.

PART II

Understanding Your Invisible Garment

Chapter Three

The Ascending Principles

The first ten principles, numbered 0–9, are called the "Ascending Principles" because they are the most basic, most elemental principles of form. They are the blueprint or grid work on which the realm of form is based. They ascend, through the consciousness of the human, toward their highest expression.

The angels who delivered this information explained to me that the Ascending Principles are the purview of the earth angels, the nature spirits, or what I refer to in these writings as the devic realm. The word deva means "god of goodwill," and it is a term commonly used to represent the nature spirits, also called faeries. Almost every time I entered into a receptive meditation with the angels to learn more about the Ascending Principles, the terms deva and devic kingdom were used by them in connection with this group of principles.

As this planet formed 4 billion years ago, an intelligent grid work also formed. Brian Swimme and Thomas Berry refer to it as the "planetary mind" (Swimme and Berry, 1992, p. 9). This grid work is metaphorically understood by many humans as an angelic realm that oversees the basic workings of the planet. The inhabitants of this realm are the angels, or devas, of nature. There are devas of the mineral kingdom, plant kingdom, and animal kingdom. Most indigenous peoples have very specific beliefs about the nature spirits as do many scholars. Rudolph Steiner, the Austrian physicist and mathematician, called them "elemental spirits." He referred to the planetary mind as the "world ether." In his occult view, elemental spirits lie hidden behind all that constitutes the physical, sense-perceptible world, making it, with their effort, truly alive (Tompkins, 1997, p. 112).

> *This planetary mind, this grid work of interacting and interdependent intelligences, is constantly evolving, reaching higher and higher levels of expression. One of the ways the devas evolve is through interaction with human consciousness.*

People who have Ascending Principles in their fabric are usually very aware of their relationship to the elements of the earth. They may love gardening. They often are attracted to jewelry with gemstones. Some work with animals and travel far to swim with dolphins or to see exotic plant or animal species. They may feel a strong urge to become ecological activists. Others may be attracted to alternative healing techniques such as hands-on healing, herbal remedies, nutritional remedies and supplements, and crystal healings.

Because our society questions the validity of most alternative health therapies and because we are not encouraged to believe in the existence of the devic world, people with Ascending Principles in their pattern often feel alienated or crazy. Learning about these principles and fully accepting the implications of their position in one's invisible garment can free a person from those feelings. Many times, I have seen tears of gratitude and relief in the eyes of my clients as I explained to them that their relationship with the devic world is a part of their gift and is a part of the reason that they took this human incarnation.

It is possible that when we work with the Ascending Principles, we are actually remembering the evolution of life on this planet. While that may be a radical idea, it is one that has been familiar to and suggested by mystical poets. Accepting this idea requires releasing any anthropomorphic concepts that dominate the human mind and stepping into a larger view of the evolution of consciousness.

We began
As a mineral.
We emerged into plant life
And into the animal state, and then into being human,
And always we have forgotten our former states,
Except in early spring when we slightly recall
Being green again.

~ RUMI
"On Resurrection Day"
The Essential Rumi
Bly and Barks, Translators, 1995

O Placement

Man follows the earth
Earth follows the universe
The Universe follows the Tao
The Tao follows only itself.

~ LAO TSU

Placement is the original principle. In other words, for something to manifest in form, it has to establish stability. It has to locate itself in time and space on the cosmic grid, and it has to be defined by the relativity of that establishment. Placement could be called the "power of limitation" or the "power of being defined by boundary."

Hildegard of Bingen says, "The firmament could not have the sun, the moon, and the stars unless the places where they accomplish their orbits had been firmly established. For such heavenly bodies could not exist without their predetermined locations in space" (Fox, 1987, p. 89). She indicates to us that first and foremost, the divine order was set. She saw in her visionary process that arrangement of the physical world was "ordained according to a definite standard" (p. 90). "Placement" is the word we use to identify that standard.

Outside the human body, Placement expresses through the natural micro universes of the earth. Our Mother Earth is composed of billions of universes, all of which operate interdependently. While they do not necessarily hold a conscious awareness of the human realm, they do hold a level of conscious communication with all sentience. They weave together the foundation of the planet.

There are laws that we call "natural laws." They are the interconnected and indivisible rules that have been agreed upon by matter, energy, space, and time. We might call them the "fibers that create the invisible garment of the planet." Each knot in the weave of this garment is tended by an energy that we call a "deva" (an intelligent force that focuses on holding these laws in place). Thomas Berry in *Dream of the Earth* refers to this interdependent connection of laws as "the intimacy of the natural world" and he emphasizes that the human's role in this wonder is to approach the natural laws with sensitivity and thankfulness (p. 14).

According to this teaching I received from the angels, our human ability to bring the devas to our awareness gives them a potential for higher expression. Naturalist John Muir shines as an example of the principle of Placement working its wonder in the consciousness of a human being. Muir's Sun was in the zero degree of Taurus—the principle of Placement in the sign of Mother Earth herself. Not surprisingly, photographer Ansel Adams's Sun was also in the principle of Placement. Each picture he took documents his ability to see the power of the natural laws and their ability to communicate to us the microcosmic and macrocosmic interconnection of all things.

Inside the human body, Placement lives in the "eyes" of the feet. These two chakra points, or points of energetic focus, are the human's rooting places. People have energetic openings in the bottoms of their feet that can potentially communicate with Mother Earth, and which one can open and close at will.

In my experience, consciously opening these root points gives me much deeper grounding and a graceful flow of energy that is connected to earth's sentience. A barefooted walk on the beach is a spiritual experience for anyone who is awake to that kind of energetic exchange. Surely, John Muir's feet-eyes were open as he walked hundreds of miles on this continent exploring its splendor, teaching farming techniques to settlers, and campaigning in Congress for forest conservation.

Native American ceremonial dances are useful metaphors for the principles of Placement (the first principle) and Movement (the last). In sacred dance, Movement is balanced by Placement. When you place your foot on the ground, you establish a relationship to the micro-universes that make up the earth. That act is Placement. Then, as soon as Placement is established, Movement (the next step) must occur in order for the next Placement to occur. Placement and Movement work hand and hand in order for evolution to forge through the realm of form.

In my dream circles, we always look for these principles in our dream images. We have learned that people who have Placement in their personal weave may have very different relationships to the principle when they are dreaming and when they are awake. For example, in a dream, it is often the job of the dreamer to help someone else find his or her right place, whereas that same person may have trouble finding his or her own right place in waking reality.

One woman in our circle almost always has trouble claiming her spot when she comes to dream circle. She either cannot decide where to sit, or she comes in, puts her stuff down, goes to the bathroom, and returns to find that someone has moved her things and taken that chair. This experience of "displacement" always stuns her. It makes her question her relationship to the principle of Placement. However, in the dreamtime, one of her primary themes is escorting people to their rightful places. She often dreams of finding people who are lost, or who have temporarily lost their way, and she assists them. This paradox is not uncommon with people who have Placement in their pattern.

Placement is the originating principle of form, and sound is the "In the beginning" movement out of the No Thing.

Another interesting observation from dream circle is that people who wear Placement often dream of songs, tones, and unusual sounds. The Gospel according to St. John, universally known to be the most mystical of the New Testament gospels, starts by saying, "In the beginning was the Word and the Word was with God and the Word was God" (John 1:1 KJV). In his remarkable book, *The Hidden Gospel,* Neil Douglas-Klotz points out that the Aramaic word for "sound" can also mean "word" or "vibration" (Douglas-Klotz, 1999, p. 134). It appears through our dreaming that Placement and The Word have an undeniably intimate vibrational relationship.

Placement, establishment in space and time, is the primal Ascending Principle. Whether one is contracted with Placement, it is by definition an integral part of any person's existence.

1 Innocence

A Brahmin should stop being a pundit and
try to live like a child.

~ THE UPANISHADS 3.5.1

Innocence may be defined as power without manifestation. It is power in its potential form. Innocence is beingness without physicality. It resides in that archetypal realm where the potential for physical expression exists. Innocence is what keeps human beings able to learn—it makes them teachable.

Watch a child who is old enough to move down from his mother's lap to explore the world. That exploration is the actual embodiment of Innocence. A pre-verbal child embraces the world as it is. He or she will move to an object and study the object with all of the senses: tasting it, touching it, banging it. A child does not need to give definition or purpose to the object. The child simply explores the object for no other reason than to learn. That is Innocence at work.

Notice, then, that this child will do the very same thing a few minutes later to the same object, as if having a totally new experience. Innocence is completely willing for the object to be something absolutely different in every moment.

Innocence as a principle idea never goes unconscious. It keeps one available to learn at all times—waking or sleeping. Even as we become more sophisticated and have mental categories, expectations, and cynicisms, if our pattern contains Innocence, we cannot totally bypass the innate influence the principle has on our lives. Whether or not our personal pattern includes Innocence, we humans never reach a point at which we cannot learn.

We are afraid to be innocent as adults because the term implies that we are naive or vulnerable. Innocence and ignorance have become synonyms in our language. "Ignorance" means to ignore. Ignoring something because we do not want to know about it is not innocence: It is denial. However, to ignore what we think we know in order to acquire deeper knowledge, or in order to see something without judgment or bias, is spiritual Innocence.

An adult, to achieve spiritual Innocence, must undergo a cleansing so that God can speak to and through his or her being.

Eckhart encouraged his congregation to ignore what they thought they knew in order to learn truth. "Thus your ignorance is not a defect, but your highest perfection, and your undergoing is thus your highest accomplishment. . . . If you wish to know God in a divine way, your knowledge has to become pure ignorance and forgetfulness of yourself and all creatures" (Fox, 1991, p. 239). Eckhart went on to say that this divine ignorance increases one's aptitude for a rich sensitivity through which he or she will be made whole (p. 240).

Spiritual Innocence, coupled with the wisdom of the mature human, is a very high accomplishment.
Innocence is archetypal. It confirms the belief that human life is a metaphor for spiritual truth. Through the eyes of Innocence, one sees the existence of something and simultaneously sees the grand design behind it. One sees the story, the blueprint, and the intent at least as clearly as he or she sees the form.

Barbara Walters is an exceptional person to me. Her television interviews and reporting are driven by her heartful, sincere interest in learning, discovering truth, and disclosing the underlying causes and motivations of events and people. Her Sun in Innocence in the twelfth house (the least personal, most philanthropic, of all the houses of the zodiac) makes it easy for us to understand the career path she chose. She is an insatiable student and a generous teacher. Innocence keeps her ever on the prowl for new learning, and her audience benefits from the results.

One of my students defined the principle beautifully:

"Innocence is the essence of any form demanding to be heard."

Many of my clients whose garments contain Innocence have real challenges with religion and organized spiritual systems because they feel that the Innocence of the original vision is often lost in the bureaucracy. These people usually either leave such organizations or go more deeply into them in order to try to restore the organizational intent to its origin.

In the immature person, Innocence does not know itself. A child is not aware of the Innocence that lives through him. However, after years of maturing, continually starting anew—leaving jobs, relationships, and situations that do not reflect authenticity—eventually that person becomes aware of the principle of Innocence as it expresses itself through his or her life. Innocence that knows itself is Love.

Innocence resides in the heart of the human. The heart chakra for a spiritually evolved person is the regulator, the thermostat, and the resistor for how God's energy flows through that person's life. God's energy comes into the heart and then is distributed to the rest of the body in accordance with the power of compassion that the person has toward all living beings. That energy is also radiated out to the world in accordance with the innocent beingness of the individual.

Many believe that the human species is evolving (Pearce, 2002, p. 54). Traditionally, the brain, the head-mind, has been our dominant thinking organ. Science is now understanding that the heart is also a brain-like organ and that we have a new emerging dominance in the heart-mind. The head-mind is a thinking organism that has two hemispheres of the neocortex. This kind of thinking keeps us in duality thinking. The heart-mind is a radiant organism that sends compassion into the world and stabilizes the body in a unity (rather than duality) consciousness (p. 58).

To walk in Innocence is to walk in safety, for one is radiating love into the world rather than trying to pull anything out of it. Innocence becomes a protective shield for anyone who allows the heart to be the primary thinking organ of a lifetime. When we walk in a needy or victimized way, we are vulnerable. When we walk in Innocence, we become strong.

One student shared an experience of Innocence and the shield of safety that it creates:

"Lately I've been going through a rather rigorous spiritual exercise that has me taking long wilderness hikes alone. Each day, as I embark on this hike, I'm very mindful that, while it is beautiful out there, there are also potential pitfalls—mountain lions being the most extreme.

Since I've started doing this, I've noticed that I'm respectful of the potential dangers, but I do not feel fearful. Perhaps this is Innocence. While I approach each hike with wonderment about what I'll discover, I've also become savvy about the dangers.

Tonight, I just realized that the posture I walk in pushes my heart forward. Since the heart is the home of Innocence, I think that walking in this strong way with my heart out front puts Innocence in front of me like a shield."

The shield of Innocence is a beautiful and paradoxical image. It is surely comforting to realize that by radiating Innocence from the heart, we become strong and inviolate. Renee dreamed the shield of Innocence:

> I dreamed I was in a small house with many adults and children of many races. I was a child (around 5 or 6) but I was also an adult and I was also a Spiritual Elder watching the scene from outside of my body. Everyone seemed happy — a celebration of some kind occurring.
>
> Then an African American man entered. He was tall, had a beard, and seemed very kind to me. He gave something to the children and we were all transforming into human butterflies. We were so beautiful, and it felt so freeing and transforming. Different children were different colors with their butterfly wings. I recall having magenta, electric blue, and maybe orange.
>
> One woman who was sitting in the corner started criticizing the man and saying he was "no good" and that he was giving us drugs or illegal substances to induce the butterfly effect. I heard her say this: I observed her to be a woman who whined a lot and criticized the food at the party. She didn't seem satisfied with life, much less the party. I was scared initially that the "peace" man may have been hurting us but decided to not listen to the woman. I realized that the butterfly effect was about transformation and that the man was "magic"—he "walked in Innocence . . . radiating Love." The woman who was cynical seemed to be afraid of being vulnerable. The butterfly certainly gave meaning to life and the "peace" man did the same.

The shield of Innocence allows us to be vulnerable and available to transformation. The above-dreamer has Innocence in the Moon position of her garment's pattern. This means that she has mastered some of the qualities of this principle and that she can call forth her "shield of vulnerability" anytime she needs to see things more clearly. The Spiritual Elder in the dream who was observing the whole scene gave her the perspective to remember how to allow Innocence to transform the cynical, pained view of life that many of us carry.

If you wear Innocence in your garment, look carefully at your dreams of children—especially the dreams when you become a child again. They are most likely encoded messages from the soul asking you to remember Innocence.

Of course, your teachings about Innocence do not come just when you are asleep. They are rampant in the waking dream, too. Cammie, with her Sun in Innocence, shares:

> "As a Montessori preschool teacher surrounded by children, I was drawn like a moth to their innocence because it helped me to feel my own. Children would run up to me on the playground to tell me their dreams that the joy of play had evoked in their bodies. 'Teacher, teacher, I dreamed of my house and when I went in the door, there was gold light shining everywhere!' One boy drew like Picasso on the chalkboard with both hands at the same time in different colors, and the other children knew what his pictures were. A four-year old wrote his name for the first time right to left in mirror script. Innocence is holy and powerful."

Another student described the enormous relief she felt about herself and her life choices when she read the definition of Innocence:

> "Over and over I've left schools, jobs, groups—you name it— when others chose to worship the form (thereby perverting its purity) and ignore the essence. Innocence gets trampled in organizations. For so many years, I've thought something was 'wrong' with me. But it was just Innocence continually reasserting itself. So what is innocence anyway? It is the essence demanding to be heard, demanding to be seen, to be felt."

2 Purity

Blessed are the pure in heart, for they shall see God.

~ MATTHEW 5:8

Blessed are the consistent in heart: They shall contemplate The One.

~ ALTERNATE ARAMAIC READING OF MATTHEW 5:8
NEIL DOUGLAS-KLOTZ

Purity is the ability to recognize the essential nature of any form. It is the ability to distill any error that has been attached to a form whether the error is ideological, psychological, or physiological. Purity is the ability to liberate oneself from patterns of error that are present in perceptual reality and instead to experience the intent of cosmic order. Purity involves being aware of the blueprint behind form. The only way one can experience the true nature of form is through the eyes of Purity.

If Purity is part of your fabric, you have a unique ability to eliminate error from any expression of life and to move (in consciousness) directly into the authenticity of the idea from which that expression (form) was manifested. To understand Purity fully, we must delve into and investigate the clarity of our thoughts. Without clarity of thought and wholeness of mind, we cannot perceive the blueprint.

Eckhart says, "Purity of heart means to be separated and cut off from all physical things, to be gathered and enclosed in oneself." He further states that this is the most direct path to God (Fox, 1991, p. 189). To be in Purity, Eckhart says, is to be in the understanding of living like a child.

When one perceives through the eyes of Purity, the inner result is Peace (one of the Descending Principles). And through the shift in perception that brings one to Purity, that person lives in a perpetually new reality. The things people do in the world take a different level of importance when seen through a Purity lens. It can be said, "The things I do in the world become statements of my I-Am-ness rather than of my Who-am-I-ness."

Dr. Matthew Fox gives us further insight into this principle in his commentary on Eckhart's sermon about Purity. "Purity is a transparency that carries us back to our divine origin" (Fox, 1991, p. 269). "Purity is that state of being that preceded original sin or the consciousness of dualisms and separations. It signifies our original freedom" (p. 269). "When God and the soul unite, the soul strives for the first purity, that is, for its divine origin" (p. 268).

It was particularly interesting for me when I discovered that both Jackie Kennedy and Eleanor Roosevelt had Mercury (mental body) in Purity. They are not two people I would automatically put in the same mental category. From external appearances, Eleanor was a brilliant thinker, a philosopher if you will, while Jackie was more focused on aesthetics and matters of family. However, what was true of both of them was their ability to clear away the clutter and cut to the essential meaning of their life experience.

One of the first things Mrs. Kennedy did in her role as First Lady was restore the White House, emphasizing its beauty, history, and importance as a national statement of American pride. Extreme times, periods of profound emotional catharsis, often create a crack in our carefully sculpted outer-selves, and in those times, the spirit works through us in amazing ways. Who of us that witnessed it will ever forget her miraculous, clear-minded way that Mrs. Kennedy created a funeral for her husband that allowed the whole world to grieve with grace, dignity, and purity?

Mrs. Roosevelt, after her husband's death, put her purity of mind to work for the benefit of all mankind by accepting the appointment as the United State's first delegate to the United Nations. Indeed, both women stand as examples of how Purity can work through the mental body of a person when he or she is willing to allow divinity to work through them.

Purity resides in the Devic Worlds.

The difference between the Archetypal Worlds of Innocence and the Devic Worlds of Purity, as I understand them, is that the Archetypal Worlds are latent thought forms while the Devic Worlds are the structural blueprint from which form emanates.

In other words, let us say you are looking at a poppy. What you are seeing is an individualization of an expression of life. Behind that poppy is a blueprint that we would call poppy-ness because all poppies operate out of the same basic plan. Behind that blueprint is flower-ness, and behind that is plant-ness, and then the entire kingdom that we know as flora. Those are the devic realms that reside behind a plant. They can be traced through the DNA of the plants. On the other hand, the archetype that plant-ness represents, or the whole kingdom that flora represents, is not scientifically proved. It is a generative thought form that is only implied.

In the human body, Purity resides in the liver, the organ that purifies the blood and allows proper nutrition to flow in the blood stream. Peace flows through our blood only when the liver is healthy and functioning at optimal performance. The liver is the only organ in the body that can regenerate itself. If you lose part of your liver to surgery, chances are the liver will recreate its wholeness. It has the ability to return to the original blueprint of itself.

One friend who is contracted with Purity dreamed that she was scouring a pot in which she planned to make a specific soup for a ceremonial meal. In discussing that dream, the circle felt it was saying that while Innocence is the container (symbolized by the pot) of form, Purity is the method through which we continuously scour the form, hoping to remove errors, flaws, and debris. When we wear Purity, we seem to be innately driven to cleanse our world and our environment just as the liver is simply driven to purify the blood. Lal Ded, the fourteenth century Kashmiri poet sheds light on this idea.

> The soul, like the moon,
> Is new, and always new again.
> Since I scoured my mind
> And my body, I too, Lalla,
> Am each moment new.

Women in Praise of the Sacred:
43 Centuries of Spiritual Poetry by Women
Hirshfield, Editor

Annette's moon is in the principle of Purity. This dream came to her, reminding her of the profound importance of remembering the Devic Worlds, remembering the garden.

At Esalen (a sacred place for me), I walk down the hill to a magnificent field of wild flowers. As I take in the beauty, the wind becomes the voice that says, "Who is the gardener?" I remain speechless and stand still. The voice continues, "Enjoy the garden." I want to stay, but I leave the garden and walk up the hill. I slip and fall into the roots of the biggest tree I've ever seen. It is polished, dark wood. It is so large that I can only see the bottom of the trunk. I grab onto it. I see that I have slipped on bits of crystal that surround it.

Annette explains why she needs to be reminded about Purity in dreams:

"I forget that God is the gardener—not me. My foundation is in the soil—in Nature—so it behooves me to remember that. I must remember not to build my life on fear but on the Purity of the blueprint."

Almost no one operates from a fear-free mind that is rooted in divine purpose. We think we are the gardeners—that we are in control. We forget how to participate in allowing pure thought to flow through systems. Our whole impetus for living has become an orbit around the "something is wrong and I must fix it" theory. Something is wrong with me, my bank account, my spouse, my career, my health, my life. And something is wrong with you. And most importantly, something is wrong with "them." Mostly them and secretly me! Collectively, we have committed to the "something is wrong" theory, and as a result, we can barely even imagine moving beyond it. It seems naive or denying to move to a way of thinking that is rooted in the original blessing of Life. However, the dreams of Purity will continue to remind us, encourage us, and call us back to source.

3 Memory

Memory is clearly greater than space....
Clearly, it is through memory that one recognizes one's
children and cattle. So, venerate memory.

~ THE UPANISHADS CU 13:1

Memory is a force that is more powerful than matter. Matter will hold more truly to Memory than to Purity. For example, if you cut yourself badly, you have a scar on your body. The rest of your life, as the body regenerates its cells, it will recreate the scar tissue. It will not bypass Memory and go back to the Purity of your original form.

Cosmologist Brian Swimme tells us that only after Memory established itself as a principle could life exist on this planet. The genetic memory, passed from the original cell forward to the future determined the evolution of life. Swimme and Berry state, "It is this power of memory that distinguishes the autopoiesis we call life" (1992, p. 87). Memory, therefore, is extremely important. Without Memory, we do not live.

Life requires a continuum; there must be a sense of past, present, and future. Memory is the interlacing of our evolutionary experience as it moves through the realm called form.

Memory is related to Flowering, the evolutionary principle we will discuss in the next chapter titled "The Containing Principles." Memory is about evolution. Biologically, life's forms continue to reproduce themselves until their usefulness in the evolutionary process is complete (p. 114). At that point, they either become extinct or they evolve into a new form, which not only carries with it all memory of the past form, but also includes new structures that will make it thrive and survive.

In a cognitive sense, humans are veiled from Memory.

We do not have the ability to "remember" dinosaur-ness. Our brains are simply not wired to access all the memory of evolution even though the patterns are stored in the DNA. Potter M.C. Richards compares individual humans to clay vases that have been designed and dried but not yet fired to the point of vitrification. If we were to pour water into our containers at this point, we would dissolve. First we must experience, as she puts it, the "ordeal by fire" in order to strengthen our forms (Richards, 1989, p. 132). Most of us do not have the containers yet that could hold the contents of full, unveiled cosmic Memory.

Mythologist Joseph Campbell's Moon (mastery) was in the principle of Memory in the tenth house (the house of career). As we look back through the enormous body of work he left as his heritage, we can see that he dedicated his adult life to the intensive study, deep understanding, and profound connecting of myth to every person's journey through life. He strengthened his vessel by telling, living, feeling, and translating the stories of other times and places that had survived the centuries. He lived the principle Memory and articulated it as story, image, symbol, dance, and art.

Leonardo da Vinci's Sun and Moon were both in the principle of Memory. He is reputed to be one of the many artists of the medieval period who encoded into his artwork the stories, myths, and truths of the ancients. Certainly, we see in his genius the imprint of access to vast knowledge.

Memory is such a powerful force that at this particular point of physiological development, humans cannot have full access to it because it would destroy the body. Humans flex their remembrance muscles by learning how to make associative mental patterns. Personal ability to remember the mundane, however, is small compared to the force that actually runs through the entire continuum. Humans could have access to past lives, for example, if they developed the body that could contain it. Full remembrance of the entire evolutionary process is in human cells. Between conception and taking the first breath, every human travels from first cell all the way through to human being. It is there in Memory.

To remember oneself fully, one has to come to right relationship with free will. Right relationship with free will involves surrender to God's will. One has to align personal authority with an impersonal, omniscient authority. At that point, one realizes that what he or she thought was unique about himself or herself was actually veiling and shielding a much larger truth. When one lifts the veils and shields and totally transforms the tendency to make separatist decisions, he or she becomes an aspect of God that has access to Memory. Then one discovers the great irony of the universe: that the physical form holds the exact same information as the whole cosmos. Within the DNA, all the information is present.

When free will is fully integrated and aligned with Divine Will, we often discover that the body and the soul are actually the same expression. Mystics of every tradition have made that discovery within their own lives. Because some people have reached that level of consciousness, because they have successfully "married" spirit and body, each of us has the ability to remember that unity. Because we are ultimately all one body, their experience is in our bones, too.

> *Memory of the earth's process of evolution is downloaded into the stones. The devas, or angels, of the stone kingdom maintain a perfect record of everything that has occurred on our planet since the minerals started gathering and crystallizing. The minerals and stones function as the skeletal system and memory banks of Mother Earth.*
>
> *Similarly, memory of human evolution is downloaded into the bones of the human body. Our own skeletal system is the record keeper of the human process. We are constantly crystallizing information into our bones, which is why anthropologists are so excited when they find a significant set of bones from ancient people. We learn more about our development from human bones than from any other remnant.*

I have found that Memory weavers have a special relationship with stones and bones. They can actually develop the ability to speak with the stone devas or at least to obtain information telepathically from them. They also appear to have a built-in memory system in their own body. When a person who wears Memory says, "I know it in my bones," it is a good idea to listen.

Jean Houston reports that once she had a discussion with Joseph Campbell about *seeing* the images of a myth in a state of deep relaxation. He admitted to her that he was not a visual person—that he does not "see" images, but instead, "I know them in my bones" (p. 94).

In fact, it is a recurring theme in our dream circles that we go to a university that is made of alabaster. This university is centered around a large stone library. Each dreamer who visits this library has a special way of accessing the information stored there. The following is a dream of mine that took me there:

I was in the university (Universe City). I went to the library. The way one accessed information in the library was to first go to a wall near the front desk and telepathically ask where to locate the material you're looking for. The answer would float forward on the wall, sort of like the answers appear on the bottom of an 8-ball toy. Then you'd go to that section of the library. There were only stone walls and big comfortable couches and tables and lamps. You'd have to intuitively find the place on the stone wall where the information was stored. You'd telepathically ask to see the information, and if you had found the correct spot, the wall would open and out would pop an ancient manuscript that contained the information. It was really neat. My teacher was there and saw me get several books in a row. He told me it was rare for anyone to know exactly where to go to get the right information. I settled down on a couch with my tomes, ready for some long hours of absorbing.

Another student came in and asked how to use the library. I showed him the 8-ball wall, and then I took him to his section, but had to leave him to his own devices from there. The walls won't give the information to someone who is not able to intuit for himself or herself.

This dream feels very affirming that what we really know is not what we learn in books but rather what is imprinted in our stones/bones. Accessing our own wisdom is a personal intuitive process. Someone can show us how to do it, but no one can do it for us. We must remember who we are by ourselves.

One very powerful dreamer related it this way in a letter to me:

"Memory is one of my Principles and I remember things I have never read about in books. In dreams, I see things I have never come across in my waking life. For example, I was taught about the Goddesses in the dreamtime, long before I read anything about the ancient cultures. Sometimes I read books about the topics I've 're-membered' in the dream, and they merely verify what I have already seen. Of course, I do not remember what I did yesterday, but ancient memories seem to reside in my being."

4 Beauty

May it be beautiful before me
May it be beautiful behind me
May it be beautiful below me
May it be beautiful above me
May it be beautiful all around me
I am restored in beauty.

~ TRADITIONAL NAVAJO PRAYER

Beauty is the harmonic of nature. It is the way forms interweave them-selves in order to create a divine harmonious oneness. Beauty is the aesthetic of cosmic order.

Moreover, Beauty is the life course on which humans move. When the Native American people talk about the Beauty Way, they refer to a path that is created by this natural harmonic. On the Beauty Way, sounds, visuals, and tactile experiences all interweave to become one multi-sensual melody—a way of walking in the world.

Matthew Fox says, "Because all beauty yearns to be conspicuous, beauty and display go together; so, therefore, do beauty and work" (1994, p. 2). In other words, what we do, how we do it, and in what attitude we do it all interweave to create our lives. If we are spiritually awake, if we have the spiritual eyes that can perceive the harmonic of life, the Beauty Way shows itself through our work in the world.

Brian Swimme says, "The human provides the space in which the universe feels its stupendous beauty. Think of it this way: Before the human arrived, the Earth and universe were magnificent realities. However, some of the depths of this magnificence were yet to be felt" (1984, p. 32). Swimme seems to be saying that it is the human's "job" to perceive beauty and reflect it back so that the Creator experiences it, too.

Beauty lives in the stone beings—especially the gemstones.

We learn from physics that gems are clusters of minerals that have found their way to this planet after spewing forth from a supernova somewhere off in the cosmos.

Gems are beauty for the sake of beauty.

Gems show us how a solid structure can let the light shine through. By virtue of the fact that we value them, they teach us about our own value. They are made, after all, from the same stardust (minerals) that we contain in our bodies. Of course, the other stones—the opaque stones—also carry the principle of Beauty. They speak to us in other ways of the Beauty Path.

Pick up a rock and ask it a question. Watch the lines and patterns on the rock form themselves into an image that answers your question.

It is an amazing relationship that humans have with the stone beings. One woman in my circle had the following dream:

I dreamed that I was somewhere strange (a stranger in a strange land). I had never been in this dusty place that also had a tropical feel. I felt lost and alone. I noticed that women were making a street/road and I went to observe and hoped I would find a community.

The women were using big, yellow machinery. I felt wary. For some reason, the street/road pulled me down—I had great difficulty merely walking on it—it was like a magnetic field pulled me down to my knees.

When I was down on the street, I noticed with great surprise and awe that the women were making the road out of crushed crystals (clear quartz) and saw that there were copious amounts of amethysts that were not crushed. They were the size of a river stone. There were other gemstones, too, but I don't recall the specifics.

This dream shows us the Beauty Way—the crystal road—being built by the dreamers with big yellow machinery of which we are almost fearful. Yellow is the color that does not define itself as much as it amplifies all the other colors. It sends its rays out to the edges of the cosmos, lighting crystal paths along the way. It is fearful because to walk the Beauty Way carries major responsibility. This road is heavy. It demands that we walk it on our knees, in humility and gratitude. The Beauty Way is not an easy way—but it is the only real way.

In the human body, the principle of Beauty lives in the throat. Every-thing about the throat gives form to Beauty: how one speaks, what one speaks, how one sings, what one sings. Beauty is the human expression of the heart coming out through the mouth. Also, Beauty is expressed through what one eats, and what one breathes, how one eats, and how one breathes. Beauty is the vibration of Creation, and it enters and exits the human body through the hollow tube of the throat.

John Lennon's Pluto (ultimate victory over life) carried the principle of Beauty. In many ways, his early life was troubled. He was raised in a lower middle-class neighborhood with not a lot of support—financial or emotional. He reached untold wealth and fame during the Beatles years, but clearly, that did not satisfy his drive to explore his life's purpose. John's Sun (primary gift to life) was the principle of Unity. It was through an underworld (Pluton-ian) journey that was unusually public that included leaving the Beatles, marrying and sometimes separating from Yoko Ono, and going through a difficult time with drug use that he apparently found his own version of the principle of Beauty.

The lyrics to "Imagine" (*You may say I'm a dreamer, but I'm not the only one. I hope someday you'll join us, and the world can live as One . . .*), as well as "Give Peace a Chance," (*All we are saying is give peace a chance . . .*) indi-cate that he did finally find his life's purpose: that Unity principle. I believe that he was supported through his underworld journey by the principle of Beauty, and his ultimate victory was that he realized the Beauty Way and wrote the songs that resonated with the principle of Unity before his tragic death.

The universe is designed according to a sacred mathematical system. Beauty is the focusing and condensation of that system into small, unique packages that can be seen, touched, and tasted. Beauty is a vibration of the divine dynamic of mathematics.

In the classes that I have taught in which we studied these principles, we have discovered that Beauty is often a confusing principle. I have also noticed this confusion in the approximately 3,000 people for whom I have done soul contract readings. Most people who have Beauty in their fabric struggle with the social definition of physical beauty. They either fit the social definition and struggle with confusion between their essence and their physical body, or they do not fit that definition and struggle with low self-esteem as a result. It is often a challenging part of their lives to learn to understand the difference between the Beauty that is the vibration of Cre-ation and the superficial beauty of the body.

Sometimes, a person's struggle with understanding Beauty is amplified by his or her narcissistic self-adoration. However, people who have engaged in this struggle, and have thereby matured their understanding of spiritual Beauty, are among the happiest and most well-adjusted people I know.

5 Extension

From the mind
Of a single, long vine,
one hundred openings live.

~ CHIYO-NI

Life loves to extend itself. Extension is life exploding out of its central seed. The plant seed has an inner drive to open, stretch, reach, and unfold continuously from that central point. So does the human seed.

The plant creates a root system that moves into the darkness in order to anchor and nourish itself. The plant simultaneously makes a stem system that reaches into the light in order to eat the light and energize itself. As deep as the one will go, the other one will go as high. This process is a metaphor for the human realm also. True growth in the seen realm (the stem system) results from deep rooting in the unseen.

I read once in Virginia Woolf's journal: "The future is dark—which is on the whole the best thing the future can be, I think." I spent many hours contemplating what she meant by this statement. Was it just the musings of a depressive personality, or was there deep wisdom in these words?

Upon looking at Woolf's pattern, I saw Extension in three different threads. Her Sun (primary reason for incarnating) and her Mid-Heaven (direct path to God) were conjunct in Aquarius. And her Saturn (the structure through which she saw the world) was in Extension in Taurus. This connection with the principle helped me understand that her "dark" was the unseen— the earth through which the roots must wriggle to find their nourishment.

In a real sense, then, I can read her use of the term "dark" to mean that which holds all potential, every possibility, and is the source of all growth. The future is unsure, unseen, full of potential, and the source of growth, which on the whole is the best thing the future can be.

Extension is the aspect of form that creates the appearance of personal space.

Form has to do with how time, space, and matter interface with each other. Quantum physics tells us that two quanta cannot occupy the same space at the same time. The principle of Extension gives them "personal" location in the time-space-matter continuum. And yet energetically, the quanta are totally connected.

The same is true of the personal space of the human.

Most humans mistakenly believe they are separated and isolated beings. But through understanding Extension, that error can be corrected. Humans are extensions and mirrors of the oneness of the human spirit. That force runs through each person continuously, powerfully, and potently. Studying the spiritual principle of Extension reminds every human being to contemplate unity-consciousness as thoroughly as one investigates self-consciousness. Extension, therefore, is the beginning of compassion, because compassion results from the true understanding of the interconnectedness of all sentience.

Compassion can be developed through gardening. The plant devas teach humans about compassion. Plants neither question their connectedness with the holistic nature of the garden nor do they remain sentimentally attached to the outcome of the garden. They demonstrate compassion—non-attached, non-sentimental, and deep connection.

Outside the human body, Extension is focused in the plant devas. These devas are the earth angels who enact the blueprints of plants. The principle of Purity contains the blueprint of life. The deva-beings of each kingdom are devoted to holding and manifesting that blueprint. If you are contracted with Extension, the devas of the plant kingdom are your friends. You can see them from time to time—you can speak with them when your attention is in the "right" dimension.

In a very real sense, we humans are the stewards of The Garden. We work with the plant devas, we build with our hands, and we tend to all the creatures on the planet. Unfortunately, too many of us have read the imperative to have "dominion" over the earth as a license to exploit her. If you have Extension in your pattern, part of your life promise is to give an example to us all of stewardship.

Inside the human body, Extension lives in the hands. Humans have chakra points—"energetic eyes"—in the palms of the hands.

Hands are the extension of the heart, because the blood vessels that extend down the arms and to the hands are directly connected to the heart. Through our hands, heart energy gets expressed in the world. When you touch something, you bless it with your heart. When you shake hands with someone, you give them energy from your heart. When you pat someone on the back, approximately at the location of their heart chakra, you have a literal exchange of energy between people's hearts. And when you use your hands to dig in your garden, you and the earth have an intimate exchange. To become conscious of the power of your hands is to become aware of the principle of Extension.

One person with Extension in her pattern had an interesting dream a few years ago that appeared to ask her to stay at home, working in her own garden, for a while. She is a naturalist by profession, and she travels all over the world to be in different kinds of natural environments. This dream seemed odd and incongruent, but her intuition made her decide to "ground" herself for six months. She cancelled all her traveling plans, changed her lifestyle temporarily, and spent a large amount of time in her own garden. She also ate as much locally grown food as possible during that period.

Her response to the experience was quite remarkable:

> "Not traveling roots me to the soil I live on and now I realize that eating local foods does the same thing. I'm just beginning to see that perhaps our primary disconnection with nature is that the matter that makes up our cells does not come from the same air that we breathe, the soil that we walk on, nor the same quality of sunlight that warms us. What makes up our bodies is trucked, flown, and shipped to us. What an astounding disconnection!"

This student is not unique. People who wear Extension seem to do better in life when they stay rooted in their own turf, connected to the devas of their own gardens, and grounded in the life force as it expresses itself in their own backyards.

6 Regeneration

The seed of God is in us.
Now the seed of a pear tree
grows into a pear tree
and a hazel seed grows into a hazel tree
a seed of God
grows into God.

~ MEISTER ECKHART

To try to define Regeneration, let us return to the plant as a metaphor. Seeds have a drive to break forth and extend themselves. They also have a drive to recreate themselves. But they do not have the drive to create something other than themselves. An oak tree will not make a pecan. An acorn will not produce a pecan tree. The oak tree will create the acorn in order to generate more oaks.

The seedness of a being does not change. The core essence does not change.

Prior to doing this work, I had somehow gotten the opinion, through studying different spiritual systems, that the soul changes as a result of an incarnation. But now I see that the seed (soul) holds the core of the being and continues to recreate its own essential self. The external expression of the soul may change. The oak tree may change because the fire comes in and hollows it out, or a year without rain gives it a mutation in its growth. But the essential oak-ness does not change.

That is not to say that the soul is not evolving. It certainly is, but that is on another plane of existence. This information about spiritual principles is specifically addressing human life in the realm of manifestation and perceptual reality.

The Regeneration process has to do with recreating the self identically. Regeneration means participating with this great unfolding drive from within but at the same time holding an essential core that is inviolate.

Eckhart maintains that regeneration occurs in the soul of things: "God is present, effective, and powerful in all things. He is only generative, however, in the soul" (Fox, 1991, p. 251).

Eckhart again: "The Father generates his Son in the soul exactly as in his own nature. He generates him in the soul as his own, and his being is attached to the fact that he is generating his Son in the soul, whether for good or for woe" (p. 401).

Outside the human body, Regeneration resides in the plant beings. Not only do the plants hold the mirror of Regeneration in the seed, but also they are the human's primary source of nutrition and healing. The plants work with the human body in the power of Regeneration. Regeneration is the energetic drive that allows information to "flow" between cells.

The plant kingdom contains the same information that the mineral kingdom possesses but in a form that is more fluid. The mineral kingdom is not organic; therefore, minerals do not have the same ability to interface directly with humans. Humans cannot swallow rocks and break them down to derive their power. However, because the plants are primarily water and humans are primarily water, the flow of information is possible between the two. The lifeblood of all forms of organic life gives those forms the ability to recreate and regenerate themselves.

Inside the human body, Regeneration lives in the breasts. Human milk is unique in the mammal kingdom because it contains nutrients and enzymes not found anywhere else in nature. It gives the human baby the power of Regeneration.

Babies who are nursed are generally known to have a longer life, a lower disease rate, a stronger immune system, and a higher chance of surviving childhood. Women who wear Regeneration need to pay special attention to their breasts.

One of my students, after seeing that she has Regeneration in her personal fabric, commented:

"I have good-sized breasts, loved nursing my children, and always wished that I could be a wet nurse. I dream frequently of nursing or having lots of milk. I wonder if all women feel this need to nourish, or if Regeneration in your chart amplifies that?"

My guess is that Regeneration in the chart most certainly amplifies the desire to nourish. I have known many people who do not have that desire!

There is magical and mystical information contained in the breast tissue of the adult human woman that can only be accessed by her and her babies. Both literally and metaphorically, breasts and the milk that they create are the physical globes of light that carry and disseminate that information. The human breasts are like little satellite dishes that send and receive information of the most divine and subtle sort. They tune in to the state of the world. They simultaneously tune in to the heart of the woman. They radiate the heart's purest desire. When we look at the human breast, we think we are looking at physical beauty. On a more subtle (and more truthful) level, we are looking at the heart energy of the feminine consciousness.

The energy of feminine consciousness has been, throughout recorded history, a primary driving force for humanitarian transformations in our societies. Coretta Scott King was the nurturing mother behind the Civil Rights Movement in the 1960s. As Martin Luther King, Jr.'s wife, she stood by him, raised their children to be loving and kind, carried on his work when he was jailed, and took the burden of meeting his scheduled speaking engagements after his assassination. She has never stopped being a generator, and a regenerator, for the movement that catapulted her and her husband into the hateful spotlight of the truth of civil rights in our country.

Coretta Scott King has five planets in the principle of Regeneration: Her Sun (primary reason for incarnating), her Ascendant (ethical body), her Mars (physical body), her Saturn (view of the external world) and probably most importantly, her Mid-Heaven (her direct path to God). While Dr. King certainly led the march, there is every reason to believe that Coretta continually regenerated the power behind the movement. She is a stunning example of how these patterns create a design for our lives, whether or not we are aware of them. Her being, her invisible garment, was the determiner of her behavior—not her willfulness or her personal mind.

During the times that we have studied Regeneration in my classes, people with this principle had many dreams involving breasts. In one particularly interesting dream, the dreamer was able to go inside the body of a client and see the convex shape of the breasts from the inside and she was able to see where the breast tissue was or was not healthy. All of these dreams contained images that connected the breast tissue with ancient, life-empowering energy. For example, one dreamer saw her own breasts as orbs of white light, and anyone who looked at them or touched them was immediately endowed with psychic powers.

I had lunch one day with one of my students, a young man. The lunch had been scheduled for weeks, and the night before our meeting, he had a most astonishing dream. He could hardly wait to tell me.

> My brother and I were meeting our mother for lunch. (His mother is in her late 50s.) When she arrived at the restaurant, she took off her jacket and sat down. We were both astonished to see that she had a milk stain near her left breast. She followed our stares and said, "Oh, sorry, I must have leaked."
>
> My brother asked our mother how she could have milk in her breasts, being so old and all.
>
> She explained, "A woman's breast never stops flowing. She can fill a bottle anytime, anywhere."
>
> We asked about her hormones. She responded, "This has nothing to do with chemistry, dear. This is about life and women's breasts."

The dream seems to be speaking of a mystical connection between the human body and life power. Regeneration literally vibrates in the cells of all beings, through the DNA's drive to reproduce itself.

People with Regeneration in their garments possess an amplified ability to perceive subtle information, to regenerate the body quickly and efficiently, and to telepathically send and receive messages to other people. I think it has to do with Eckhart's idea of "seedness and sameness." If we are truly connected to our seedness (soul essence), we are more likely to be able to connect with that which we perceive as "other." I wonder if oak trees talk to each other?

7 Generosity

The gift, to be true, must be the flowing of the giver unto me,
correspondent to my flowing unto him.

~ RALPH WALDO EMERSON

Generosity is integral to the success of life. Generosity is a principle that
stirs a deep knowing of the importance of giving and receiving as it relates
to the perpetuation of life. The principle of Generosity reminds one that
giving and receiving are actually the same. The reciprocal nature of energy
works in that way.

Generosity brings one closer to the Reflective World. The Reflective
World mirrors a person's deepest thoughts and desires. If one lives in
a scarcity mentality, the Reflective World constantly mirrors fear and
lack. If one lives in a mindset that is in awe of life, the Reflective World
impeccably shows unparalleled beauty and wonder.

In *The Universe Is a Green Dragon*, Brian Swimme reminds us of the deepest level of this principle by saying, "The ultimate source of all that is, the support and well of being, is Ultimate Generosity . . . the root reality of the universe is generosity of being. . . . Ultimate Generosity retains nothing" (p. 146). We are that Ultimate Generosity expressed in human form. When all is said and done, when the incarnation is ended, we retain nothing, and we have given all.

Eckhart says that one of the qualities of a good person is that "one gives freely of one's material and spiritual gifts. . . . Gifts must be given because someone wants to receive them, because someone desires to improve the quality of his or her life for the sake of God" (Fox, 1991, p. 339).

A pure being comes into an incarnation solely to deliver the gifts of his
or her soul to any and all who want to receive. Generosity is one of the
foundational principles on which form is built.

> *Generosity is about sending out and taking back in. However, the*
> *master of Generosity must remember that the taking back in does not*
> *necessarily come from the expected direction. One gives freely, know-*
> *ing that it will come back in some other way.*

As Eckhart points out, we must be prepared at all times for the gifts of God—and we must be surprised by them (p. 340). If we feel that we know what gift we should receive in exchange for our giving, we are off base, and the "giving" is not really giving but bartering!

> *The animals teach humans about Generosity, especially domesticated*
> *pets. There is an unconditional outpouring of love from a domesticated*
> *animal that does not alter with any amount of inattention or abuse.*

I was surprised to hear this praise of domesticated animals from the angels. But I certainly know the deep truth of this statement from my own pets. I can forget to give them a cookie one day, or I can forget talk to them when I enter a room, and they still adore me. There is nothing conditional about the love a pet has for his or her owner. That is the kind of generosity a human needs to learn: not doormat syndrome but generosity of spirit.

Native American teachers often speak of the buffalo and the deer as being the great teachers of the giveaway. In the hunting days on the Great Plains, when the buffalo went down, all of the parts of the buffalo became a gift to the people. They used the meat, hide, sinew, bones, organs, and blood. Everything was used because it is the way to say "thank you" to the animal for laying down his life so that the people might live. Of course, we do not know what the buffalo may have felt about giving his life to the tribe, but the indigenous people felt that the way to express gratitude for the gift of a life was to use all of the gift.

Our scientists tell us that millions of years ago, the animal kingdom evolved in order to save life on the planet. Before animals, there were only the plants on Earth. An oxygen cloud of exhaust fumes created by the plants had surrounded our planet so severely that light could not penetrate, and life was endangered. Through the emergence of creatures with lungs, that oxygen became useful to a new type of being, and life was saved. In addition, these oxygen-breathing animals ate the plants, so that the plant kingdom could no longer over-proliferate. Further, animals ate each other for the same reason. Truly, the breathing animal gives the gift of life to the planet.

Interestingly, Charles Darwin had the principle of Generosity three

times in his pattern. One cannot help but wonder whether this natural alignment with the spirit of the animal kingdom might have guided his curiosity
about the human animal and its evolutionary journey. If he had been
equally as connected to the plants, might his focus been less "controversial"?
Might he have concentrated on the regeneration of life rather than the
evolution of life? How would his focus have changed without his deep
spiritual connection to the devas of the animal world?

> *Generosity is the spiritual gift of life. Giving the gift of Life and receiving*
> *life from Life is the generosity of spirit in which life lives itself.*
>
> *Inside the human body, a new chakra point is opening just below*
> *the heart at the base of the sternum. It is called the point of generosity.*
> *Spiritual energy spirals into the heart from the heart of the cosmos, and*
> *then out of the heart into all the parts of the body. The first point it hits*
> *is this point of generosity. People who are not generous of spirit, who*
> *do not live in the deepest understanding that all of life is a giveaway,*
> *struggle with restriction and limitation.*

For many who wear Generosity, this point on the body is often sore to
the touch. It is constantly reminding us to open our heart chakras more fully.
In order to deliver the gift of human spirit into form, we must be "heartful" and we must give with a heartfelt attitude.

> *It is time for all spiritual practitioners to become the agents of trans-*
> *formation. One's participation with the principle of Generosity*
> *demands that one not only transform oneself (by igniting the point of*
> *generosity), but also that he or she give that transformation a form of*
> *expression. By living in a transformed state of consciousness, one*
> *helps create patterns in the world that allow for a larger shift of con-*
> *sciousness.*

Like the animals who first breathed oxygen—which was at that time poi-
soning the world—and transformed it into something useful, it is our job
to gather the negativity of our cultures and transform it into a "yes" to life.

In this dream, a student learned abut the power of transforming energy
and the potential of saying "yes" to life from her cat.

*I was in my car in a familiar neighborhood. Zeus, my cat, was with
me. We stopped at a stop sign. Zeus leaped out of the car and jumped
on a nearby roof. He turned into a white bird. He squawked and fright-
ened off some crows which were eating the fruit of a nearby tree. He stood*

there regally for a while and then morphed into a mourning dove. He fell off the roof! I ran to pick him up screaming, "No, No." His neck was broken. Suddenly, I knew to say "yes." "Yes, yes, yes, yes." I pressed him against my chest. He morphed back in to Zeus—healthy and alive.

This dream is complex and could possibly have many levels of meaning. However, in the most direct sense, the cat taught the dreamer that each action is sacred, and that nothing—not even death—is to be denied. When the dreamer changed her "no" to a "yes," life was regenerated in her arms. The generosity of the cat and the dreamer kept life flowing.

In the classes I have taught, the students who interface with Generosity state that they feel the need to transform the concepts of giving and receiving. It is not so much a matter of learning to make sure you take care of yourself as well as others (in other words, it is not about creating a better form of an old pattern), but it is more a matter of creating a new paradigm for giving. This new paradigm needs to start with the concept that life is a gift, so the "receiving" has already taken place the moment one is born. The giving, then, becomes a gift back to life itself.

Ironically, following this line of thought, if Generosity is in our pattern, we need to transform our concept of giving so that Generosity becomes a natural outflow of our daily expression of life. Stated simply, this new paradigm requires that we *be* Generosity, not that we *do* generous acts.

8 Goodness

What is the mark of a good person?
A good person praises good people.

~ MEISTER ECKHART

Goodness is very similar to "Godness." Goodness is a knowing that one is made and carried by God's loving kindness. Humans are expressions of God. Each human is one of the many faces that God wears. To be contracted with Goodness is to live in the constant awareness that one is made in God's image. Real Goodness requires a profound connection to the level of soul that connects spirit to matter.

As I first began to meditate on the principles in 1995, I was continually amazed at the subtle and yet significant differences between our ordinary use of these words and their spiritual definition. In contemplating Goodness, we especially experience the paradox of that difference. It is hard to stay out of a mundane understanding of "goodness" as an act worthy of praise and move toward a comprehension of "Goodness as Godness," or of Goodness as a spiritual force that under girds all of creation.

If one is truly connected to Goodness, then one is deeply moved by the Goodness in other people.

Our culture teaches us, paradoxically, to look for badness—to look for what is wrong with people. It teaches us in the most incipient and subliminal ways that to praise someone else somehow diminishes us. That is one of the many lies woven into the fabric of our society.

Goodness sees goodness; Goodness praises goodness; Goodness is augmented by goodness.

Joseph Rael, Beautiful Painted Arrow, shares the Pueblo perspective of what Goodness is. He says that wood is the most consistent expression of the principle of Goodness in form. The tree itself (and the product of the tree) is God's expression of Goodness. There is no judgment in wood; there are no shoulds. There is just the Divine Perfection of the tree. When you walk on a wooden floor, your path is one of goodness. When you eat from a wooden spoon, you nourish yourself with goodness. In fact, he says, "Life is the road of Goodness" (1993, p. 13).

He also says that in his tradition, the horizontal plane represents Goodness. That is why it is important for us to go to the horizontal plane (to lie down) to dream. Literally, our chemistry changes when we recline from the vertical plane to the horizontal plane. We carry ourselves on the vertical plane; God carries us on the horizontal plane (p. 17).

Also, Rael speaks of the kiva ladder and Jacob's ladder as metaphors for the upward movement in consciousness that requires the horizontal plane's goodness. In other words, it is the horizontal step of the ladder that makes the vertical movement possible (p. 24).

Goodness is also expressed in the animal kingdom. Animals have no judgment—discernment and choices, yes, but no judgment. They do not have a sense of how things should be. They are not particularly concerned about whether "my coat looks as good as her coat." They are the masters of "as-isness."

I always laugh when someone tells me I "should" be a vegetarian. Can you imagine someone's saying to a lion: "You'd be much more healthy if you only ate lettuce"? There is a "not shouldness" in the animal kingdom that is good.

J.K. Rowling, author of the infamous Harry Potter books, carries Goodness as her primary purpose for living (her Sun principle). This brings a smile, as I think about the Harry Potter stories, and the author's particular talent for creating magical animals like the randomly exploding *skrewt*, the flying half-horse-half-bird *hippogriff*, and the buried-treasure sniffing *niffler*. More importantly, her special fondness for the massive Rubeus Hagrid, the Keeper of Keys and Grounds at Hogwarts School who teaches The Care of Magical Creatures class, is a dead giveaway that she is hopelessly enveloped in Goodness. And of course, the over-all tenor of the books invites readers to examine the power that Goodness has over every attempt to destroy it.

Animals are much better at beingness than humans. Goodness involves not judging but simply being.

The spiritual principle called Goodness is hard to define because it lives on the border between knowledge and instinct. Instinct is a kind of knowing—but it is involuntary and therefore unexamined in animals. The Goodness that is the invisible force on which both human and animal instinct are founded, however, is a force that can be examined. Humans can "feel" Goodness/Godness.

The fine line between human and animal consciousness evokes the idea of control. Control is not a bad thing—it is THE thing that identifies humans. Consider the metaphor of a mounted horse as the body being ridden by the soul. The soul MUST be able to control the direction and intention of the ride. Otherwise, it is not a ride of wisdom.

I had the following dream as we were focusing our study on the principle of Goodness in one of my online classes.

I go for a bareback trail ride on a bright azure blue horse. I've never seen a horse this color before. The trail is rugged and steep. Sometimes we go off trail and bushwhack. It's tricky for me to stay on.

We arrive at a log house with a corral and barn. I try to brush the horse. He is wild and acting nervous. I leave him in the corral and go in the house. There are four kittens by the hearth, one of which is my kitty.

Delighted to see my precious kitten, I start over to pick him up. I notice two bobcats stalking the kittens. I dream-know that they are going to eat them. I try to position myself between the bobcats and the kittens but too late. I rescue the female kitten, but not before she's been badly injured. I look up just in time to see the bobcats escape out the cat door—the two male kittens in their mouths.

I lose control of my emotions. A young boy tries to calm me, but I become absolutely inconsolable, screaming hysterically that they are killing my kitten.

Soon, my kitten comes bouncing back in the cat door, happy as can be. The other kitten follows him. They begin to play and roll around in their kitten way, as if nothing extraordinary had happened.

Recovering my emotional stability, I gather my things knowing that I need to get back on the horse and down the hill quickly. I take the kitten with me.

We saw in this dream the reminder that Goodness and instinct are almost synonymous. The horse reminds the dreamer to ride her wildness with ease and dignity. The dreamer loses control of her emotions when facing what she judges to be the certain death of her kitten. The kittens apparently did not die, did not experience emotional or physical trauma, and in fact behaved as if the threat of death were nothing extraordinary. This dream marks the line that has been drawn separating humans from instinct and encourages all who hear the dream to "ride" the wildness of their instinctual selves with dispassionate control.

In the traditional tarot deck, the major arcana card entitled The Chariot depicts a charioteer (soul) riding in a chariot (body) and holding the reins of the cats or horses (instinct) that pull it. In card #8, called Strength, the woman has woven a belt of roses. She has wrapped that belt round her waist and then twisting it into a figure 8 or infinity sign, she has also wrapped it around the neck of the lion. Again, the symbolism speaks to us of the need to take human control over, or to tame, instinct in order to use it with wisdom. However, this control in no way kills, eliminates, or denies instinct; it merely harnesses it.

Another interesting thread I see connecting people who wear Goodness is a "call to the wild." One of my students described it like this:

"In the 80s, I was a hot-shot, super-powered exec with a flashy degree, a big salary, and a big future. I went up to Alaska to chase their billions like all of the slick 80s investment firms were doing and ended up with some free time between business meetings.

I decided to go on a flight with a bush pilot—mostly because it was glamorous and would make for good dinner party conversation. But we got up there and the power of the landscape got to me. At one point, we circled high above the mountains and overlooked an expanse of wilderness that stretched to the horizon and beyond. Out of nowhere, I had the sudden thought, 'I belong out there.'"

She goes on to explain that after that experience, no matter how she tried, she could not control that wildness. She had to leave her job and move into a career that suited her Goodness.

In the human body, Goodness is focused in the kidneys. All organs are miraculous, but kidneys are masters at filtering the "good" from the "needs to be recycled."

Each time I awoke from a dream with information about the focus of the spiritual principles in the human body, I was surprised. This revelation especially surprised me. I had never thought about kidneys as organs of Goodness/Godness. However, in my readings, I have found that almost everyone who is contracted with Goodness has a special history of "kidney-ness." Many have had kidney disease or kidney stones. Others have donated kidneys for transplants or have received transplants. This connection has been an amazing discovery.

9 Awareness

When all my awareness is Yours,
what can there be to know?

~ MAHADEVIYAKKA

Awareness evokes the arousal of consciousness. The first nine spiritual principles exist "beneath" ordinary consciousness. Their impact on the process of life and the realm of form is pre-conscious for the most part. However, at this turn of the spiral, consciousness reaches a new level. It now becomes not only possible but also imperative for consciousness to begin to understand itself as a participating aspect of evolution. Awareness awakens life to a self-conscious perspective.

Mahadeviyakka, the poet who wrote the epigraph I have chosen for Awareness, was a twelfth century Indian mystic and a devotee of Shiva. Legend says that she died by disappearing into a burst of light. Her words here convey to us that Awareness is more than just an awakening of conscious attention; it is indeed a spiritual awakening to the vast possibility of oneness between the self and the Divine.

Rabbi David A. Cooper in *God Is a Verb* states that Awareness is our most precious gift. Contrary to many spiritual systems that suggest that the mind is the enemy, the Kabbalistic system teaches that it is through healthy use of the mind that we will reach our highest levels of enlightenment. Cooper reminds us that Awareness is that which differentiates us from average animal life (p. 33). He reminds us that through human Awareness, we achieve the continuum that makes a conscious evolutionary process possible (p. 34). Cooper suggests that routines and mundanity dull our expanding Awareness (p. 174). He warns against boredom, stating that the process of expanding Awareness of ourselves and the world is the fundamental reason for our existence (p. 180).

Entrepreneur and talk show host Oprah Winfrey has three planets in the principle of Awareness. She became, in many ways, the "Queen of Information" by creating *The Oprah Show*, dedicated to educating her audience to the many ways in which they could take responsibility for their lives. Oprah believes that information is power. The influence of the spiritual principle of Awareness in her life is overt.

> *Awareness is most acute when one is drifting into sleep. That moment of total blackness, unaware of self as ego but simultaneously super-aware of sounds, smells, and sensations that have no literal translation—that is the moment of most heightened Awareness. That is the moment that embodies the energetic frequency of this principle.*
>
> *The same thing happens as one slowly awakens from sleep. In that moment when everything is amplified, another period of "pregnant Awareness" occurs. Of course, one carries Awareness to greater or lesser degrees at all times. But in those particular moments on the horizontal plane, residing in the plane of Goodness and outside of one's own mental judgment, there can be flashes of truth that expand Awareness. Awareness is paradoxical.*

In this way, Awareness is a metaphor of itself. We are most aware in those moments between what we call "waking" and what we call "sleeping"—a time that we would normally call "unaware." Awareness is paradoxical. It broadens us, yes, but in ways that we may not expect or understand.

> *Human Awareness awakens the Earth's understanding of herself. It is through the self-reflective nature of the human thought process that Earth and Nature begin to feel and sense their own Awarenesses. We are a dynamic—a dimension of consciousness, if you will—that awakens a cosmic Awareness.*

Poet Yeshe Tsogyel, a second century Buddhist nun, says it magnificently:

> If you recognize me,
> Queen of the Lake of Awareness,
> who encompasses
> both emptiness and form,
> know that I live in the minds
> of all beings who live....

> *Women in Praise of the Sacred:*
> *43 Centuries of Spiritual Poetry by Women*
> Hirshfield, Editor

Awareness lives in the realms of form that are paradoxical. If one is contracted with the principle of Awareness, he or she is able to contain paradox more easily than others.

If you have Awareness in your weave, you can expand your perspective so that you include both ends of the spectrum when a duality or dilemma presents itself. If Awareness is strongly aspected in your chart, you do not have the tendency to polarize and take an unbendable position on an issue.

On the other hand, because Awareness does require one to experience both ends of a pole—both sides of a question—it is not always a comfortable principle.

Because Awareness requires that one open the spectrum of consciousness, it may actually evoke fear and cause one to intentionally close down—to put on blinders.

We do not generally like the idea that spiritual maturity may bring emotional or physical pain. Yet it is true that when we expand enough to encompass all of humanity, we encounter the suffering of humanity.

Awareness calls one to the mirror of humanity—to the mirror of the collective lack of a compassionate heart.

One dreamer was deeply puzzled to have this dream when we were studying the principle of Awareness.

> *I'm observing a large room where chickens are slaughtered and hung from hooks or ropes from the ceiling. At first I see only chickens. Then I see that they are women. Actually they seem to shift back and forth from plucked chickens to flat-chested, expressionless women. I assume they're dead but then I see one of them move her leg in discomfort as something drips down from her bowels.*

As we discussed the paradox of her having such a "dark" dream while we were studying the light and expanding principle of Awareness, one student recognized the dream as having similarities to the story of Inanna. In this story, Inanna enters the underworld in search of her sister who is apparently ill. Compassion takes her to the depths of consciousness. She ends up being stripped of all self-identity in this journey but eventually re-emerges with a new strength and a profound sensitivity to the nature of suffering. When we go into the underworld (into the hell of human suffering) with the Awareness of an awakened dreamer, we bring compassionate relief to the entirety of the human condition. Awakened dreamers can bridge the paradox between the depths of human suffering and the truth of our divine origins.

Oprah Winfrey's early life was certainly not enviable. She was passed from household to household, primarily because her mother was a single parent who did not have the time or energy necessary to give to parenting such a bright and strong-willed child. At age 14, she was sent to live with her father, whose high expectations and strong disciplinary hand helped her harness her rebellious tendencies and use them to her (and her eventual fans') benefit. Of that time she says, "If I hadn't been sent to my father, I would have gone in another direction. I could have made a good criminal. I would have used these same instincts differently."

While we do not usually look at the principles as having a "dark" side, this comment from Oprah gives us pause. Each of us does, indeed, have freedom of choice, which includes the choice to turn our blessings into curses!

In the human body, Awareness lives in the pancreas. The pancreas is the most paradoxical organ in the body. It creates a kind of sugar to balance one's sugar intake. It measures imbalances and does what it can to balance the bloodstream. Pancreatic function is Awareness expressed in organic form.

One of my friends states that her physical body is her most reliable source of information:

"It's like having the Dreamtime inside all the time—but the information is given through actual physical sensations and feelings."

She is a therapist, and she states that she can often feel the emotions and stresses of her clients as they walk in the door. People who learn to expand their awareness in this way find that their lives have meaning and purpose. Awareness allows us to bridge the gap between feeling that we are small and insignificant and uninformed, and knowing that we are also omniscient and omnipresent.

Although I have never discussed her principles with her, I, like most people in America, have followed Oprah Winfrey's public relationship to her weight gain and loss. I have often wondered if because her pattern includes the principle of Awareness, her pancreatic ebbs and flows keep her always on her toes. When the stresses of her busy life overwhelm her and seduce her away from being on task with her life's purpose, her body pulls her attention! While this is certainly conjecture on my part, it is a possibility that we might all consider as we look at our own patterns. It is a question worth considering: In what ways does the body focus points of our principles work to keep us focused in our spiritual essence?

Another client shared the following story:

"When I was four and a half, I remember finding myself in the family bathroom. The room is misty and pink in memory. I can remember the claw-footed tub and the layout of the room. I remember looking in the mirror and being given a profound awareness that I was alive. I also remember that my inner proprietary voice spoke up saying that this was a big moment. This experience has always felt foundational to me, pivotal in my awareness of myself as awake or perhaps in tune."

For this client, the principle of Awareness is in the very personal part of her chart (the first house of the zodiac), so this waking up at such a young age has functioned as a very personal, and as she calls it, pivotal experience of being embodied.

Awareness is the principle that bridges us out of the elemental (Ascending) principles of form, and into the more human (Containing) principles.

Chapter Four

The Containing Principles

The middle ten principles, numbered 10–19, are called the Containing Principles. Using a tree as a metaphor for all 30 of the principles, the Ascending ones would be the roots, reaching deep into the earth and then ascending, bringing her nurturance up toward the light. The Descending ones would be the branches and leaves, reaching high, eating the sunlight, snatching moisture from the air, and then descending in order to interrelate the tree with the heavens, so to speak. The Containing Principles would be the trunk, which create the vessel allowing for the flow of energy and the exchange of information between roots and branches.

The Containing Principles are more familiar to the human than the other two sets, because they are the principles that interconnect with human minds. These are the principles of the intellect. These are the principles that give humans their unique role of marrying heaven and earth. These are the principles of thought, creative expression, and genetic make-up.

Of course, most people have all three levels of the principles in their pattern, but usually one of the three is dominant. I have found in my work with clients that people who are heavily contracted with the Containing Principles are generally very practical. They have strong manifestation skills and they are highly creative, but they are also grounded in their ideals. These are the "doers" of the species. They provide the fuel, as well as the labor force, that keeps our societies developing.

This does not mean that they are not capable of profound spiritual work and growth, but I have found that the Containing Principles demand that the spiritual practitioner be as concerned with application as with theory. The people with dominantly Containing Principles and are the "chop wood and carry water" practitioners.

The angels of the earth reside within the Ascending Principles. The angels of heaven reside within the Descending Principles. The Containing Principles provide their connection. The angels are "programmed" to perform their functions in the cosmic order. The human must choose to do so.

When the messenger angels said this to me that winter of 1995, I did not fully understand. But as I studied the Containing Principles more closely, I realized that through these principles, which involve Creativity, Intelligence, Evolving, Resistance, and Focus (to name a few), the human is able to make the choice to do good works in the world, aligning with the angels.

Hildegard of Bingen says something similar: "Our inner spirit so announces our power in both earthly and heavenly matters that even our body can foster an intimate association in its creative power over these matters. For wherever soul and body live together in proper agreement, they attain the highest reward of mutual joy" (Fox, 1987, p. 82). In this statement, I see that Hildegard felt that the body's agreement with the soul is of highest importance in one's experience of a rewarding life. Her message to her spiritual followers was always a message of "living one's divine calling" (p. xii).

The Containing Principles help us to find the actions in the world that allow us to live our divine calling. This idea is not to be confused with "doingness." My angel messengers were clear in stating that as we truly strive to perfect our "beingness," the appropriate "doingness" will present itself to us. However, it does seem to follow that most of our actions must filter through some of the Containing Principles in order to be expressed in alignment with our soul's intent. Our Intellect, Creativity, Resistance, and Focus all contribute to the expression of spirit in form.

10 Reciprocity

For what is inside you is what is outside you,
and the one who formed you on the outside
is the one who shaped you within.
And what you see outside you, you see within.
It is visible and it is your garment.

~ THE NAG HAMMADI LIBRARY IN ENGLISH

Reciprocity, like Generosity, has to do with giving and receiving. Reciprocity is a higher octave of the principle of Generosity. But it is more than that. It is connected to karma, the great balancing force of the universe. Reciprocity guarantees that "what goes around comes around."

For example, let us say you touch a tree. Does the tree touch you as well? Yes, in a way, it does. It responds to your touch by touching back. There is a reciprocal relationship between you and that tree.

Reciprocity is also connected with vision. When you see an object with your physical eyes, you are being touched by the light it reflects to you. Also, when you see that object, the object is being touched by your mental "light," and it is therefore granted beingness through your eyes. Although an object does not literally see a human being with physical eyes, there is an exchange of light energy between the two that constitutes Reciprocity. Seeing and being seen are reciprocal.

I particularly love this idea of seeing and being seen. We are taught that we see because light strikes an object and is reflected from that object into our eyes, which then sends visual information to the brain, which then interprets the vision.

The angels indicated that there is also a light that comes out of our eyes and that through our eyes, we grant beingness to an object. The act of seeing creates an interchange of information between the person and the object. We are not sophisticated enough to know exactly how we are "seen" by that thing that we see. However, it is reasonable to understand that some form of communication occurs between the human and the perceived object.

Similarly, when we hear a sound, we allow a hearingness to happen by exchanging information with a sound frequency. The music that you hear when you go to a concert reverberates back into your body, and it literally affects your atoms. We have been able to measure the change in brainwaves created by music scientifically. We are not sophisticated enough to know how our hearing affects the frequency itself, but it is reasonable to feel that it does. The question: "When a tree falls in a forest and there is no one to hear it, does it make a sound?" has long been one of the great philosophical questions.

There is a reciprocity to every expression of life. That is because we are all One, expressing ourselves in diversity.

In one of her poems, Mechtild of Magdeburg, a thirteenth century Christian mystic, states that Reciprocity is the flow of energy between God and man.

Effortlessly,
Love flows from God into man ...
Thus we move in his world,
One in body and soul,
Though outwardly separate in form.

Women in Praise of the Sacred:
43 Centuries of Spiritual Poetry by Women
Hirshfield, Editor

Reciprocity is said to live between dimensions of consciousness—it is inter-dimensional. It is the glue that holds various levels of form and consciousness together. Think of the yin/yang symbol. It consists of the light, which contains the seed of the dark, and the dark, which contains the seed of the light. But what most people do not notice is the curved line that separates the two. That curved line is Reciprocity.

People who have Reciprocity in their soul charts often find themselves living "outside the norm." For example, Reciprocity renders argument useless. If one clearly understands Reciprocity, he or she will always search for a point of view that bridges, includes, and satisfies the greatest number of dynamics.

This comment on the principle of Reciprocity reminds me of the Native American tradition of sitting in council to solve community problems. In council, each member is like a point on a circle; therefore, each has an equal say. It has been apparent to me in the many years of holding dream circles that this form actually contributes to an expansion of group consciousness and that in this kind of expansion, we experience the magic of the principle of Reciprocity.

It is said that the core of the civilizations of the Andes (both present and ancient) is the principle of Reciprocity. The indigenous people of that land understand this principle in very profound ways, for they see themselves and all of mankind as a bridge builder between the living world and the unseen realms. Through embodying the dream, the Andean people walk their daily lives in total partnership, both with each other, and with the vast mystery of the great unknown.

I traveled once to Peru with a group of people who were there to experience our dreaming in the profoundly spiritual environments of the ancient temples there. One of the first dreams reported came from a man, who, in his dream, encountered a woman who said she would now take him to the Temple of Reciprocity.

The symbol that most clearly represents Reciprocity is the infinity sign. A linear viewpoint does not suffice when trying to understand this principle. Mirrors, figure eights, and multiple dimensions are necessary. This is the first gift humans offer to creation: the ability to see inter-dimensionally, the ability to experience life folding in on itself and then expanding again, the ability to observe breath, the ability to know that what is inside is also outside and that what is inside time is determined by what is outside of time.

This amazing statement gives each of us a profound imperative to self-investigate. What is in each of us that allows the appearance of injustice in the world? What is outside our mental reach that is choreographing our life-dance?

In the human body, Reciprocity lives in the lungs.

I understood this statement immediately, because I once heard a scientist say that on a normal breath, a human breathes in 10^{22} atoms, and then exhales 10^{22} atoms. The exact same number is inhaled and exhaled. However, they are technically "different" atoms. We primarily breathe in oxygen, we primarily breathe out carbon dioxide, but the volume is the same. This process is a perfect metaphor for Reciprocity.

One student had a friend who was suffering with pneumonia. The student consulted with her Tibetan lama teacher about what kinds of prayers were appropriate for someone with such an illness. He advised her to pray not just for her one friend but also for all people with this illness. She prayed that prayer before bed, and that night she had the following dream:

I was standing in a hospital corridor. I saw some hospital volunteers coming out of a room. They were pushing wheelbarrows full of blood. The scene was so awful that I woke myself up.

In discussing this dream, we considered the possibility that these hospital "angels" were taking her friend's blood out for a little fresh air. The two wheelbarrows suggested the two lungs that cannot properly oxygenate the blood of someone who is suffering with pneumonia. And indeed, even though she had prayed for all people suffering with the disease, her friend's pneumonia was significantly better the next morning after this dream.

Through Reciprocity, humans consciously enter Oneness. With the emergence of this principle, people become aware of the illusion of separation.

Of course, people are individualizations of the One, but Reciprocity gives us a tool to understand that Oneness. With a thorough understanding of this principle, we also gain a thorough understanding of interconnectedness. We realize that while our senses tell us we are experiencing life in separation, we can also hold the perspective that we are contributing to a great collective experience. Our sense of separation is really a gift to Unity.

One of my students, an attorney, feels that Reciprocity and the perspective that it gives her are responsible for the enormous success she has in her practice. She realized very soon in her career that she thinks differently from most people—or at least from most other attorneys. She finds arguing, polarizing, and playing tug of war to be a waste of time—boring in fact.

"I see the way around an issue or problem; I never get stuck in the prescribed routes. I don't feel bound by many conventions. I see what will work for the whole, and then I find the little people-oriented details that can make it happen."

She says that even as a little child, she knew that there had to be balance in life somewhere, somehow. As a result, she learned long ago to think "outside of the box."

"I simply could not—would not—accept that I was a victim of life."

Many people also state that they see that balance as a pendulum swing and that in the last few years the pendulum does not take as long to swing as it used to. For example, if they criticize someone for running a red light, they will accidentally run a stop sign in the next five minutes. This is one principle that easily makes itself known in our daily lives if we learn to look for it.

His Holiness the Dalai Lama has his Moon (his mastery) in Reciprocity. This discovery made sense to me on many levels. First, if our invisible garment says anything to us about reincarnation, it would be through the moon's principle. In some other time, in some other dimension, we have mastered a principle (enough) so that we carry it in this incarnation's garment as our primary threading tool.

If this information says anything to us about the Buddhist idea of karma, the balancing force of the universe, it would be this principle of Reciprocity. Who better to be the past life master of Reciprocity than the Dalai Lama himself? In his many years in exile, he has continued to preach the principle of Reciprocity, and he has encouraged his followers to treat every living being, even their enemies, with loving kindness and compassion. And finally, the Dalai Lama's Moon is in his second house, the house of personal possessions. He is known to have revealed himself as the newly born Dalai Lama and was able to identify the personal possessions of his last incarnation. Surely, this principle guides, instructs, informs, and powers his present incarnation.

11 Flowering

Near your breastbone there is an open flower.
Drink the honey that is all around that flower.

~ KABIR

This word, "Flowering," surprised me when it came through. In fact, all the words of this principle surprised me: unfolding, flowering, reptilian memory, thymus gland. They all seemed vague and almost unreachable to me as their explanations began to develop. This is the only principle that has three names. "Flowering" is used most often. "Unfolding" is also commonly used. And then occasionally, "Evolving" is used. My sense is that "Flowering" is a gentler, more sensual way to name this principle, while "Unfolding" is scientific or emotionless, and "Evolving" is a metaphysical term. In my readings, I use the words interchangeably.

Unfolding/Flowering is the evolutionary drive. It is that aspect of life that impels humans to experience themselves in higher and higher states of consciousness. It is imprinted in the atom.

Sufi poet Rumi says:

Grass agrees to die
So that it can rise up
and receive
A little of the animal's enthusiasm

Esctatic Love
Bly and Barks, 1989

The longer poem from which this verse comes expresses the idea that each level of consciousness longs for its highest expression and will lay itself down to death in order to be consumed by that higher expression. We human beings forget that we are here to lay our small selves down to be consumed by the higher expression of who we are.

Eckhart speaks of Flowering as God's delight in giving:

"It is not because of God's righteousness or strength
that he asks a lot of human beings. It is because of his great joy
in giving when he wants a soul to be enlarged. God enables the soul
to receive much so that God himself has the opportunity to give much."

~ Fox, 1991

As I understand it, Eckhart is saying here that our Unfolding, our Flowering, our Evolution as beings is God's gift to us. It is the reward we receive for taking human incarnation and participating in the great universal unfolding.

From the soul's perspective, each individual is an eternal flower in a great garden. Each human is a unique expression of oneness and a part of a great pattern of wholeness.

Hildegard of Bingen says, "The soul . . . is the firmament of the whole organism. By saturating the body with its power, the soul achieves and carries out all its dealings with us. We become, in this way, gardens in bloom . . ." (Fox, 1987, p. 117). We are constantly unfolding our soul's intent for us. In addition to being the personal imperative for our life, this intent is also universal and collective in nature. We are each inextricable parts of a pattern of wholeness.

Inside the body, Flowering is focused in the thymus gland. The thymus gland, located behind the sternum, is becoming a new center of evolutionary energy in the human.

From studies in pre-natal development, we learn that because of the size of their heads, human babies are born in a less mature state than offspring of most other mammals. Almost all other mammal babies are able to get up, walk around, and find food within a few hours of birth. Human babies take months to reach that level of sophistication. They have what is called an "extrogestation period." The thymus gland participates in the development of the body's immune system during that time, and the thymus continues to grow until puberty (Pearce, pp. 31-33). After its job is done, the thymus more or less atrophies.

However, in my meditations on this principle, I saw that the thymus gland is the position of a new energetic chakra point. Physiologically, there is not much evidence to prove that the thymus remains active in adults. But I have gathered quite an impressive amount of anecdotal evidence that the region around the thymus gland is a profoundly sensitive area in people who are contracted with Flowering.

People who suffer from various immune deficiency diseases are especially affected. We are a generation of people who are experiencing a change in the human body. The immune system is breaking down in many of us. It is either becoming more sophisticated (in the sense that it incorporates more viruses, bacteria, and so forth, and rejects fewer), or it is disappearing altogether and giving the responsibility of disease control to the central nervous system.

After discussing the idea of this new chakra point with many people, I have come to some fairly radical conclusions. My understanding of this new opening—this new energetic center that is activating an evolutionary shift—is that we are moving toward a consciousness that can access wider ranges of biological information. It appears that we are not going to be living with so much unconsciousness about our bodily functions anymore. To the extent that we so choose, we are going to be able to access more memory of evolution. We will be able to know where we have come from, how we have gotten here, and where we are going as humans.

Flowering lives in the "reptilian memory." Reptilian memory is that aspect of human consciousness that remembers the entire development and evolution of all the species on this planet. It is the Akashic record, the total memory of all that has been as well as all that could have been as well as all potential for all futures.

Reptilian memory is unconscious memory. The reptilian brain is the innermost part of the human brain. It is not a cognitive aspect of the whole organ but rather a source of instinct and image. Our connection to the evolution of life is stored in the reptilian brain. It is with the reptilian memory that humans communicate with the whales and the dolphins are the keepers of the frequency of the planet. It is with the reptilian memory that one sees angels, faeries, and ghosts. Destiny is written in the reptilian memory.

These are some of the most radical statements I heard from my messenger angels. It is certainly not common to believe that we have access to memory of evolution. Nor is it popular to believe that we can remember our future—that we have access to destiny. However, whether this information is endorsed by science or politics, most of us know that life is changing, species are evolving, and indeed, human beings are transforming.

When clients come to me for readings and I see that they have Flowering in their charts, I humorously refer to them as "cosmic lab rats." They laugh, but they almost always agree that this phrase accurately describes how they feel. If Flowering relates to their physical bodies, they have often spent most of their lives dealing with undiagnosed pain or with "atypical" disorders. If Flowering relates to their mental bodies, they have felt alienated much of their lives because they think differently from others. If Flowering is in their emotional bodies, they have struggled with anger or shame and have not really understood why. When I assure them that their job is to lay themselves down on the altar of transformation so that their highest expression of humanity can emerge through them, I literally see the tension melting away from their countenances.

Bill Clinton is double contracted with the principle of Flowering. His Pluto (his journeys into the underworld) and his Venus (emotional body) are both in Flowering. In light of the fact that it was a relative immaturity in his emotional body that led to his humiliation and impeachment, this principle shows an interesting, and unusual "dark" side. It is fascinating to contemplate the possibility that, in spite of his extreme intelligence on one level, the "cosmic lab rat" syndrome and his not-yet fully evolved reptilian unconscious brain overwhelmed him.

Clinton's entire presidency was surely filled with not only the stress of being the most powerful man in the world but also the stress of being under constant attack from his political enemies. Stress and attack evoke the involuntary memory of survival techniques in us animal beings. Clinton's emotional Flowering and his personal encounter with the underworld of his own consciousness was possibly ironically amplified and accelerated by his sexual improprieties. History has not finished writing his story.

Flowering is not an easy principle because it does involve change. However, when we understand the change, see value in it, and allow ourselves to be comfortable with it, it becomes a part of the awe of our lives rather than a dreaded aspect. When we embrace our physical, mental, or emotional processes as part of our spiritual agreements with life rather than viewing them as psychological issues, our lives become awesome and full of wonder.

One client said it this way:

"Physical pain and emotional angst have been my *twin companions* since the age of eight. I've had more diagnoses than Carter has liver pills. I think a lot of women have been crippled—not so much by the physicalness of diseases—but by our perceptions of what pain is about. Viewing pain through the lens of the principle of Flowering is the most liberating and healing experience I've ever known."

12 Creativity

Creativity is neither a rational deductive process
nor the irrational wandering of the undisciplined mind,
but the emergence of beauty as mysterious as the blossoming
of a field of daisies out of the dark Earth.

~ THOMAS BERRY

Creativity is the mental ability to go beyond the information or empirical data that is overtly present in a situation. It is the ability to juxtapose ideas, forms, and matter in ways that result in new expressions or new frequencies. Human creativity is unique because it results from the vast development of personal imagination that no other species possesses.

In many ways, the ultimate example of this principle was demonstrated by Albert Einstein, whose Mid-Heaven (his access to the level of soul) sat in Creativity. He spent his life transcending the apparent or popular understanding of empirical data, and he gave birth to an entirely new paradigm of human understanding. Of course, his great mistake came when his own mathematical investigations took him beyond the beyond, into the possibility of an ever-expanding universe. That concept over-extended his own power of comprehension, and at that point he altered his formulas (placing a constant in them so that the universe "could not" expand).

According to the story, when this creative genius looked through the Hubble telescope and saw beyond a doubt that his original unaltered equations were correct—that the universe is indeed expanding—he is quoted to have said that alteration was the greatest error of his life. Indeed, Creativity will, if we let it, take us beyond our own boundaries.

Creativity is at the heart of a deep understanding of the human's role in the cosmic unfolding.

The angels constantly remind me that we humans have the ability to dream up realities and manifest them. We contain a drive to improve and develop. In *A Spirituality Named Compassion*, Matthew Fox says, "The very heart of being creative is seeing relations between matter and form that no one has ever imagined before or that people deeply want and need to see" (p. 127). Later he expands the concept: "Creativity is the search for interdependence which is, in our terminology, the search for compassion" (p. 128). Certainly, we have not always used our creative genius to carry us to improved and compassionate ends. But at the core of the principle we find benevolence and deep connection to be the driving force for creative expression.

> *Creativity needs the innocent mind—the beginner's mind. Creativity may be seen as a higher octave of Innocence. One must always be curious and available to whatever information is present but simultaneously not be stopped by it the way a toddler can be available to whatever he or she is experiencing and exploring, but not be in any way limited or diminished by it.*
>
> *Creativity requires the confidence of a scientist's questioning mind. In addition, it requires faith. When a creative being encounters a set of phenomena, there must be a willingness to question its validity objectively, and there must be a greater trust in the experience than in the data. This is the faith of the mystic—one who first and foremost trusts his or her experience.*
>
> *This combination of innocence, questioning, and faith results in a new expression of the life force.*

As I contemplated these statements, I realized the truth of them. The only person who can truly create something is the person who is not afraid to question and not afraid to trust his or her experience. The person who is afraid will stay within the safety of that which is already created.

Walt Disney's Sun principle was Creativity. Does that come as a surprise? He maintained his dedication to the innocent mind, child-like curiosity, and an awe-struck fascination with the possibilities technology offered throughout his whole life. His true passion was Disneyland, "The Happiest Place on Earth." His gift to life, more than Disneyland or Mickey Mouse or animation or movies of the fairytales, was his creative connection to the wonder and sacredness of happiness.

> *Creativity can occur on the human level, but it can (and does) also occur on all levels of form.*

If we had a microscope that would allow us physically to see an atom of hydrogen or an atom of oxygen, we would not see anything that indicates "water-ness." But the right bonding of hydrogen and oxygen results in something that is not visible from viewing parts. That is how creativity works on the tiniest levels. This idea amplifies itself all the way through all levels of consciousness. As previously unrelated ideas or objects interrelate, new expressions are created that both include and surpass the parts.

Because Creativity is such an important part of creation spirituality theology, Matthew Fox, the prevalent champion of that philosophy, discusses it in almost all of his books. In *Coming of the Cosmic Christ*, he says, "The creative person then is a Maker of Connections who has first seen these connections at some almost unreachable level of awareness" (p. 131). In other words, the creative person has the inner microscope that perceives "water-ness" without needing to see it physically. And the creative person is driven to make those connections and manifest their results. Fox, therefore, considers the principle of Awareness to be an aspect of Creativity.

He also states that wisdom is a necessary ingredient. "Wisdom is present in creativity" (1988, p. 22). Wisdom requires connectedness; creativity requires wisdom.

Dr. Fox also encompasses Ecstasy as a part of Creativity. "Energy whose human name is ecstasy, is the proper product of authentic creativity" (1979, p. 127). According to the angels who shared these principles with me, Ecstasy—as we will see later—is the principle that reconstructs form after it has been deconstructed by Resistance. In the evolutionary process, matter continually restructures, recycles, and reconstructs itself. Ecstasy and Creativity are the forces that drive that process.

One can understand Creativity as a part of our cellular makeup through studying the new creation story in the works of Brian Swimme and Thomas Berry. The first single-cell organism lived and procreated happily for thousands of years on this earth. Then rather suddenly, its food supply ran out. The first food shortage crisis led to a massive mutational era to find a way for life to continue. One of those mutations resulted in photosynthesis— the living cell's ability to "eat" light. The plant kingdom then evolved and procreated happily for millions of years.

As mentioned in the "Generosity" section, exhaust fumes of the plants (oxygen) eventually surrounded the planet like a killer cloud. Again, the cry for creative problem solving went out, and the first air pollution crisis was resolved when an oxygen-breathing creature crawled up out of that ocean (1992, p. 62). This drive to be creative is in the DNA of our very cells.

Outside the human body, Creativity lives in the astral level of consciousness. This is the realm of psychic phenomenon, telepathy, and clairvoyance. Astral consciousness originated in the mindstuff of the cosmos that caused early life on this planet to mutate and reinvent itself. Astral consciousness is also a product of the human mind.

I found the concept of "astral consciousness" to be difficult to understand. This aspect of the angel's teachings inspired me to research the metaphysical systems that use this term. I learned that the Theosophists believe that the astral plane is not divinely inspired but is made by human imagination and intelligence (Bailey, 1955, p. 377). This level of consciousness is fraught, therefore, with error, so we must be careful when we explore the psychic realm. We must remember to question every thought and every idea to see if they feel truthful before we fully endorse any psychic information.

However, the angels indicated that the astral mind is also the *source of all new things, all potential waiting to burst into form. The creative person's imperative is to explore that realm.* Creativity, therefore, demands that one access a plane of consciousness in which new potential waits to be perceived and manifested. However, one must also know how to recognize and eliminate flawed thinking and error in the process of bringing potential into form.

We might think of such creative geniuses as Beethoven, Mozart, Hemingway, Van Gogh, Leonardo da Vinci, Warhol, and hundreds of others who struggled mightily with their "inner demons" in the process of bringing their masterpieces into the world. The astral plane is full of shadows, caves, and crevices infused with error and terror. Creativity is not for the weak of heart.

Inside the human body, Creativity is focused in the stomach. In the stomach, magical decisions are made regarding the human body: what to process, what to discard, what to break down, what to pass on. People who are contracted with Creativity have stomachs of great sensitivity and wisdom.

The concept of the stomach's being the most creative organ in the body reminded me of the spider that pulls the fibers out of her spinneret to weave her web. Perhaps, our stomachs are the organs that weave our web of physical reality, working almost totally involuntarily and unconsciously, so that we may use our conscious energy to develop our imaginations.

Bestselling author and psychologist Jean Houston's Ascendant (ethical body) is in the principle of Creativity. Along these lines, she has said, "The world is too complex for linear thinking now. To be smart in the global village means thinking with your stomach, thinking rhythmically, thinking organically, thinking in terms of yourself as an interwoven piece of nature (Ray and Anderson, p. 9). She seems to be suggesting that we must let our thinking become so organic as to be involuntary. Removing thinking from the realms of cellular consciousness strips Creativity from our living.

During one of my classes on the principle of Creativity, many of the students' dreams involved capes. We were surprised at this "uniform" of Creativity but soon realized that we had all dream-agreed on a very appropriate symbol. The cape is a *visible garment* that marks us as royalty, and it simultaneously hides us. It can serve as a signal of metaphysical authority, such as that worn by a high priestess or Merlin, or it can serve as the trappings of the dark trickster, villain, or vampire. It evokes both the hidden-ness of the most precious or sacred self and the insidious nature of secrets, errors, and lies. It can be our garment of starlight, calling attention to us— or it can be our security blanket, hiding us. It can allow us to fly or to disappear. The cape is truly the garment of Creativity.

Near the end of our Creativity class, one of the dreamers summarized this principle beautifully:

> "Creativity is a principle that insists on human incarnation. After Flowering, which suggests our place in evolution, Creativity becomes very particular and personal.
>
> As humans, we take on the huge task of organizing an immense body of energy and information and of keeping that information open to new developments. We know that every atom in our body could be 'split' to produce enormous amounts of energy, and yet all those billions of atoms are organized and interrelated in amazing ways, resonating rhythmically with one another all the time. We manage tremendous quantities of data, which include—and must include for the species to continue—the information of astral realms and beyond, and we are remaining constantly open to the ever-evolving new knowledge which is ready to be integrated into human consciousness. This particular place that we call 'me' is an amazing concentration of information and energy—consolidated, focused, 'wrapped up' in the cape of Creativity, yet also expansive, ready to fly or run and traverse other realms."

Creativity is one of the principles that allows humans to determine, guide, and influence all of Creation.

13 Intelligence

As a human being, one has been endowed with
just enough intelligence to be able to see clearly
how utterly inadequate that intelligence is when
confronted with what exists.

~ Einstein

*Intelligence is the ability to respond to information. It is the ability that
two atoms or two subatomic particles use to communicate data to
each other and to respond accordingly.*

*Atoms respond to each other, subatomic particles respond to each
other, and larger organisms respond to each other through the principle of Intelligence. They all share information. Intelligence is an
information-management system, interfacing with all the other principles. It exists in the spirit of a being, not in his or her biology.*

Meister Eckhart says, "The intellect is capable of receiving the universe. . . . Man's similarity with God consists in his openness to the totality
of what is . . . the intellect is naturally connected with the universe" (Fox,
1991, p. 119). Human intelligence is both limited and boundless. Our belief
systems and our perspective limit it. It is boundless because we are cellular
constructions.

As was discussed in the section on "Beauty," the materials that make
up our cells have come from the stars of other galaxies and solar systems.
We are literally beings of the heavens and anything that has happened in
the universe is embedded in our cellular consciousness. In another sermon,
Eckhart says, "The pure and unadulterated power of the intellect is what
the masters of the spiritual life call receptivity" (p. 390). In other words, our
ability to receive the information of the cosmos comes from the power of
our Intelligence.

Intelligence exists in the micro-universes of the human species. Forms are constantly interacting with other forms, seen and unseen. Whatever has bonded together through shared information is interactive. Sodium interfaces with chloride and salt results. Iron interfaces with oxygen and iron oxide results. You interface with another person and friendship results.

There is always an exchange of information and an exchange of energy in the realm of form. In the human realm, this interaction becomes even more sophisticated—or at least more observable. Humans are a configuration of micro-universes that bridge all appearances of separation. Humans experience psychic knowing, telepathic communication, and clairvoyance. Humans are like a hologram of the earth, and they have the unconscious ability to exchange information with every aspect of form.

Rupert Sheldrake's theory of morphic fields of resonance helped me to understand Intelligence as the angels seemed to be describing it (1988, p. 106). Morphic fields are invisible rhythmic patterns of activity that store information (p. 108). Much like a field of gravity, any form that comes into resonance with a morphic field operates according to its rules. According to Sheldrake's theory, we do not store data in our brains, but rather we have specific DNA programming that allows us to resonate with certain morphic fields of information, thereby accessing the data stored there (p. 136). This concept seems to align with the angel's spiritual definition of Intelligence as an information-management system that allows interaction between atoms, cells, organisms, species, and so forth.

This thought-provoking definition of Intelligence reminded me of the story of the hundredth monkey. As reported by Ken Keyes, Jr., a certain species of Japanese monkey was observed in the wild for a period of over 30 years. In 1952, on the island of Koshima, scientists were dropping sweet potatoes in the sand for the monkeys to eat. The monkeys liked the taste of the raw sweet potatoes, but they apparently found the dirt unpleasant. An 18-month-old female primate named Imo found she could solve the problem by washing the potatoes in a nearby stream. She taught her mother and her playmates to wash their potatoes, and her playmates in turn taught their mothers.

This habit was gradually transmitted to many monkeys on the island, and the scientists noted when each new primate learned the skill. Eventually, all the young monkeys learned to wash the sandy sweet potatoes.

The older monkeys were a little slower than the younger ones to grasp the new idea.

Then something startling happened: A certain number of these monkeys were washing sweet potatoes. The exact number is not known, but for purposes of the story, Keyes says that one day there were 99 monkeys on Koshima Island washing their sweet potatoes. That day, one more monkey—the hundredth monkey—joined them. Suddenly, on that very day, the habit of washing sweet potatoes jumped across the water. Amazingly, monkeys of the same species living on other nearby islands began washing their sweet potatoes (p. 12).

The story has been used to demonstrate that when a critical number of embodied beings integrates a new level of consciousness or a new habit, the information may be communicated from mind to mind. Apparently, the rhythmic pattern of a behavior amplifies as more and more beings participate, giving that pattern enough intensity to entrain other rhythms. Sheldrake might say that the information penetrated a monkey morphic field and became universally available to all monkeys who had similar DNA resonance.

Jane Goodall, the famous and revolutionary researcher of chimpanzees, is contracted with Intelligence (Sun principle). Because when she began her research she was not a trained scientist, she used highly unconventional methods to gather information about the chimpanzee's social structures, physical environments, and their personalities. Her findings disproved many of the "scientifically based" conventional ideas about chimpanzees, including the long-standing myths that only humans made and used tools, and that chimps were passive vegetarians (indeed, they murder and eat the meat of their victims).

Most importantly, because she suspended traditional learning techniques in favor of direct observation and interaction with her "clients," Goodall's use of the principle of Intelligence discovered the intelligent nature of the lives of chimpanzees. She has documented their complex social structures, sophisticated tool-making and lifestyle-determining systems, and advanced organizational structures within their family and clan groups. Intelligence recognizes intelligence. It bypasses linear learning and incorporates direct experience. It allows information-sharing to be the driving factor in the learning process.

Intelligence is not a mental process. It is an information-sharing process that transcends time and space.

Having Intelligence in your pattern indicates that one of the gifts you are delivering to life is the ability to interface clearly with information. Giving, receiving, and responding to data are easy and natural to you. However, in order to mature your use of this principle, you must learn to listen and search dispassionately. You know you are using the principle of Intelligence to its highest spiritual advantage when you are able to recognize error and eliminate it quickly and ruthlessly from your web of beliefs.

In the body, Intelligence is concentrated in the nervous system. The human nervous system, without judgment or bias, gives and receives data intercellularly in the body.

When a group of us studied the principle of Intelligence together, we learned some interesting things about the physical bodies of people who have it in their charts. Intelligence seems to create super-sensitive bodies. These sensitivities are not just local. In other words, these bodies seemed to react as violently to change in atmospheric pressure or to a hurricane hundreds of miles away as they did to eating something disagreeable to their system. Learning to trust this kind of sensitivity and "flow" with it has been a life-long challenge for these students.

Interestingly, the people who were Intelligence had a greater propensity for dreams that contain no stories but instead are simply images of geometric forms, grid lines, swirling eddies, and sparks of brilliant color. It appeared to us that these people could literally interface with the morphic field and its storage banks directly in the dream.

The largest struggle for people with Intelligence in fused garments seems to be differentiating between mental capacity and raw intelligence. This class occurred during the election contest between Al Gore and George W. Bush. We had some good laughs when we discovered that Bush, not then known for his mental sharpness, has his sun in Intelligence. At the time, he served as a good example for us all to remember the difference between the spiritual and the social definitions of this principle.

People who rely on their wit to guide them through life will sometimes override the abilities and wisdom of their physical bodies. Instead, they lean on mental beliefs and linear thinking to guide their choices. As we studied this principle, many of the students commented that they realized that they had trained themselves not to allow pure Intelligence to have a voice in their lives. However, by the end of that phase of our study, most students had begun to realize that listening to their body's Intelligence, by paying careful attention to their physical intuition, they held the key to all the other principles. Indeed, the morphic field of human wisdom can best be opened by allowing one's spiritual Intelligence to develop.

14 Ecstasy

We came from the light,
The place where light came into being
Of its own accord
And established itself
And became manifested through their image

~ Gospel of Thomas, Logion 50

Ecstasy is simply the Divine flow of energy. It is energy (or light) flowing with absolute freedom to express itself and experience itself.

Phenomenology is the study of immediate experience. According to the theory of phenomenology, what you are experiencing through your body in the present is the only reality—everything else is theoretical. It is the "be here now" theory of the 1960s; it is the basis for Eckhart Tolle's popular *The Power of Now*. It claims that we experience a good portion of our lives by remembering, analyzing, re-thinking, re-structuring, and projecting what has already occurred and is no longer present. Phenomenology is about being perfectly present to what is happening now. Phenomenology is also about Ecstasy.

To live the principle of Ecstasy does not mean that you are a Rumi-esque mystic wandering around in eternal spiritual bliss. It means that you are carrying the potential to be always new, always awake, always creating the present. Life is living itself through you very intensely in every moment.

Ecstasy occurs when all of one's bodies (physical, emotional, mental, spiritual, and energetic) are perfectly aligned so that energy is able to express itself truthfully though you. It is not so much an experience of orgasmic proportion as it is an experience of deep wakefulness. Your whole being is alive and alert—awake to its reality.

People who wear Ecstasy often find that slow, intentional physical movement gives them a strong sense of being present to the Divine. Body prayer and other types of moving meditations are sources of Ecstasy for these people.

Ecstasy is the experience of a personal God. Each being is a unique configuration of energy. When one's physical, mental, emotional, and spiritual bodies are in alignment with their principles, the ecstatic experience of now occurs.

In a very real sense, this information gives us a way to define a personal God. The principles show us that each person has a totally singular way of defining or creating a boundaried arena through which God can speak. When we experience an alignment with our pattern, we create a definition—a vehicle—through which God's energy can move into expression more perfectly. That creation is the experience of Ecstasy. You do not need Ecstasy in your chart to have this experience, of course, but if you do have it, the ecstatic experience also helps define you—your individuated self—more clearly.

Poet, actress, playwright, civil rights activist, and educator Maya Angelou's Sun is in Ecstasy. Her talent with crafting words to create transcendent experience is the vehicle through which she delivers Ecstasy to the realm of form. Her rhythm and grace with words create for her readers a universe in which racial division and class hierarchy dissolve. Wholeness, oneness, the kinship of us all resonate in every piece she has written. She spoke the words of Ecstasy in an interview for *Mother Jones* magazine: "The most delicious piece of knowledge for me is that I am a *child of God*. That is so mind-boggling, that this 'it' created everything, and I am a child of 'it.'" It means I am connected to every thing and every body."

Art patron Gertrude Stein's Sun was in Ecstasy. She is particularly interesting, because it was not her direct talents but rather her eye for talent that became her primary vehicle for embodying Ecstasy. Without her generosity and philanthropy, many of the great artistic masters of the impressionist, cubist, and early modern period may have been unnoticed.

In the human body, Ecstasy expresses itself through the adrenals.

The adrenal glands, tucked above the kidneys, keep a human balanced in the face of fear and stress. As soon as a signal comes from any part of the body that there is distress, the adrenals pump out the needed hormones to create balance and right use of energy.

The adrenals are an extension of the central nervous system; therefore, Ecstasy is connected to Intelligence through this physical connection.

The messenger angels seem to be saying that Intelligence, which is focused in the central nervous system, and Ecstasy, focused in the adrenals, work hand-in-hand within the physical body. These principles inform and communicate with each other so that when the physical body is healthy and not over-stressed, it can be a clear vessel for experiencing the awe and wonder of life without the burden of misinformation.

Ecstasy is the white hole of creation out of which everything spews toward manifestation. For anything to exist, it must experience itself as ecstatically connected to its source.

Again, we and all life-forms are made of light (stardust). The more fully we understand this concept, not as a poetic analogy but as an actual fact, the more clearly we align with our purpose for living. When one is simultaneously aware of the connection to Source and fully present in the mundane world, the energy flows without blockage: Ecstasy occurs.

The following dream was one shared in our circle during the week that we studied Ecstasy:

I feel heavy, in pain, burdened. Someone is moving my body from side-to-side. Someone else is holding my head—like in cranial sacral work.

Suddenly, I drop down into the ocean. Strange mutated dolphins float by and then a most grand turtle takes me to her home. I feel awe. I see my dream circle there also. She smiles at me and says, "My dear sister, listen and know I have taken you and your sisters deeper than you've known or remembered." She hands me a hollowed-out stone cylinder, which was formed from broken stone millions of years ago. Within it is a spectrum of colors never imagined. I then take the dream group inside and—oh— the colors—very vivid—very vivid and swirling against darkness. There are red, purple, green—every color. We all became the color that suited us; we turned into fishes—electrifying, flying fish! God appeared in the form of a woman whose face was hidden by a veil that was heavily beaded. She said, "I am She—I am She—be my breath—be my whisper—be my body." She then took the stone and it became a beam of red light, which seemed to take us back, back, back through all civilizations.

One member of the class responded to this dream like this:

"I feel that this dream was truly a message of the truth of Ecstasy. If any of us feels a burden, emotional, physical, or even a burden of schedule and mundane stress, it is possibly because we do not remember that all form is light. Our mantle is the mantle of light. We are bodies of light."

In our group study of the principle of Ecstasy, we were surprised to find that some people who wear the principle experience ecstatic feelings more in dreaming, while others experience them more in the waking body. We were not able to discern the clear reasons for the difference. But we did find it interesting that unlike the other principles, this one seems to be dominantly felt in either the dreaming body or the waking body but not in both.

One of the students described her experience with the principle this way:

"The body can take me to Ecstasy, and therefore to clarity, more easily than any level of consciousness. There have been stressful times in my life that would be physically difficult for my friends. Those times didn't seem hard to me at all because I was intensely involved with movement. I was either teaching aerobics, running, walking, or in some way working up a sweat everyday. This daily movement kept me in the present moment, and I knew that none of the dramas around me were real."

Because her mental, emotional, and physical bodies were in alignment with her spiritual body, she experienced Ecstasy rather than pain and anguish during these rough times.

Ecstasy is a principle of high energy, profound creativity, and deep aware-ness. It gives every spiritual practitioner access to awe. It brings every human to the threshold of Creation.

One question that comes up often for students of this information is, "Do the principles ever have negative effects on personalities?" In other words, is there a shadow side to the principles? My contemplations on the princi-ples and direct transmissions from the angels about them indicate that the answer is no. The principles are blessings, not curses. The principles hold us in blessing no matter what happens to us in our lives. However, I must also say that I have noticed that my clients who struggle with addiction to drugs and alcohol often have Ecstasy in their charts.

Although he is not a client (I have never met him), I found it fascinating to see that Robert Downey, Jr. has Sun, Moon, Ascendant, and Pluto in the principle of Ecstasy. His notorious battle with addiction, in fact, is what prompted me to look at his chart in the first place. The question then is this: Does Ecstasy's relentless pull toward experiencing divine connection also drive a personality to finding alternative routes there? Does Robert Downey, Jr.'s urgent and essential need for the experience of connection to what Maya Angelou called the "it" that created everything also create his helplessness in avoiding the use of mind-altering drugs?

We do not know the answer. My feeling is that Ecstasy is what holds addicts to life, not what drives them to use drugs. The power of the energy of Ecstasy is the web that keeps them from disappearing into their dependency. However, I must admit that of all the principles in the chart of 30, Ecstasy is the one that appears in the charts of my most troubled-by-daily-life clients.

15 Resistance

Jesus was perhaps the most active resister in known history.
This was non-violence par excellence.

~ GANDHI

In order for you to understand Resistance as a spiritual principle, we must redefine it. The classic meaning of the term (opposition or defensiveness) is deeply embedded into your consciousness because of your psychological association with the word. From the spiritual point of view, however, Resistance is something else altogether. Resistance is a friction that causes energy to experience itself, transform itself, and realign itself with greater purpose.

The spiritual definition is similar to the physicist's understanding of the word. Resistance, from a scientific point of view, is an interference pattern. It is that which creates the opportunity for quanta (little teeny tiny pieces of matter) to feel themselves.

According to Newton's law of movement, if something is projected in a straight line, it will continue in a straight line until it meets Resistance. Therefore, it will not even know itself until it meets some sort of force that redirects its movement.

Resistance in your chart means that you are acting as an insertion (interference pattern) into the collective. You are inserting something that interrupts the flow of energy and allows a creative interfacing with form.

Because Resistance is a strong thread in my weave and because the term is particularly meaningful to me, I received much of the information about this principle in the second person. Usually, the angels spoke to me in the third person, but with this principle I often heard "you." I felt that I needed to hear this information personally. I began to wonder exactly what kind of interference pattern I was establishing.

I immediately thought of Rosa Parks, the amazingly brave woman who, after a long day's work, refused to stand up and give a white person her seat on a racially segregated Birmingham bus. Imagine my surprise when I looked up her chart and discovered that she is double contracted with Resistance. Her Sun is conjunct her Mid-Heaven at 15° of Aquarius. In that important moment in December of 1955, she established an interference pattern that came from the depths of her own integrity. At that point, the entire Civil Rights Movement crystallized, organized, and harmonized around the philosophy of nonviolent direct action.

Forty-three years later, when he gave her the Congressional Medal of Freedom, Bill Clinton said of Rosa Parks: "Her action that December day was in itself a simple one, but it required uncommon courage. It . . . began the remarkable journey that has brought the American people closer to the Promised Land we know it can truly be."

One hundred and thirty seven years earlier, President Abraham Lincoln made a similar statement about another female resister. When he met Harriet Beecher Stowe, author of *Uncle Tom's Cabin*, he said, "Is this the little woman who made this big war?" Harriet Beecher Stowe's Uranus is in the principle of Resistance. The Uranus principle lets us know ourselves authentically; therefore, Resistance was a natural course for H.B. Stowe. Harriet's father and all seven of his brothers were respected ministers who put great emphasis on morals and ethics. She, however, was the loudest voice of ethics in the country at that time, selling over 3,000,000 copies of her provocative anti-slavery novel.

We who are students of the path of peace are mystics—here to interfere with the old patterns.

In quantum physics, the perceiver and the perceived cannot be separated. They are reciprocal because the perceiver "interferes" with the perceived by simply observing. Then the question is this: Until there is a perceiver, does the perceived even exist? The resister is the perceiver who creates the tension or friction that allows the perceived to impact itself.

Physicist Wolfgang Pauli created a mathematical explanation for something called the "exclusion principle." In a nutshell, it states that two things cannot exist within the same quantum space—they resist each other. Things develop a resistance to each other because they have rights as creative aspects of the universe—the right to be. The fact that something *is* gives it a place in the physical universe (Wolf, 1984, p. 141).

Technically, we only experience anything—or anything only experiences itself—through relationship. If there is no "friction," there is no calling up of the experience of self.

Think of an electrical circuit. There is a source of energy—say a dam. The energy is harnessed and runs through a circuitry that involves a resistor. The resistor is the interference object that takes the power from the dam and transforms it into appropriate units so that you can plug in appliances at your house without receiving the full energetic potential of the dam.

Because you have Resistance in your contract, you are a "resistor" in the flow of divine energy. You receive energy from the cosmos and transform it into appropriate messages and/or information for humanity. You play a role in the efficient use and expression of cosmic energy. Your goal is to transform the energy, not to conflict with it.

Resistance is integral to Creation. Resistance provides the avenue through which humans can feel otherness. This otherness allows humans to experience self-consciousness.

Resistance resides in the realm of self-consciousness, which is the realm of understanding self—being aware of self. One of the many ways in which a human being can experience himself or herself is as an individuated self with a higher Self to serve as guide and inspiration. Resistance lives in the level of consciousness that allows humans to contemplate themselves as self.

As a resister (one who is contracted with Resistance), you have a special "place" in the universe story. You help define the "isness" of things as they bump up against each other. You give particles, (or ideas, or energy) a definition that allows them to experience themselves in form. You help protect the viability of the "things" in the universe.

Sometimes, this experience leads to painful or even violent interaction among things. When systems close and no longer accept new energy (transformation), they begin to kill themselves by clashing violently with other systems. As a resister, you then become a diplomat, a negotiator.

Resistance is the principle that constantly deals with the marriage between spirit and matter. One energy is fine and subtle, the other dense and gross. They often cannot find ways to merge gracefully within the human system. That is your job: finding pathways within self-consciousness for energies to marry and therefore bring out their potential.

When Gandhi made the statement I used at the beginning of this section, he was, of course, speaking of Jesus as a nonviolent demonstrator against the injustices of his day. However, if you apply the esoteric definition of Resistance and resister to Jesus, it also fits very nicely. Jesus is our most powerful human example of the marriage between spirit and matter.

If you have the principle of Resistance in your chart, you may be destined to be a spiritual teacher. If you can, in fact, learn to understand the principle and harness it correctly (beneficially for yourself and for others), you can become a transmitter of power to other people.

Llewellyn Vaughan-Lee, a Sufi teacher, describes this idea in his book *Catching the Thread.* "The teacher is the transformer, transforming millions of volts into the one or two hundred necessary for individual use. Through the teacher, the seeker can connect with the energy of the Absolute" (230). Of course, if you have Resistance in your chart, you will not necessarily reach the stage of spiritual teacher in this lifetime. You may be practicing—building up your mastery for future lifetimes.

> *In your body, Resistance lives in the muscles. In order to lift something, in fact, in order to move at all, a complex system of muscles resisting gravity and other muscles must occur. Your muscles, their strength or lack thereof, will tell you about your self— your ability to identify as self and Self. They will also tell you about your power in the realm of form.*

During the portion of our class when we studied Resistance, I had a personal realization that has changed my self-concept profoundly. I worded it thusly to my students:

> "Resistance is a word used often in the psychological field—
> and in that context it means that you're not doing what you
> should be doing—that you are being willful in the choice not
> to do or experience or feel something. During this time of
> studying Resistance as a spiritual energy that transforms,
> modifies, and makes cosmic energy appropriate for human
> consumption, I have come to understand myself in a totally new
> light. Everything about this information is liberating for me, but
> nothing is so freeing as being liberated from the psychological
> 'brand' of being resistant and being delivered into the concept
> of myself as a transformation tool for spirit."

Another student responded and summarized beautifully:

> "Resistance has always felt like an energetic allergic reaction to me,
> one that has sent me into intolerable waves of frustration and
> irritation, which made me want to run away and withdraw and
> resist the Resistance. Yet I can see how it is the push of Resistance

that moves things and makes the space to create anew. The interplay between Ecstasy and Resistance truly is what creates everything. Is that why it is smack in the middle of the Containing Principles? In fact, isn't all form the manifestation of Resistance?"

16 Unity

All that exists in the universe traces back to an exotic, ungraspable
seed event, a microcosmic grain. . . . Every being in existence
is integrally related to this primordial Flaring Forth.

~ BRIAN SWIMME AND THOMAS BERRY

*To define Unity, let us start with the metaphor of the seed. The seed of
anything has its core, and to get to that core—the shell has to be broken. A seed creates what it is programmed to create: An acorn will not
ever create a peach tree because life regenerates sameness.*

In *The Universe Story*, Brian Swimme and Thomas Berry present a
comprehensive creation story that is predicated on the fact that everything
in perceptual reality is made of the same "stuff" because it all—rocks, fish,
fliers, crawlers, minerals, atoms, humans, orangutans, oceans, stars—came
from the same seed. We are all the children of the original flaring forth of
perceptual reality out of the great cosmic void. While we take multiple
forms and while each of us is faithful to recreating our individuated form,
we are still a "multiform development in which each event is woven together
with all others in the fabric of the space-time continuum" (p. 21).

*Each human being is the result of a genetic line, which is one of the strands
that sews the fabric of the cosmos together.*

This strand—our own genetic lineage—gives us an opportunity to
know our sameness with other humans. We know our unique self as being
the result of our genetic lineage. We are in Unity with our lineage.

In indigenous tribal cultures, this lineage is called a clan. In our modern society, we are not so clan-conscious. In fact, most of us are more or less
separated from our extended families. But none of us can separate from our
biological Unity.

Life longs to see itself mirrored in itself. Life, through DNA, is pro-grammed to recreate itself in images of itself. This principle of Unity is the expression of life that identifies itself in partnership with itself.

Thomas Berry also speaks of Unity in his book *Dream of the Earth*: "Our bonding with the larger dimensions of the universe comes about primarily through our genetic coding. It provides the constant guidance in the organic functioning that takes place in all our sense functions: in our capacity for transforming food into energy: in our thought, imaginative and emotional life" (p. 108). He goes on: "The human, we must understand, is genetically coded toward a further transgenetic cultural coding whereby we invent ourselves in the human expression of our being" (p. 200). In other words, our very humanness *is* Unity. We are one because we are like each other. Our genetic lineage guarantees that we will mirror that likeness to each other.

Eckhart explains it in a more complex way: "Unity is a negation of nega-tion and a denial of denial. What does unity mean? Unity means that nothing has been added. . . . All creatures carry a negation in themselves; one denies that it is the other.

. . . But God is the negation of negation; He is one and denies every other, for outside God there is nothing" (Fox, 1991, p. 190). Eckhart is saying that Unity negates our belief that we are separate and non-alike. People who wear the principle of Unity are here to develop, evolve, and share that under-standing.

Matthew Fox further explains what Eckhart is saying, "Unity is some-thing purer than goodness and truth. Goodness and truth add something—but unity and purity subtract" (p. 196).

Rabbi David Cooper in his book *God Is a Verb* uses the human body as a metaphor for the principle of Unity. If we look at the human body through a microscope, we see hundreds of millions of individual cells, each performing its own task. Yet each has a set of chromosomes identical to every other cell in the body. We can choose to focus on the separation of each cell or on the unity of the wholeness of the body (p. 39).

Outside the human body, Unity lives in the genetic lineage—in the gene pool. People who are contracted with Unity are often cleansing or purifying the gene pool. Aspects of the lineage that are not serv-ing the greater family of man will be eliminated through these people. Aspects of the gene pool that are strong, benevolent, and important to the evolution of the species will be amplified in them.

A surprising number of the late twentieth century First Ladies of the United States have Unity in their invisible garments. Every principle, depending on where it appears within the pattern, affects behavior and life experience in different ways. It is interesting to compare these women, as they all had a profound impact on our culture.

Eleanor Roosevelt's Ascendant (ethical body) was in Unity, which perhaps sheds light on her choice not to divorce FDR when she discovered his affair, and it also speaks to her complex decisions between holding her family together and becoming the ultimate spokeswoman for the family of humanity. Lady Bird Johnson's Mars (physical body) was in Unity. Pat Nixon's Saturn (the way she perceives the realm of form), Rosalyn Carter's Pluto (her deep introspection), and Hillary Clinton's Mercury (mental body) were there, too. Mrs. Johnson, Nixon, Carter, and Clinton all had teenage-becoming-adult daughters while in the White House. Their fierce protection of their daughter's privacy is noteworthy. Barbara Bush's Moon (mastery) and Mid-Heaven (direct connection to the soul) are in Unity. Her loyalty to family is unquestioned. Nancy Reagan (like Hillary Clinton) had Mercury (mental body) in Unity. Although the two of them are rarely compared, they were both certainly strong-minded First Ladies who had profound influence on their husbands' politics.

Each of these woman had unique challenges during her White House years. Some had marital difficulties to overcome. Some (perhaps all) received harsh criticism from the press. Some had addictions that overwhelmed them. Some encountered the deep and tragic social issues of our spiritually arid culture. But all of them had a strong genetic background—a lineage of faith, family, commitment, and unbending strength of character. Unity brings those characteristics to people who have it woven into their personal garment.

Inside the human body, Unity lives in the ribs. The rib cage is the sacred container for the vital organs. It protects the delicate parts of the body so that they can do their work. This is the same function that the genetic patterning plays in the being. The basic structure is strong and protective so that the nuances and subtleties can emerge.

In our class study of Unity, one of the participants expressed the paradox she feels with this principle:

"Unity is an unusual double-edged principle. It involves understanding ourselves as a unique result of a genetic lineage. It also involves transcending any sense of separation so that we can envelop Unity Consciousness in its purest form. But it's as if first we must understand our separateness and our special-ness before we can comprehend the Unity of all beings."

This dream speaks to that genetic lineage aspect of our beings.

I see a Princess dressed in a lavender flowing gown; the whole atmosphere is faintly lavender. She is being told her life story and is rather bored. She doesn't want to be a Princess. However, she is instructed that lineage is very important if understood correctly. I don't know if she's getting it, but I as the observer hear the information: It's all the special connections that are made through the generations, the serendipitous events that lead to people meeting and matching. It's portrayed not as a straight line or a genealogical tree, but as a zigzag going from one bright point to another, like lines that connect the stars to make constellations— with no beginning and no end.

As the study of Unity unfolded, we encountered more dreams in which the dream character "did not want to know" or "was bored" by what the dream was revealing. One student commented:

"It seems to me that Unity combines both the absolute uniqueness of each of us (the prince or princess—in Hasidic tales, the princess is always the beloved daughter of God) and our simultaneous total connection to the universe."

The princess who does not want to know—does not want to be contaminated with crumbs—is like a person trying to hide the skeletons in the closet.

Another student shared an interesting story of a client of hers who is married to a Jewish man. Although she has not converted to Judaism herself, she has spent most of her adult life celebrating the Jewish traditions. She has been plagued with the horrors of the holocaust, and she feels a profound sorrow when she contemplates the events in Nazi Germany.

Her mother died just a few years after she married, and this client went to clean out her mother's home. In looking through a box of pictures, she found a photograph of her great-great grandfather—in a Nazi uniform. She realized, as her eyes locked onto his, that indeed we are all one, and that what any of us does reflects on and in all of us. That moment helped her understand the importance of healing any shred of racism, hatred, violence, fear, terror, and agony in herself so that it may be healed in generations past and generations to come. This story is a story of Unity.

17 Attraction

In the branch of mathematics known as dynamics,
attractors represent the limits toward which dynamic systems are drawn.
. . . The attractors are not fixed for all time. . . .
Their structure depends on what has happened before.

~ RUPERT SHELDRAKE

Humans believe they are lacking. Humans seek life partners who possess the qualities they wish they had. However, the deeper truth is that humans are holistic— parts of a greater Whole. They lack nothing.

It is true. Almost every human feels that he or she is lacking something. That something can be physical, material, psychological, or spiritual. We put a great deal of our energy, consciously and unconsciously, into obtaining what we think we lack. How ironic to consider the idea that we lack nothing.

In polarized or dualistic reality, opposites attract. That is a law of gravity—it is a mathematical, scientific fact. However, it is also a magical and mysterious fact. Brian Swimme describes it this way: "Gravity is the word used by scientists and the rest of us in the modern era to point to this primary attraction. . . . The attracting activity is a stupendous and mysterious fact of existence" (1984, p. 44).

Attraction is one of the truly magical and mysterious aspects of form. Attraction brings us together and holds us together. It is that inexplicable, yet primary, force that motivates all relationships. The Earth's relationship to the Sun is determined by Attraction; your relationship with your lover is determined by Attraction. In a very literal sense, we exist because Attraction exists.

On a level of truth that transcends psychology, humans are naturally attracted toward that greater Wholeness and toward a consciousness of human wholeness.

In just the last few years, the human genome code has been broken—

or at least cracked. We now know something that devastates our smug, racist, separatist, egocentric belief systems: We are all one. Biologically, we are all but identical. We came from one mother, so to speak, and she came from Africa. In a very real sense, everyone in America is African-American. It diminishes racism to an illusion, does it not?

However, the human genome code does not tell us about our spiritual DNA. It does not tell us what that early African Mama cherished and valued, and it does not tell us why we place importance on certain behaviors, ethics, and ideals. Many esoteric and mystical systems give us clues about the human's spiritual DNA. And in fact, the principles of this system are a study of that encoding.

Attraction is the strand of the human soul's DNA that encodes humans to remember wholeness.

Rupert Sheldrake explains that in the mathematical system known as dynamics, there are attractors that are affected by history, and they affect the present as it moves into the future (1988, p. 304). Attraction, then, is affected by the past, and it pulls us toward the future. In the realm of physics, Attraction is gravity. In the realm of soul, however, it is something else entirely. When viewed through a spiritual lens, Attraction becomes the power that calls us to remember our wholeness, to remember unity, to remember that we are all aspects of the One.

During our class on the principle of Attraction, we discussed our desire to "go home"—that nagging pull we all experience to find our seed-selves and reside in that state of consciousness. We came to the conclusion that in a sense we are all "divinely homeless." We left *home* to come into the realm of form to deliver a divine message. Most of us have forgotten the message, forgotten the purpose of the mission, and become very lost in the process of "making a home" (gathering money, things, security, bank accounts, houses, careers, families, personal identity).

Attraction expresses the active interplay between the perceived and the perceiver.

Once, a Native American elder took me on a long, magical walk. We came upon a little natural dam in the river. Water dripped through a teeny tiny space in the dam. There was a recognizable, even drip-drip-drip pattern. He stopped me and told me to put my head down next to the water dripping, and listen carefully to the pattern. Then he said, "Now, change the pattern with your ears." By sending energy out my ear, the drip-drip-drip pattern changed to drip-drip, drip-drip, drip-drip. The interplay between the perceiver and the perceived determined the pattern. My hearing and the movement of the water interrelated in this way.

> *Attraction is the ability to interweave and merge with that which is perceived as "other."*
> *Attraction resides in humanity's cross-cultural understanding of life.*

Yes, we see ourselves as individuated selves. Yes, we see ourselves as extensions of our gene pool. But beyond that, we also see ourselves as members of the Human Family. No matter what color our eyes, we can recognize kinship in the eyes of another human. When African shaman Malidoma Some looks into my eyes and calls me mother or sister, I recognize my deep kinship with him. He says he is speaking from a past life memory—that he literally remembers me. Whether that is true, a deeper truth is that he recognizes me as a member of his family, the family of humanity. He knows that we came from the same Mama.

Margaret Mead may be the most well-known and well-loved cultural anthropologist of the twentieth century. She was fascinated with human life, as anyone can see from her never-dry, never-scientifically-boring books. She had Attraction in her pattern five times: Ascendant, Mars, Jupiter, Uranus, and Pluto. This means that her behavioral body, physical body, sense of being supported by the universe, sense of authentic self-knowing, and journeys into deep self-investigation all depended on a cross-cultural frame of reference. In a very real sense, everything that Margaret Mead contributed to the world through her studies of anthropology also contributed to the unification of the world's thinking about race. She argued and demonstrated tirelessly that there is one human race, not many races that make up a species.

In addition to being an attractor, she is also known to have had an uncanny ability to "read" attractor-like energy in others. Jean Houston tells a story of going to a party with Margaret in which Mead would watch people's interactions and then in whispers to Houston predict something like: "See that lone man over there. These two people are going to drift over to him shortly. Then that triangle is going to pull these three people across the room, and that will be the hub of the next interesting interchange in the room." And she was right. It was a matter, to her, of observing kinesics and body signals. Houston found herself wondering, "Was Margaret doing cultural anthropology that evening, or was Margaret doing Margaret Mead, or is there any difference?" (1996, p. 230). With five planets in the principle of Attraction, I would say there is no difference.

Attraction is seeing the likeness in the not alikeness. Attraction is recognizing the impersonality of the forms Life Force actually takes. It recognizes self and other as One.

In the human body, Attraction demonstrates itself in the intestines.

The intestines are called the "abdominal brain" by Theosophists and other esoteric schools of thought. Actually, intestines and brains do look alike. The abdominal brain makes the decisions about what to assimilate. What do we need? The intestines absorb needed nutrients into the body. These nutrients are aspects of the "outside" world that we take in as food or drink and that resonate with our inner physical body and nurture it. The intestines, then, assimilate what is "like" us (anything that carries a resonant frequency), and they discard what is "unlike" us (anything that carries a discordant frequency).

The metaphor of the abdominal brain helps us understand that it is on the gut level that Attraction as a spiritual principle operates in us. We may have a visual experience of someone or something. Initially, we may want to possess that person or thing, believing that it will make us happy. However, unless we are very immature, looks alone do not determine whether we are really attracted to him or her or it. It is the deeper (gut) perception that determines spiritual Attraction. Attraction calls to us only that which resonates and enhances us.

In our group study of Attraction, we all agreed on one aspect of this principle: Attraction roots us deeply in the truth of ourselves. If we choose to ignore the power that we have to magnetize what we need, then we also ignore our essential selves. It is extremely important, especially for the person who is contracted with Attraction, to understand the interconnectedness of all beings, all thoughts, all prayers, and all actions; and to realize that in her seed-self she is a part of all those things. Each of us helps create the world by attracting energies, taking action, sharing thought systems, and participating in cultural behaviors. It is important for each person to fully understand Attraction. How else can each person become fully accountable to the world we create?

18 Focus

Concentration and clear focus are essential on the Direct Path....
The more wholeheartedly we can plunge into (spiritual) practice,
and the more completely we can gather all the powers of our being
and focus them, the more richly it can reveal its power to us and in us.

~ ANDREW HARVEY

Focus is the ability to place one's perception intentionally in a specific frequency and thereby call forth certain responses. Focus is the natural state of the scientific mind. One uses Focus to cut off all other data input in order to examine a specific idea or object.

In the early 1900s, Einstein proved that light or energy is made of particles (photons), or little bitty bullets of matter. The problem with his experiment, for which he received the Nobel Prize, was that 100 years earlier, another scientist named Young had proved that light was made of waves, or little bitty vibrations of energy. Wave and particle are mutually exclusive. A substance is either energy or matter, not both simultaneously. While Einstein could prove that light is made of photons, he could not disprove that it is also made of waves (Capra, 1975, p. 56). This problem created a big duality in the field of physics known as the "wave/particle dilemma." Does light come as little packets of matter, or does light come as waves of energy? What is light?

In the late 1920s, Neils Bohr demonstrated that light has no properties of its own at all. Light will demonstrate itself in whatever form the perceiver wants to see. If you want to see matter, you set up a specific kind of experiment, and light demonstrates its *matter-ness*. If you want to see vibration, you set up another kind of experiment, and light demonstrates its *vibration-ness*. This phenomenon is the marriage between "perceived and perceiver": The perceiver has decision-making control over what is perceived (p. 55).

Focus is the human ability to determine what is perceived and experienced and then to evoke it. Focus is very powerful because it allows for the understanding of humans as co-creators with God.

Some say that this idea touches on the "reason" the realm of form came into existence. Perhaps in wanting to be perceived, God set up a system in which The All could be perceived in infinitely different ways. We, *Homo sapiens sapiens* (which means "one who knows that he knows"), may be the most sophisticated of the perceivers. (There is a possibility, of course, that dolphins, whales, and other creatures are more so, but we have not yet found a way to examine that possibility.)

Focus resides in the realm of planetary consciousness. Homo sapiens sapiens know that they are beings, observing themselves and nature in the evolutionary process.

Planetary Consciousness means that we know that we are an integral part of the planet and that the planet Herself is in an evolutionary movement. This aspect of the principle implies that when one has Focus in his or her chart, there is the possibility to pull one's attention to the minutest detail, but there is also the ability to cast one's attention wide. One can chose near-sightedness, or far-sightedness, or any perspective in between on which to focus.

Eleanor Roosevelt's primary principle (Sun) was Focus. A look at the accomplishments of her life can give us an amazing picture of this principle. She came from wealth and privilege, but like no other First Lady in our history, she took the burdens of the nation's poor as her primary point of attention.

Although she nearly divorced him when she discovered he was having an affair, she chose to stay with her husband, encouraging him to seek and escorting him to the most powerful political position in the world. His position during the Great Depression created for her the opportunities to bring women into public life in profound new ways. She headed up many women's organizations, she hosted over 350 for-women-reporters-only press conferences in the White House, she wrote a daily newspaper column "My Day," she broadcasted her own weekly radio program—all the while raising five children and attending to the social obligations of hostess of our nation.

After FDR's death, she became the American delegate to the United Nations. When she needed to isolate specific problems and solve them, she did. When she needed global perspective, she had it. Surely, Eleanor Roosevelt is the poster child for the spiritual principle of Focus.

Focus is concentrated in the human body inside the pineal gland.

Dr. Jacob Liberman, author of *Light Medicine of the Future*, calls the pineal the light meter of the body. He claims that this gland assists us in becoming synchronized with nature and thus one with the universe (p. xxv). It is from the chakra called the "third eye" that we are able to activate the one-pointed attention that allows us to concentrate our awareness. The pineal is a very powerful gland; it moderates the imaginal aspect of human consciousness. Any of us who has experienced an out-of-body experience or any other unusual or spontaneous expansion of consciousness knows the power of the pineal. It manages the energetic flow of otherwise-inaccessible information that is made available during these out-of-the ordinary times.

Hellen Keller's Moon (mastery) was in the principle of Focus. When we consider the amazing accomplishments she made and the seemingly impenetrable barriers she overcame in her lifetime, we can see the power of this principle at work in her life. Without being able to speak or hear, she conquered the world of communication far better than most of us and spoke to the world in a language that needs no translation.

In order for energies to experience themselves, they must interface with themselves. The human has the unique ability to predetermine what that interfacing is going to be.

Focus is a principle that requires deep discipline from a human. Animals have an ability to concentrate, but theirs is instinctual programming. Humans, however, have to use personal discipline to achieve a mastery of the principle of Focus. People who succeed in mastering Focus constantly hone their meditative and concentration skills.

In our class, when we studied this principle, we discovered a pattern of dreaming among the people who have Focus in their charts. They all have recurring dreams of being in high school. Indeed, we realized that studying this body of information had put us all in high school in the sense that we felt as if we were in some ancient mystery school examining some of the higher concepts of human life. Most of us will never reach the planetary-citizen status that Eleanor Roosevelt and Helen Keller achieved. However, having the principle of Focus in your pattern certainly guarantees that your mind and heart must stay open to the largest and the smallest of details of life. You are a student of the high school truth of the "as above, so below" paradox. Your life embodies the microcosm, and your invisible garment carries threads of the macrocosm.

19 Service

God's peace prompts service among brothers and sisters.
In that way one creature sustains another.
One enriches the other, and that is why
all creatures are interdependent.

~ Meister Eckhart

If you fully understand life as energy bonding to itself and experiencing itself, then you truly understand yourself as a being who is in a mutual interaction with Life. That is Service.

Semantically, the word "service" often means humbling yourself before other people. Socially, "service" is defined as seeing what other people need and meeting their needs. It means serving other beings, nurturing them, and taking care of them.

Service as a spiritual principle, however, is more sophisticated than that. It has to do with knowing that every form is an intelligent form. It means that every bonding of molecules is a sentient expression of life. It means that every human being is first and foremost an individuation of human soul. When one lives in that consciousness, one is serving form. Service, when understood as a spiritual principle, is a state of consciousness, a state of being—not an action or a state of doing.

The related concepts of "being" and "doing" apply to every principle. The angels gave them special emphasis, however, in connection with Service. This message from the angels was very clear: You are serving life by *being* who you are—bottom line—that is it. Life is a mutual interchange of sentience. Life is Itself, bonding Itself to Itself in order to exchange information. When you, as a human, live in that consciousness, you are living in Service to life.

When you are perceiving life or interfacing with life, if you know your own tendencies or your own probability factors, then you understand that you are perceiving that which you have agreed to "see" in this lifetime. You know that your perception is a contribution to the collective. Your perception becomes holy, because you know who you are, how you perceive, why you perceive that way, and what that gift is to the greater community.

Both Martin Luther King, Jr. and Gandhi had the Moons (mastery) in the principle of Service. Even though neither of them had access to this information as I present it in this form, surely, the above statements are true of them both: They knew that their perceptions were contributions to the collective; they knew the holiness of their perceptions; and they knew that their only real choice in life was to give their lives to the greater community.

Dr. King spoke eloquently of his understanding of himself, and indeed everyone, as a servant to life in a speech made at his church, Ebenezer Baptist, on February 4, 1968:

> Jesus gave us a new norm of greatness. He said, 'He who is greatest among you shall be your servant.' That means that everybody can be great. You don't have to have a college degree to serve. You don't have to make your subject and your verb agree to serve. You don't have to know about Plato and Aristotle to serve. You don't have to know Einstein's theory of relativity to serve. You don't have to know the second theory of thermodynamics in physics to serve. You only need a heart full of grace. A soul generated by love. And you can be that servant.
>
> *A Testament of Hope: The Essential Writings and Speeches of Martin Luther King, Jr.*
> Washington, Editor

None of this is about doing. The doing outflows as a result of one's understanding oneself as a perceiver.

In other words, if you are consciously aware of yourself as a servant to life, you do what you do because you perceive that in the doing you express the truth of life more fully.

Gandhi said it like this:

> It is because we have at the present moment everybody claiming the right of conscience without going through any spiritual discipline that there is so much untruth being delivered to a bewildered world.... A person cannot do right in one department of life whilst he or she is occupied in doing wrong in any other department. Life is one indivisible whole.
>
> *The Words of Gandhi*
> Attenborough, Editor

As human life has evolved, it can no longer be a statement: "Look what I did, look how great I am, look what I have accomplished." It is, instead, knowing that through authentically living one's personal potentialities and probabilities, one contributes the greatest possible gift. No Enlightened Being ever did more. We do not call them Enlightened Doings—we call them Enlightened Beings.

Humans are potentially becoming a species of Enlightened Beings. The Beings of the Age of Peace will be beings who know their contract and live it. The New Experiment will involve finding answers to these questions: How much love can one being express? How much light can one being carry? How much truth can one being speak?

As I understand it, Service, more than any other principle, involves action. However, it is about the attitude rather than the performance of action. Service is the way (attitude of action) through which you discover wholeness. Your doingness connects you to wholeness. Gandhi, again:

> What I want to achieve—what I have been striving and pining
> to achieve these 30 years … is to see God face to face.…
> I live and move and have my being in pursuit of this goal.
> All that I do by way of speaking and writing and all my ventures
> in the political field, are directed to this same end.
>
> ~ GANDHI
> *Prayer*
> Strohmeier, Editor

Outside the body, Service lives in the consciousness of Soul. Humans have a unique ability to see themselves multi-dimensionally. Humans are conscious of the individual self through the principle of Resistance. You know yourselves as part of a genetic line through Unity. You know yourselves as part of the human family through Attraction. You know yourselves as part of a part of a planetary organism through Focus. And you know yourselves as extending and individuating from a level that we call Soul. That level is slightly beyond human mental comprehension, but it is definitely within your intuitional reach. You may each define Soul differently, but you know that "soul" means "home."

Service is the principle that emanates from a knowingness that we are all temporarily away from home. Eckhart says, "And when I return to God and to the core, the soil, the ground, the stream and the source of the Godhead, no one asks me where I am coming from or where I have been. For no one misses me in the place where God ceases to become" (Fox, 1983,

p. 13). When we unite with soul, we realize we have never been anything other than fully united with soul although we feel separated because of the appearance of form. Eckhart continues, "God is at home. It is we who have gone out for a walk" (Fox, 1983, p. 15).

> *Service lives in the knees in the human body. The knees are new chakra points just opening. They are the parts of the human body that give it the greatest level of flexibility and variety of movement. They carry the energy of the future, for they carry one's potential for walking gracefully toward his or her destiny. People who are contracted with Service need to spend time on their knees. When you pray, kneel. When you garden, get those knees dirty. When you lean over or bend down to pick something up, squat. Your knees are energetic points that need to be honored, recognized, and exercised.*

In our course, to my surprise, the principle of Service brought the most animated conversations of all the principles. Apparently, women have a hard time really grasping the principle of Service because culturally, the word has a "doormat" connotation. So many women are literally exhausted by the term. One student wrote about that:

> "I think merely saying the word 'Service' puts me into a state of being tired. Although I feel it on an emotional level, I didn't realize the depth of my fatigue until we began to study the spiritual meaning of the principle. I've been a pleaser/giver. Because of this class, I made the decision to let go of my career in the healing arts. That was Service for me."

Other students were not as fatigued by the principle as they were confounded by the apparent paradox that our truest Service is really found in our own self-knowing. One student reported that she had made a commitment early in her life to creating a career that allowed her to "follow her bliss":

> "But following my bliss didn't turn out to be so simple. My definition of 'bliss' is in a constant state of evolution. I can't feel bliss without feeling that whatever I'm doing serves some higher purpose. The challenge through my life has been in identifying the true higher purpose and separating it from my small-self desires, so that I can find the bliss. This course has really 'Served' to show me how much I need to discard all of the 'shoulds' in my life and pay close, close attention to my inner knowing and intuition. It's the quiet voice that seems to know where to lead me."

We all agreed that the paradox of "To thine own self be true" is a big one. One can spend one's entire life trying to be *true,* only to realize eventually that being myopic is not being true. We learned that "To thine own self be true" is impossible without adding, "and to thy tribe, thy neighbors, thy soul cluster, thy dreams, thy cosmology, thy God!"

Another student "confessed" that studying Service had helped her understand something about how her mind works:

> "I apply information to the whole of society first, and then to myself. It used to frustrate me *so much* that others didn't do that. It just seemed logical to me, for information became so much more available and useful to me in the context of the greater perspective. This course has really helped me understand what other people's minds are doing, so I'm not so frustrated any more."

We all learned what one student pointed out so beautifully: that Service calls us to humble ourselves, not before others but before ourselves. Doing so shakes us to our core, for the only gift we can really give is ourselves. We must each learn our patterns and wear our spiritual garments gracefully, for if we do, our soul will give itself through us.

The dreamer who is truly in Service is one who knows that her job is to bridge the potential we can dream and the matrix of ordinary life. A true dreamer is always in the principle of Service, for she is always dreaming the new dream.

At the end of the study of Service, we adopted some lines from Rumi as our motto:

> Love, make me your servant!
> Slavery to You is the door into the Garden.
> My door into eternity is exactly the shape I make
> When I walk forward, headless, on my knees.

> *Light Upon Light: Inspirations from Rumi*
> Harvey, 1996

Chapter Five

The Descending Principles

The Descending Principles evoke and choreograph evolutionary move-
ment. They descend from the transcendental planes to interface with
the realm of form. As they interface with forms on the denser planes,
they simultaneously inspire all forms to elevate to transcendental
consciousness. The Descending Principles create the environment that
allows individual forms to join together to create more sophisticated
structures.

For example, an atom that is bonded into a molecule is simulta-
neously an atom and a part of a greater structure. The glue that bonds
atoms together is Love (one of the Descending Principles). Atom-ness
does not dissolve into the molecule. The singular atom maintains its indi-
viduality as it simultaneously moves forward in the evolutionary
pattern, in partnership with other atoms, to create a more organized
structure or form.

An evolved form includes everything that has preceded it, and yet
it is greater than the sum of its parts. A form that has evolved from pre-
vious forms is a structure that is more sophisticated than its predecessors
could have predicted. There is nothing in either oxygen or hydrogen that
"predicts" water. And yet when bonded in the right proportions, hydro-
gen and oxygen atoms indeed create this magical form from which all
other Earth life springs.

These Descending Principles work in the human realm to evoke greater organizational structure of consciousness. They urge humans to remember that they are embodied souls and that their embodiment is a gift. Humans are gifts given to the realm of form from the realm of soul for the purpose of delivering gifts to the realm of form. All the energies of the cosmos joyously participate with humans in the act of delivering these gifts.

In their book *The Physics of Angels*, Rupert Sheldrake and Matthew Fox discuss the concept that the angels of the cosmos assist and in fact praise humans for delivering their unique gifts into form. Angels do not have choice: They have to love. They *are* love. Humans have the gift of choice, so a human act of loving kindness has the power of choice behind it. Angels admire this ability to choose, and they endorse it, assist us with it, and spread word of it throughout the cosmos (pp. 165-167).

These Descending Principles are the work of the angels brought into form through human beings' behaviors, attitudes, language, and deeds. They are hard to define—who can truly define Love, Peace, Humility, Silence?—and yet they are forces that truly merge with human lives and inform human choices.

Brian Swimme speaks of the galactic realms as the "ground of the universe." By placing the "ground" in the heavens, Swimme turns our normal perspective upside down. He might agree with the Kabbalists who say that the Tree of Life is rooted in heaven. Swimme says, "The ground of the universe then is an empty fullness, a fecund nothingness" (1996, p. 93). He refers to the massive potential that lurks in and constantly springs from what appears to be a massive void. He goes further to inspire his readers to become co-creative with the cosmos: "The challenge is in identifying our deepest personal reality with the powers of the universe" (p. 105).

People who are contracted with the Descending Principles find the challenge of embodying them to be difficult. The principles are overwhelmingly powerful, and yet they are difficult to define, hard to bring into form, and sometimes impossible to live. Yet as each person who studies these principles begins to accept the ideas that they present, the challenges of living them become intriguing.

One of my students pointed out to me that oxygen and hydrogen, after they are bonded into a molecule of water, cannot get a divorce. People can, however, because Love for us does not always function as a binding force.

It is more difficult for the human being to live the principle of Love, because the free will, the ego, the power of choice will often seduce the individual away from alignment with Love. Each of the Descending Principles offers this kind of challenge to the spiritual practitioner.

20 Gratitude

If the only prayer
you say in your entire life
is "Thank You"
that would suffice.

~ MEISTER ECKHART

*Gratitude is the most universal of all of the spiritual principles. Every-
one has to learn to live in gratitude in order to transcend the mundanity
of life, whether it is in his or her contract. If one is not living the principle of Gratitude, he or she is not able to access Creator and Creation.
Gratitude is the principle that continually points to Creator. When one
experiences Gratitude, one remembers the wonder of Creation.*

*Someone who is specifically contracted with Gratitude carries a spe-
cial ability to mirror it to the greater community. In other words,
someone who walks in Gratitude for life brings the awareness of life's
gifts into every circumstance.*

Anne Frank's Sun was in Gratitude in the eleventh house (the house of
the brotherhood of all humanity). Through the legacy she left in her diaries,
the principle is mirrored to all humanity. Her diaries were not documen-
tation of the horrors of the holocaust but rather the inspired observations
of a woman/child who felt the deepest passion for life. Her postings were
testimony to the alikeness of all beings and fly in the face of racist and elit-
ist philosophy. Gratitude undergirded her writings and her life.

*Gratitude is the deep understanding that life is a gift, not a burden or
an assignment. To live in Gratitude is to know that even the angels long
to experience the realm of form. The gift of becoming human is God's
generosity made manifest. Humans are God's companions. God was
lonely until humans joined the cosmic dance.*

To live in Gratitude is to live in prayer. As Eckhart says, "Thank you" is the only prayer that is ever really needed (Fox, 1983, p. 34). To live in the constant state of "thank you" is perhaps the most noble and spiritual goal of any human.

> *Outside the human body, Gratitude is focused in sentience itself. All of life is sentient; all forms have intelligence; all cells and parts of cells are aspects of the cosmic expression. To understand these concepts is to understand oneself as a complex aggregate of many sentient beings.*

Julia Butterfly Hill, whose Moon (mastery) is in Gratitude, so deeply understood the sentience of the trees that she opted to sit in a tree for 738 days in order to keep the foresters from cutting it down. She named the tree "Luna," and her little platform high in the branches of Luna became an international hub of communications during the time that she was there. Julia and Luna became friends, speaking to each other in the language of all sentience, the language of the dream. In her book *The Legacy of Luna*, Julia defines Luna as the symbol of hope that love will always win out on this beautiful planet, reminding us that there are no "sides" but instead only life and love (p. 253).

Every human is an expression of cosmic life force. To be fully aware of our human-ness, then, we must live in Gratitude. All of us must remember that we are simultaneously an individual self, a part of a genetic lineage, a part of a cultural lineage, a member of one of the Earth's species, an individuation of the human soul, and also a cell in the vast intelligent sentience of the cosmos. These ever-expanding ways of seeing ourselves connect us to the great weave of life. Gratitude is the natural result of this awesome awareness.

> *Inside the body, Gratitude lives in the spleen, which is one of the blood-purifying glands. It eliminates any residue in the blood that has been chemically changed by anger or ill humor. The spleen restores balance to the bloodstream.*

As mentioned earlier, the Descending Principles are difficult to embody because they demand that we experience ourselves in a galactic or cosmic sense as well as in an individual sense. In our class discussion of the principle of Gratitude, we made a very interesting discovery: Several of us experience chronic physical pain. The difficulty of living a life that involves daily pain is unimaginable to pain-free people. One of the most common results of living in constant pain is that the person who experiences it is self-judging. We feel that we "deserve" to be in pain, we are somehow doing something "wrong," and our bodies are different or "special" in some way. This feeling results in an inability to feel Gratitude at work in our lives. As long as we feel separated or isolated from life, we cannot merge into it and be thankful for it.

One dreamer summed it up for us:

"From my own experience, Gratitude is certainly something that will elude us forever if we admonish ourselves to experience it. Gratitude is an energy that is always there. We just need to let go of enough of our 'junk' (to let our spiritual spleens clear our metaphorical blood) to experience it."

21 | Harmony

One day in your wine shop I drank a little wine
And threw off the robe of this body:
I knew, drunk on you, this world in harmony—
Creation, destruction, I'm dancing for them both.

~ Rumi

People who are contracted with Harmony are the people who integrate the is not. They work in the negative space of the piece of art that is life. They find worship in the sacred darkness because they know the power of the unseen work.

Hildegard of Bingen says, "Humans have empty spaces as well as full ones, as does the cosmos" (Fox, 1985, p. 48). Hildegard points out that we humans are duplications of the cosmos in this sense. This idea means that emptiness is essential to the human being.

To describe Harmony as a spiritual principle, I often use the metaphor of jazz. The jazz musician brings dimension to a tune. If a musician just plays a single-note melody—a single-note progression that is a little tune—the listener experiences one level of hearing the music. But when the notes that do not belong to the melody get emphasized, then the melody takes on much greater dimension.

A good jazz pianist will often start with just the melody. Next comes the melody with harmonic undertones or overtones. Eventually, the pianist plays everything but the melody, and the listener is required to hear what *is* (the tune) by listening to all the what *is not* (the harmonic). The jazz musician toys with a melody by bringing it to a minor, dirge-like dimension or by making it laugh at itself by playing notes that seem to skip all around it. A really good pianist or horn player brings depth into the musical experience through his or her choice of how to express the harmonics of a piece.

Similarly, the person who wears Harmony presents the melody of life by emphasizing the counter-melodies.

Harmony resides in the dark spaces of pre-consciousness. The dark takes us out of control. Matthew Fox says, "We cannot control too many of our ideas in the dark. We are forced to listen more keenly in the dark and to strain to see more deeply in the dark" (Fox, 1979, p. 96). Of course, please understand that this "dark" does not refer to the repressed, denied, or psychological resistance one has to memories of painful events. This is not the dark psyche but instead the unseen realms, the mystery, the black sun behind the sun—the spiritual foundation of all that is.

> *People who are contracted with Harmony have a certain imperative to bring out the dimensionality of whatever with which they are working. Whether it is music, whether it is thought, whether it is form—whatever it is, they bring forward the invisible.*
>
> *One who understands Harmony loves the unseen aspects as well as the seen aspects of any experience, any form. It is a profound principle, for it calls the being to constant attention. When one masters Harmony, one becomes aware of the totality of every situation and combines that awareness with the compassion invoked in every situation. Compassion, therefore, becomes extremely important in the understanding and embodiment of Harmony.*

Really talented musicians often are crazy in the sense that they do not normalize. What they hear and what they experience come from a dimension that most ordinary people never access. And this aberration is true of people who wear Harmony. Within their incarnational pattern is woven a commitment to the unseen—a promise to remain faithful to the "is-not-ness" of appearances. They dedicate their lives to the descending realms. The "dark night of the soul" is familiar territory to them, for they must periodically encounter emptiness in order to be full.

> *In the human body, harmony lives in the colon. That is the organ of the body where darkness is the most prevalent. The materials that need to be recycled move through the dark insides of the colon and are massaged on their way out of the body.*

This concept of recycling waste rather than rejecting it is important in the consideration of this principle. When any creature excretes waste matter, according to divine plan, that matter then becomes the fertile soil in which new things (or ideas) can grow. Harmony is the spiritual principle that, as Rumi says, dances with both creation and destruction.

Studying Harmony in the principles class proved to be very interesting. We realized that many of us struggle with the difficulty of living this principle. Because femininity has been dishonored in almost every society on the planet for many hundreds of years, women bear the burden of much of the so-called collective darkness. We are familiar with the "dark" side of manipulation, competition, jealousy, and greed. Generally, male manifestations of these experiences are raw, visible, and predictable. Female expressions of these kinds of experiences, however, are often unclean and unhealthy, hidden and secretive. In the class, we discussed the idea that our most important contribution to society is to liberate ourselves and our sisters from the burden of carrying that shadow of the collective psychology.

However, we also mutually agreed that it is an exhausting imperative. One of the class members dreamed she saw a woman being kidnapped and taken under a bridge where she was to be murdered. Although the dreamer wanted to help liberate the woman, she knew she did not have the energy. Her exhaustion prevented her from moving. We often feel this way in our society: Combating the issues that need changing is too fatiguing for us.

Like all the Descending Principles, Harmony is difficult to understand and even more difficult to embody. Harmony is a principle that invites us into the Great Mystery. It is a principle that asks us to be comfortable in the dark, be okay with not being able to understand everything, and rest in the knowledge that we are not required to engage with every shadow that appears. Our challenge in embodying Harmony is not to eliminate the darkness but rather to be comfortable in mystery.

William Wordsworth's Ascendant and Venus were in the principle of Harmony.

> While with an eye made quiet by the power
> Of harmony, and the deep power of joy,
> We see into the life of things.
>
> ~ WILLIAM WORDSWORTH
> *Lines Composed a Few Miles Above Tintern Abbey*

22 Dreaming

I sleep but my heart watches...

~ Song of Songs 5:2

Spiritually defined, Dreaming is the ability to shift into non-ordinary states of consciousness. Dreaming is a direct encounter with energy in the dimension of truth. It does not necessarily require being asleep to experience Dreaming. It does, however, require a relationship with the Void—the sacred whirlpool of primordial energy. It requires being able to pull information out of that which is unformed.

Meister Eckhart says, "You can never be better off than when you are completely in the darkness." He goes on to define this darkness as "an aptitude for sensitivity that is not at all lacking or devoid of being. It is rather a rich sensitivity in which you will be made whole" (Fox, 1991, p. 239). Eckhart was not speaking specifically about being asleep in this particular passage, but he was speaking about the ability to move one's mind and attention into the Void to be sensitive to beingness. This is *Dreaming*.

The Void is the darkness from which all manifestation occurs. It is the place of all potential. It is the womb of the cosmos. Each human starts life's journey in the holy darkness of the mother's body cavities. Your physical creation came out of your mother's dreaming organ—her womb—the location of that Void within the human body. The womb is the dreaming organ for men and women. In men, it is the chakra area around the metaphorical womb. Dreaming comes through the internal, secret knowledge of the womb.

Makeda, Queen of Sheba, was one of King Solomon's many lovers. She is known as a great poet. This poem, dating nearly 3,000 years ago describes dreaming:

> While in the dark sea,
> I slept,
> and not overwhelmed there,
> dreamt: a star
> blazed in my womb

Women in Praise of the Sacred:
43 Centuries of Spiritual Poetry by Women
Hirshfield, Editor

As a dreamer, you work with the "angels of the unseen potential" to help anchor all that is unfamiliar (all that has not been known) into the realm of the known. The "seen" holds within it the "unseen." The dreamer travels into the darkness in order to resonate with the tension between the seen and the unseen.

Dreaming makes co-creation possible. The dreamer works closely with the dynamics of creation and destruction, energies that "expose" themselves in the process called Dreaming. The dreamer works in the dream with the Divine to create the manifested world.

Of course, the implications of this statement are huge. We dreamers must be fully accountable to the world we inhabit, for we have co-created it. It is our dream, and all the species on this planet are required to live within our dream. As Thomas Berry points out: "Our entire modern world is itself inspired not by any rational process, but by a distorted dream experience" (1988, p. 205). This does not mean that Dreaming, as a spiritual principle, is responsible for the troubles in this world. It is not the Dreaming that is distorted; it is the dreamer. If we truly accept ourselves as spiritual beings, we must learn to recognize and correct those distortions in ourselves so that we can co-create a world that is in alignment with truth.

Abraham Lincoln was double contracted with Dreaming (Ascendant and Jupiter). Certainly, he did not run for president on an abolitionist platform. But when in office, he was submerged into the realization that ownership of another human being is ethically horrific. With Dreaming in his Ascendant (ethical body), it became abhorrent to him that this crime against humanity was not only happening in his beloved country but that it was dividing the country to the point of civil war. The tortures of his position kept him simultaneously depressed and acutely energized throughout his administration.

In addition to Lincoln's being a dreamer who worked in the unseen realms to bring truth and light to manifestation, we also have reason to believe that his night visions, the stories of his dreamtime, were highly influential experiences for him.

According to his close friend, Ward Hill Lamon, Lincoln had a precognitive dream of his own death about two weeks prior to the assassination. He reported to his wife and a few friends that he dreamed he was upstairs at the White House asleep. He woke and heard sobs. He became aware that there were hundreds of people (all invisible—he could see none of them but only hear their weeping) in all of the rooms of the house crying as if their hearts were broken.

He wandered from room to room and eventually found his way to the East Room, where he saw a catafalque with a corpse wrapped and resting on it. He was able to see the guards who stood at attention nearby and asked them: "Who is dead at the White House?" The answer came, "The President, killed by an assassin." Lincoln reported that the wailing of the mourners woke him from the dream, and it apparently haunted him up to the last minutes of his life.

This kind of prophecy is rare, of course, and only available to the most sophisticated of dreamers. I cannot help but wonder if Lincoln's dream did not come as much to forewarn Mary, his wife, as anything else. According to the story, after hearing the dream, she determined to pull out of her own depression and join her husband in celebrating the end of the war and the survival of the Union.

All that resides outside the typical band of human consciousness is Dreaming. The dreamer travels into that unknown universe to participate in the process of manifestation. Those journeys are often not translatable into words or images. In fact, many people who wear Dreaming do not remember their night dreams on a regular basis. It is a process that is so far outside the consciousness of humanity that sometimes it cannot be transliterated.

Often, people who are contracted with Dreaming awaken with awareness of nothing more than a fragrance. That may be as close as the human experience can get to the memory of the dream. Think of trying to verbalize the fragrance of a rose. It is literally impossible to explain it to someone who has never smelled a rose. So it is with Dreaming—it is sometimes impossible to explain the energetic experience even to yourself.

Eckhart says, "The soul cannot create or draw an image of itself. Of nothing does it know so little as of itself because of the necessary intermediary" (Fox, 1991, p. 295). The angels have taught me that the dream is the intermediary. The soul gives the dreamer hints of itself through dreams. Therefore, we cannot fully interpret our own dreams—because they come out of the darkness of our potential and therefore cannot be fully seen by us.

Eckhart goes on to say, "No image aims at or points to itself. It rather aims at and points to the object of which it is the image" (p. 297). Our dream images give us clues as to our soul's intent and potential. The absoluteness of the soul, however, cannot be fully revealed.

Rumi expresses it beautifully:

> Humankind is being led along an evolving course,
> Through this migration of intelligences,
> And though we seem to be sleeping,
> There is an inner wakefulness
> That directs the dream,
> And that will eventually startle us back
> To the truth of who we are.
>
> *Poems of Rumi*
> Bly and Barks, Translators
> Barks, Reader

In our class, we discussed how the principle of Dreaming demands that we work "consciously" in the Void. This is a paradoxical statement. Since the Void is unknowable, Dreaming also cannot be fully known. All the definitions and words we use to discuss the principles are simply pointers, not really definitive. But the words about Dreaming are uniquely elusive because Dreaming involves extracting information from—as Brian Swimme calls it— the "not-yet realms."

One student spoke of Dreaming by metaphorically describing it as "dancing in the dark." In one dream, a woman burst out of a dark hole wrapped in bright colors and invited the dreamer: "Come dance, come dance." Another student saw that this woman may be the Earth herself and reminded us that she, Gaia, invites us to dance with the beauty and music of the planet.

The class discussion also included our realizing that everyone has the experience of the Void: everyone dreams. People who are conscious of it are dancing with the power of the darkness; these people are not struggling with trying to understand and control the visible world.

We concluded that the ability to dream and manifest our dreams is an aspect of human life that is a unique privilege. If we learn to hear the information of Dreaming correctly, we will be guided by our soul-selves, and we will live rooted in divine potential and possibility. If we ignore the information of Dreaming, our lives will be controlled by personal will, false-self goals, and the limitations of our personal minds.

23 Randomness

As far as the laws of mathematics refer to reality,
they are not certain,
and as far as they are certain,
they do not refer to reality.

~ EINSTEIN

Spiritually speaking, Randomness occurs in that moment when all potential is present and nothing is certain. Randomness is chaotic in nature.

I like to use the kaleidoscope as a metaphor for Randomness. When you look through a kaleidoscope, you see a pattern. When you turn it slightly, everything is totally chaotic momentarily, and then another pattern crystallizes. That next pattern is something that you can hardly believe was potential in the pattern before. The new pattern can have completely different colors and completely different structuring.

It is in that moment between crystallized patterns that the widest range of possibility presents itself to be manifested.

Quantum physicists refer to an "ambiguity barrier." There is a "veil" that separates an idea from its manifestation in form. That veil—that barrier—cannot be fully perceived by human consciousness. For example, one of the most interesting concepts in quantum physics is the particle and wave duality. Scientists have been able to "prove" that light is wave-like. Other scientists have been able to "prove" that light is particle-like. And yet neither can disprove the other. Light is both wave and particle, but it can only be observed as one or the other.

Even Einstein, the undisputed greatest genius of our time (whose Sun was in Randomness, by the way) could not bridge this profound paradox.

When one observes the wave, the particle disappears. Conversely, when one observes the particle, the wave phenomenon stops, because the particle has to be frozen in time and space to reveal itself. The ambiguity barrier prevents an observer from seeing both simultaneously. I see the ambiguity barrier as analogous to the spiritual principle of Randomness.

> *Randomness is the bridge between light and dark. It is the bridge between what is and what could be. Light and dark are not two distinct forces. They are, rather, one force that expresses itself in multiple forms in order to differentiate its qualities. Randomness differentiates spiritual qualities just as light and dark differentiate forms.*
>
> *Randomness creates balance between the seen and the unseen realms.*
>
> *Randomness is the Void being stirred. Randomness begins its expression the moment potential begins to stir itself and move toward becoming. How and when that stirring occurs is a part of the Great Mystery.*
>
> *Out of Randomness comes mutation. All genetic mutations— therefore, all evolution—have come out of Randomness.*

Brian Swimme and Thomas Berry speak of Randomness and mutation in *The Universe Story.* They explain that a group of cells washed up on the shore from deep within the sea millions of years ago, and they were pushed too far to return to the water. They realized that they were going to starve (for their nourishment was in the waters) unless they journeyed into the possibility of all things and developed a way to "eat" the sunlight. The plant kingdom had its first beginning through odd, spontaneous, vitally necessary genetic mutation (p. 116).

> *Randomness lives in the ovaries of a woman. They are the most random organs of the body. You never know which seed will come out of which ovary—and whether it will bring new life or purging of the stored blood in the body of the woman. The testicles for the male also illustrate Randomness. Millions of sperm come shooting out (at random times), and there is no predicting which of them may penetrate the seed and create life.*

The dreamers who took the principles class noted a particular kinship between Dreaming and Randomness. It seemed to us that the night dreams we experienced during the week that we were discussing Randomness were the most vivid dreams of the entire course, and they seemed to point directly to the principle. Almost every dream involved singing or some other sound vibration that altered the feeling and outcome of the dream.

We discussed the possibility that sound pulls order out of chaos.

Sleep takes us into the Darkness—before the flaring forth—where we have an energetic experience with divine potential. That experience is closely related to Randomness because it is not controlled or restricted. Eventually, we create a story to try to help us understand that experience more clearly. That story is what we call the dream. In many cases, during our week of studying Randomness, that dream story involved beautiful sounds that seemed to create order and a sense of peace in the dreamer.

Almost everyone who wears Randomness agrees that it is a hard principle to live. When one is fully participating in Randomness (i.e., when one's life is in chaos), he or she cannot see the new patterns emerging. The antidote is to let love flow through and around the chaos and to trust that the new patterns will reflect that loving energy.

Martin Luther King, Jr.'s Ascendant (ethical body) was in the principle of Randomness. Surely in him we can see a shining example of a man who used it well. It appeared that the more trying and chaotic the times became, the more powerfully he spoke of the ethical and moral imperative to stop the evil forces of racism and human cruelty. Out of every chaotic event, King rose like a phoenix to lead the black people of America forward in a mighty battle of morality.

Even when we know intellectually that Randomness is chaotic, we still feel a deep need for order. In the midst of our most confusing times, we try to project order into the chaos because we have such a strong desire for structure. We participate in decomposing old patterns, hoping that new, better ones can emerge. One student mentioned that during the week of studying Randomness, she had the realization that we cannot use our will to force Randomness into order:

> "Faith in the movement of Randomness allows the old picture to
> surrender, the gems to roll, and the new picture to expand. And I
> am personally astounded at the sweetness I feel when I look at,
> perceive, and focus on the movement of this amazing Randomness
> in my life—I can feel the presence of all potential."

24 Humility

Humility is the mother of all the virtues.

~ HILDEGARD OF BINGEN

There is a place within you that is sacred and that remains untouched by anything earthly. It was born the moment the universe was born, and it has traveled with you in consciousness in various forms ever since. It is not a physical location but a time/space location. It became authentically perceivable only after you came into human form. When you remember that time/space, you are experiencing humility.

Humility is one of those words about which people can become semantically confused. In our Western cultures, we equate humility with poverty and low self-esteem. Those are not the meanings intended when discussing it as a spiritual principle of form. The word "humility" comes from the Latin word *humus* or "earth." Matthew Fox says, "Authentic humility . . . is our dependence on the Earth" (Fox, 1994, p. 141).

To be humble is to be authentically aware of the true nucleus of the essential self. It is arrogant to think yourself grander than you are. It is equally arrogant to think yourself less than you are. You are nothing less than the perfect Child of God, born simultaneously with the universe itself. No one else has ever come to form to do what you have come to do. No one else has ever held the same configuration of energy that you do. The nucleus self has held a pattern and has waited throughout all the history of the universe for the time to be right for you to be born to bring the gifts to form that are unique to your highest self. It is the authentic knowing of that self that allows you to live in Humility. That Humility evokes your godlike beingness.

When one has that authenticity, then he or she is able to integrate information directly from the light. When one does not have that authenticity, he or she is so veiled that the light is never directly perceived.

Humility has to do with lifting your own veils and telling the truth to yourself about yourself. Matthew Fox reminds us that humility is "not a putting down of oneself or one's gifts, but . . . an acknowledgment that the developed use of those very gifts leads to the awesome awakening of how ignorant we are of this very complicated and beautiful web we call life" (Fox, 1979, p. 157).

The Tibetan, the Master quoted in the many volumes of Alice Bailey's books, says that humility involves having a sense of right proportion about yourself within the context of life. It requires a balanced point of view, a dispassionate attitude, and a truthful recognition of the assets as well as the debits of one's character (Bailey, 1955, p. 256).

Thinking that we know what *should* be true about ourselves or the world is the opposite of humility. Fox says, "Humility is letting go of our compulsion to prove we know more than we do" (Fox, 1979, p. 157).

Meister Eckhart also has some beautiful insights on humility:

> True humility (occurs) when a person embraces
> complete abandonment while remaining in grace.
> ~ Fox, 1991

> For the virtue which is called humility is a root in the ground of divinity
> where it is planted so that it has its existence only in the eternal . . .
> all things come to perfection in the truly humble person.
> ~ Fox, 1991

> For the more purely humble beings are free from themselves
> and in themselves, the more simply they know all diversity in themselves
> and remain unchangeable in themselves.
> ~ Fox, 1991

Rabbi David Cooper, in *God Is A Verb* says, "Humility means to be clear, confident, and accepting without pride, self-interest or ambition" (p. 211).

Humility also allows one to see other sentient beings as unique expressions of an energy that has coagulated around their own gifts.

Jean Houston is triple contracted with the principle of Humility. It comes as no surprise then, that she has dedicated much of her life to her mystery school in which she teaches people to become aware of the interweaving of history, philosophy, the new physics, psychology, anthropology, myth, and many levels of personal potential within their own lives. Teaching humility—teaching authentic self-knowing—are encoded in her very beingness. She uses her own story to evoke others: *The mythic quality of my life is by no means unique. It is only my individual version of the pattern . . . everybody and everything is being woven together into a new world myth* (p. 4).

Interestingly, one of Jean Houston's primary teachers was the mythologist Joseph Campbell. His Mid-Heaven was in the principle of Humility. It seems clear that his "path to God" evoked his student's Humility. The principle of Humility, when fully actualized in a being, insures that the world we experience and the internal world we are sourced in are reciprocal. Jean Houston and Joseph Campbell both knew the deep power of living a mythic life—of understanding one's personal life as an out-picturing of an ancient story.

> *The experience of knowing oneself authentically gives one the sense of being supported by the Universe. In future humans, the new way of experiencing energy through the chakra systems will be through a spiraling of energy out from the heart rather than a rising of energy from the base of the spine as it has in the old Kundalini system. Energy will come directly from Creator into the heart and spiral out to the extremities. As one evolves more fully, he or she will find authentic self-knowing. When one is in absolute Humility, his or her heart will literally vibrate.*
>
> *Humility involves integrating information directly from light (specifically the sun) through the skin. Light itself has no properties. Humans grant light properties by their sentient interrelationship with it.*

As was discussed in the section on Randomness, scientific experiments can prove that light is made of photons (teeny tiny particles of matter) or that light is made of waves (vibrations). So, light is particle and/or wave, depending on how one decides to experiment with it and see it. Either way, light appears to have intelligence. It interfaces with the scientist. It changes its appearance based on the desired intent of the observer.

When the angels say, "You can integrate information from the light," they are basically saying that one can, with consciousness and sentience, interact with light in such a way that intelligence is activated, and that one can exchange and integrate information directly from interacting with light.

> *Humans can also exchange and integrate information directly out of the dark—or that which is pre-conscious. However, these two processes are slightly different. Pulling information directly out of the dark (in Dreaming), or bridging light and dark (in Randomness) involves*

moving consciousness into a more fundamental level—a pre-conscious level. Integrating information from the light requires moving to a trans-conscious level and allowing light to penetrate one's intelligence.

Simply put, if you wear Humility, you have the ability to sit in the sun and absorb the nutrients of the light. You can gain deep wisdom by simply relating to the sunlight. This absorption occurs literally through your skin. We could say you are part person, part tree. Your skin knows how to photosynthesize—only you do not grab photons and use them for food. Instead, you grab information and translate it into wisdom. You are a sun dancer whether you have ever been to a ceremony.

Our primary discussion during the time that our class studied Humility centered around one's inability to "know" Humility. One dreamer stated it this way:

> "I think it's humanly impossible to sit down and say, 'Okay, I think I'll be humble now.' To think you're humble is to prevent yourself from experiencing Humility. It's the reverse of 'Don't think of a pink elephant.' Once you've had the thought, the process is inevitable."

In order to experience Humility, one has to be unaware of its presence.

25 Desire

All desires are the desire for God, obscured and veiled.
When you go out of this world and see the King face-to-face
then you will know that everything you longed for here—
whether women or men, wealth or palaces, things to eat,
political or religious power—all these things
were veils and coverings of Him.

~ Rumi

The Desire Principle is addressed in almost every form of religion. It usually is considered to be synonymous with greed. Spiritual use of the word is markedly different from the ordinary use of the word. Spiritually defined, Desire provides a never-ending call toward home. Desire drives one to be Whole—to be reunited with Creator. All things and all beings have this drive.

Eckhart speaks often of the principle of Desire. In one sermon, he says, "Earthly things desire to be equal to those in heaven"(Fox, 1991, p. 498). He refers to the *call toward home* when he says, "Just as every created thing follows and pursues its end, so likewise it follows its beginning" (p. 62). Fox expands on that idea by saying that all creatures seek the homeyness and warmth of their divine origins (p. 62).

For a very practical look at the principle, picture yourself on a shopping spree. You see something that you desire. On some level, you believe that by owning that object, your life will be more complete. On that level, ownership of a "thing" stirs the Desire principle.

Obviously, it is not true that owning a material object makes a human life complete. Any of us knows in our deepest self that consumerism does not make one's life "more whole." As Rabbi David Cooper points out in *God Is A Verb*: "If we stay at the level of the human eye's desire, we will never reach the spiritual level of the principle. The human eyeball represents desire that can never be satisfied. The desire of human beings is immeasurably weightier than all the gold and silver in the world" (p. 49).

The goal is to mature the Desire Principle in yourself so that your true desire is to become the fulfillment of life rather than to possess the fulfillment of life.

Brian Swimme in *The Universe Is a Green Dragon* connects Desire with the principles of Generosity and Goodness. "Our deepest desire is to share our riches . . . our desire to flood all things with goodness. Whenever you are filled with a desire to fling your gifts into the world, you have become this cosmic dynamic of celebration" (p. 148).

Eckhart contrasts our sense of longing to "share our riches" to God's desire for us: "Never has a person longed after anything so intensely as God longs to bring a person to the point of knowing him" (Fox, 1991, p. 141).

A Native American teaching tells us that anything that we can see, we actually possess. To see is to own, for one grants beingness to the object with the eyes. Natives believe that if something is perceived, it exists. When a Native American teacher sends you out on a vision quest, they will usually tell you to first find your power spot. Then from that spot face each of the four directions. "Own" everything that you can see in the South. Now turn. "Own" everything that you can see in the West, and so forth.

The intent and meaning behind this teaching is profound: If one gives visual attention to something, one grants beingness to that thing. By seeing it, one gives it life. (Of course, one has to hear this teaching through the ears of Humility.) Conversely, the observed thing has to send a visual clue back to the observer: it has to send its light toward the seer's eyes; otherwise, one cannot grant it visual focus.

Seeing requires the exchange of light. Desire, as a spiritual principle, is based on the integration of the interchange of light.

Eckhart says, "There is one power that helps the eye to see and another power through which it realizes the fact that it sees" (Fox, 1991, p. 517). He takes it a step further, in fact, agreeing with the Native American teaching by saying, "The eye with which I see God is the same eye with which God sees me" (Fox, 1983, p. 21).

A person who is contracted with Desire has special energy in the eyes that allow the seeing of the unseen.

Goethe states that the physical eye was called forth (in evolution) by light. Eyes evolved to perceive light. In addition, he states that the eye has a light of its own and that the light within the eye can correspond and interact with the light from outside (p. iii).

Everyone possesses these etheric eyes, or the "within" eyes, but few use them. The etheric eyes endow the physical eyes with vitality and fire but normally do not function independently. (In other words, you have to train yourself to use them.) Humans are so used to using the retina for ordinary sight that you have programmed yourselves not to respond to delicate vibrations of light, such as those put out by fairies and nature spirits.

The eyes are the gateway between the "in here" world and the "out there" world; they are the door to the soul.

Hildegard of Bingen says, "The eyes are the windows through which the soul knows external nature" (Fox, 1987, p. 126).

When there is no difference between the "in here" and the "out there," when there is no difference between the soul and the embodied being, then we are fully reunited with Creator. Desire no longer has an object.

Rumi says,

> Do you pray any longer to wooden idols?
> Then why do you pray to your Desire?
> If you become the one you long for
> Then what will you do with your longing?

> Poems of Rumi (Audio)
> Bly and Barks, Translators

Desire is actually an extremely sophisticated principle that sometimes gets distorted in the human mind. It is a sacred longing.

Matthew Fox describes it as a longing in the soul—"longing that grows in the soul. Longing is wider than all the angels . . . immeasurably wide" (1991, p. 132). When that longing is misunderstood, it becomes materialism.

Princess Diana's Moon (mastery) was in the principle of Desire in the second house (the house of personal possessions). She stands as a shining example of one who matured that principle throughout her lifetime. As a young bride, she was notoriously materialistic. Even the Queen was apparently complaining about the expense of her shopping sprees. Eventually, however, Diana became more and more philanthropic. She divorced Prince Charles in 1996, and in so doing, one would think she would be divorcing her role as princess. To everyone's surprise, she became even more generous and more humanitarian as a single woman. By the time of her tragic death in 1997, she was known no longer as the Princess of Wales, but as the Queen of Hearts.

Jackie Kennedy-Onassis also had her Moon in the principle of Desire in the fifth house (the house of children). Jackie Kennedy is famous for many reasons, of course, but she is probably most well known as an incredible mother who fiercely protected her children from the public eye and from the cruelty of the American public's ravenous hunger for information about them. It would appear that the principle of Desire came to its most mature usage through her after her children were born. Truly, her greatest desire in life was for them to be allowed to live authentically—in happiness and in peace.

One of the students in the course described her own life-long development and the maturing of Desire in her life:

> "The principle of Desire has been my greatest friend and teacher. Like all young people, I grew up worrying/wondering what people thought of me. I longed to be liked, to be desired, to be validated. I also longed to own, possess, have. As my 20s, 30s, and 40s unfolded, however, I became steadily less interested in what other people thought of me or in what I have and don't have. Desire changed me from longing to be *loved* to longing to be *Love*. So in an ironic sense, I find myself less interested in the physical body and more interested in the loving body. And yet acting with love, as love, in love requires a physical embodiment. Desire and patience are synonyms in that one must be still and know that one's personal will can override true Desire. If we plunge forward achieving, gathering, consuming, taking, we never learn the nature of our truest Desires."

26 Silence

Be silent at last! You've been talking a long time.
Let silence transform your mind.

~ Rumi

Silence is really a paradox. Absolute Silence is impossible as long as one is in form. If one obtains the discipline and ability to quieten the mind and stop the inner dialogue, then the bones of the skull attune with the music of the spheres and begin to resonate their sound. The bones of the skull actually vibrate with the sound on which form is based. To achieve Silence is to go into a direct, holy integration with sound. Silence is the sound of the spheres, the sound of God, the sound of Life Itself.

The Bible says, "In the beginning was the word" (John 1:1 KJV). As was discussed in the section on Placement, a more authentic translation of that statement would read, "In the beginning was the sound."

Silence is being with beingness. Silence is sitting still and listening to the beingness of yourself, your environment, your cosmos. It invites the mystic in you to come forth.

Rumi says:
> Ground yourself, strip yourself down,
> To blind loving silence.
> Stay there, until you see
> You are gazing at the Light
> With its own ageless eyes.

"One One One"
Light Upon Light: Inspirations from Rumi
Harvey, 1996

Eckhart is clear that silence is a profound spiritual experience: "Understand this truly: that remaining quite still and for as long at a time as possible is the best thing you can do" (Fox, 1991, p. 241).

Silent times and silent spaces are absolutely necessary for truly experiencing the connectedness and profundity of life.

Gandhi's Ascendant (ethical body) and Mid-Heaven (access to God) were both in the principle of Silence. Indeed, his daily meditation and prayer time, taken in absolute silence, were oft noted to be the foundation of his strength. "My faith is increasing in the efficacy of silence. It is by itself an act—perhaps the highest act, requiring the most refined diligence" (Strohmeier, p. 95).

Eckhart says, "You have to divest yourself of all your activities and bring all your powers to silence if you really wish to experience the birth within yourself" (Fox, 1991, p. 257). In this statement, he refers to the internal birth of God's image. In another sermon he reiterates, "Understand that it is the best and most noble situation you can attain in life when you are silent and let God speak and be effective" (p. 297).

Brian Swimme's new creation story speaks of the "great silent fire at the beginning of time." Everything that exists now existed in potential at the beginning—in that profound silence—that burning explosion of light (1984, p. 27).

True healing—indeed the healings of Christ—occur in silence.

Matthew Fox says they "flow from a deep sense of silence" (1988, p. 71).

Outside the human body, Silence lives in the outermost dimensions. One has to expand one's consciousness all the way out to the edges of the cosmos to truly understand profound Silence—the sound of the spheres.

The bones of the skull hold the responsibility for carrying and protecting the organ that runs the whole shebang—the brain. The spherical shape of the skull is a metaphor for the container of the universe. The bones of the skull contain the Silence of which we speak.

Hildegard of Bingen says, "The sphere of the human head indicates the roundness of the firmament, and the right and balanced measurements of our head reflect the right and balanced measurement of the firmament" (Fox, 1987, p. 91). She is indicating that when we allow the bones of the skull to attune with the firmament, we not only balance ourselves, but we participate in balancing the firmament. The persons who wear Silence are participants in that balance.

When you are able to cease your internal dialogue so that your own personal will and mental body are not overriding it, you move into that state that is in full alignment with all the information of the universe. You have access to this information.

Once, I did a reading for someone who definitely wore Silence. Master Lee is a master at kung fu, and he is also a talented healer. Earlier in his life, he took a 20-year retreat from the world. He learned kung fu, not from a teacher, but from the silence in his own physical body during those 20 years of solitude. He brought back a teaching that he learned through his energy body rather than through his physical or mental body. This teaching involved using energy to heal and be healed, and it related to allowing himself to move and be moved by cosmic energy.

The manifestation of every one of these principles varies, of course, according to the development of the being who wears them. But in my experience, Silence shows the widest variation. I have known some people who are contracted with Silence who literally never stop talking—as if they were afraid of silence. I remember a reading for a woman whose Sun was in Silence, and she interrupted me so many times during the reading that we never got past the Moon (the second clause out of the twelve) in an hour and a half. Others, like Master Lee, can use Silence to its utmost potential.

Earlier I described cultural anthropologist Margaret Mead's multiple agreement with the principle of Attraction. As importantly, Mead's Moon (her mastery) was in Silence. Jean Houston describes her as "a different order of being. . . . In pursuing the mind of Margaret Mead, I was crossing a forbidden threshold, entering, it seemed, an area of women's mysteries in which silence was the rule . . ." (1996, p. 233). I expect that Mead's success in becoming a trusted sister, in many cultures around the world, could be attributed to her mastery of Silence.

In her brilliant book, *Silent Thunder,* naturalist and bio-acoustics researcher Katy Payne brings elephants and their unparalleled ability to communicate across miles to the attention of readers. She speaks passionately about the elephant's use of silence:

Watching these animals who achieve silence when it is called for—
never mind that there are dozens or even hundreds together and that
some weigh ten tons, which makes silence of the feet difficult, while others
are but a day or two old, which makes silence of the voice unlikely—
you remember that in humans as in elephants,
communication is only as good as what is received.

To use silence so well: If I could choose for people one attribute
of elephants, I would choose this.

27 Peace

Blessed are the peacemakers
for they shall be called the children of God.

~ MATTHEW 5:9 KJV

Peace is not the absence of war. Peace is emptiness—absolute and Divine Emptiness. It is an emptiness that is so filled with holy energy that it does not need to be expressed. It is not the emptiness that says, "I lack." It is the Emptiness that says, "I have no need." It is the emptiness that allows for the experience of Oneness with All.

There is no relativity in this Peace.

Meister Eckhart states it simply: "Insofar as one is in peace, one is in God; insofar as one is outside peace, one is outside God" (Fox, 1991, p. 179).

Peace runs through the blood. The vessels that carry the blood in the human body are full. They are not lacking, and they are not empty. They carry in them the nurturance that one needs, and they carry away the toxins. It is a system that is so whole and complete that it just is. Of course, from time to time, the physical body can get out of balance with this system. But when the body is working appropriately, the last thing you worry about is whether your blood is flowing.

I think Eckhart would agree with this "runningness" of peace in the blood. He said, "People should run to peace, and that when the lord said 'Vade in pace,' he didn't mean 'go in peace'; he meant 'run to peace.'" Eckhart continues, "What is born of God seeks peace and runs into peace. Therefore, the Lord said: 'Vade in pace, run into peace.' The person who runs and runs, continually running into peace, is a heavenly person. The heavens are continually running and in their running they seek peace" (p. 440).

In his book *The Biology of Transcendence*, Joseph Chilton Pearce includes modern research showing that the heart has as much (and in some instances more) communication with the body cells and neurons as the brain. The blood, as it moves through the body under the rhythm of the heart, carries not only nutrients, but also other kinds of information based on the heart's electromagnetic field of communication with the environment. Heart intelligence, as he explains it, is a silent intelligence that underlies our experience of our world (p. 70).

Pearce suggests that the heart is a brain that is presently evolving into the dominant brain in the human system (p. 73). The primary energy of this new brain system will be compassion and understanding. For people who wear the principle of Peace, this brain is already becoming dominant. In this new brain-system, the deeply underlying gestalt through which humans will experience life is Peace—the new food on which our cells will thrive.

The term "metanoia" comes from Latin roots and means "change of heart." If you have Peace in your spiritual pattern, this lifetime is probably a metanoia for you. Your heart has ceased to be just an organ among many in your body and has become a brain—a radiant thinking and communicating system.

Ironically, if that is the case, you may be experiencing a sort of "inner war." Your head-brain and your heart-brain may find themselves in conflict for dominion. We still live, after all, in a world that preaches logic—reason and dualism as being the preferred mode of thinking. Part of your lifetime work is to find Peace within your own self in order to radiate it into the larger world system.

Satprem is a modern mystic who lives in France. He was once a student of Mirra Alfassa, who later in her life became known as simply "Mother." In his book about Mother's profound life, *The Mind of the Cells*, Satprem explains how he observed Mother's body evolving during her last 15 years of life. Of his observations, he states simply: "We are not the end of civilization. We are at the Time of Man's imminent birth" (p. 12).

In evolution, it is the weakness of the old species that opens the door for the new. In our case, that weakness appears to be in the rational brain. We have created, through our minimalism, reductionism, and rationalism, a birth canal through which the heart-brained species can and must be born. Peace is the spiritual principle that calls forth that evolution. It is the spiritual hormone that evokes new birth.

Peace is an "isness" that does not lack anything. Therefore, it does not need anything. It exists on a dimension of consciousness that is beyond duality. Peace is found before division, separation, and polarity were possible.

One night, several of the students studying the principles were in my living room. We were having a lively discussion about how Peace does and does not manifest itself in our lives. We made a remarkable discovery: Every person in the room who had Peace in his or her pattern (which was a majority of us) had been a debater in college. We are, "by nature," arguers. This tendency does not necessarily evoke the principle of Peace, so we were very curious about why this connection occurred.

When I reported this fact to my family, my son (who was only 11 at the time) pointed out that my daughter and I both wear Peace, and even though Peace is not in his pattern, he is the peacemaker in the family. He further pointed out that it is his wearing the principle of Gratitude that brings Peace out in us. Out of the mouths of babes! I suggested to the class at our next meeting that we need to see Peace as a principle that is evoked by the authentic expression of other principles. Why are we debaters? Because we are looking for truth; and when truth is expressed, Peace is present.

These kinds of ironies led to some deep insights in our online classroom about the difficulty in manifesting these Descending Principles.

One student made some important observations:

"Perhaps in the real world we can only experience Peace in contrast to conflict. And/or perhaps we should re-imagine Peace as dynamic rather than (as I tend to do) a static state on the order of thank-God-nothing's-disturbing-me-now. I don't claim to know how to do this, but if we think about how Peace emerges, how it is *created*, inwardly and outwardly, maybe we'll get some insights."

In response to her, another said:

"Understanding Peace as a spiritual principle is like trying to grab mercury from the thermometer when it breaks. I know there are some schools of thought that put forth the idea that Peace is always present all around us and all we have to do to experience it is to choose it. I myself have not had a great deal of success with this approach. It does not seem as though the Descending Principles can be grabbed or chosen directly. But perhaps Peace is always potentially present in the cosmic soup, and as we deliver our gifts to the world, we bring it forth. This would explain why we cannot hold on to it but must constantly create it anew."

And a third summed up our discussion:

"Our struggle with Peace does seem to be a struggle between understanding it as a state of being and understanding it as a never ending flow of blessings."

Mother Teresa was a healer, missionary, and perhaps the most outstanding humanitarian of the late twentieth century. She was triple contracted with Peace. Her Moon (mastery) and Mid-Heaven (connection to God) were conjunct at 27° of Taurus, and her Pluto (avenue into the underworld) was at 27° of Gemini. Certainly, she embodied the metanoia—the change of heart—that we, as a species, must all accomplish. She lived in the "underworld" of India's poverty-stricken society. And like the debaters in my dream circle, she constantly searched for truth. She was neither known, in fact, for her softness nor her diplomacy. She served God fiercely and according to the message she received (she believed) directly from the Divine. Her mission was neither to change institutions nor to save the world, but to evoke peace in each person she served.

28 Love

Love gleams and shines in the sublime lightning flash of its gifts
in such a way that it surpasses every insight of human understanding ...
none of us can grasp this abundance with our minds.

~ HILDEGARD OF BINGEN

*Love is the primary pattern and is beyond description or definition. It
is the glue that holds the atom as a unit. What is it that keeps the elec-
tron from spinning off and becoming its own universe? Love. Love
contains the hologram of the unified principles of form.*

Rumi would agree with Hildegard of Bingen and with my messenger
angels in the assertion that Love is beyond description or definition.

Whatever I say to explain or describe Love
When I arrive at Love itself, I'm ashamed of my words ...
Only Love itself can explain Love,
Only Love can explain the destiny of lovers.

Teachings of Rumi
Harvey, 1999

The angels said relatively little about the definition of Love as a spiritual principle. They seemed to imply that Love just *is*. However, in a feeble
attempt to try to understand more deeply, I have searched other sources.

Matthew Fox calls Love the pattern that connects—the Cosmic Christ
in each of us (1988, p. 18). Fritjof Capra (the physicist) says life is "a web
of interrelated events, interwoven by love" (1975, p. 43).

Even though she states that Love surpasses our ability to understand it,
Hildegard of Bingen does provide some indications of what Love is: "Out
of the original source of true Love in whose knowledge the cosmic wheel
rests, there shines forth an exceedingly precise order over all things" (Fox,
1987, p. 53). This order, she goes on to say, preserves and nourishes

everything. Love, for this mystic and visionary, was indeed the same ordered web of interrelated events that the scientists are only now discovering.

To experience Love requires an authentic experience of self-love. Love ripples out from the first dynamic to the ends of the universe—the first dynamic being self-love.

Dante claims that it is Love that moves the universe. "Through love, nothing is trivial because everything is moved by Love and connected through Love" (Fox, 1988, p. 143).

Eckhart says, "Love is so pure, so simple, so detached in itself that the best teachers say that the love with which we love is the Holy Spirit" (Fox, 1991, p. 311).

Love's synonym is grace. Grace is full reconciliation with God. True experience and understanding of Love render death not only not frightening, but impossible. To become the embodiment of Love is everyone's ultimate destiny.

How do you know when you are "in love—in grace"? Eckhart has some very clear measuring sticks: "We must love our fellow human beings like ourselves. We must rejoice in their joys as much as in our own joys, we must long for their honor as much as for our own honor, and we must love a stranger as our own relatives" (p. 399).

The principle of Love is not a sentimental or emotional attachment to a person or thing. It is, instead, the sourcing of our very existence. Humans are creatures of Love. The primary challenge of a human being is to expand his or her awareness in order to understand Love's magnitude.

Father Anthony de Mello has some beautiful analogies of unconditional love. He reminds us that unconditional love is like a rose that shares its fragrance with all who stop to smell. It is like a tree that provides shade for all who stop to rest. It is like the lamp that shares its light with all who enter the room. The rose does not decide not to share its fragrance with the wicked. The tree does not withdraw its shade from the wrongdoer. The light does not withdraw itself from those it deems undeserving. Love exists before judgment—beyond opinion—outside boundary (1989, Tape Five).

Love is focused on the angels. This means that the angelic realm is programmed to love unconditionally. They do not have universal permission to interfere with a human's free will. However, they can and do hover nearby, waiting for human minds and hearts to align with an attitude of Love. At that point, they reinforce every loving act that is chosen by the human.

We are known to be the envy of the angels, because as mentioned earlier, they *must* love, while we can choose to love. Accordingly, the human choice to love carries more power, more authority, more energy than the angels can imagine. Rumi says:

> There is no angel so sublime, He whispered,
> Who can be granted for one moment
> What is granted you forever.
> And I hung my head, astounded.
>
> *Light Upon Light: Inspirations from Rumi*
> Harvey, 1996

When we wear Love, it is our imperative to understand the power of the human choices as it relates to the spiritual principle. We must "hang our heads, astounded" each time we realize and actualize the profound energy of Love in our lives.

Healer and modern-day prophet Edgar Cayce's Sun was in the principle of Love in Pisces in the ninth house. This thread in his pattern draws an unusually clear picture of how and why he lived the life that he lived. Being dominated by the principle of Love, his natural tendency was to heal. Love, according to my angelic messengers, is the principle that lives in the angelic realm. And the ninth house, according to their charting system, is the house of the avatars—the advanced teachers. Through this placement of his Sun, Cayce had a unique relationship with both the angelic kingdom and the master teachers of the human species.

In addition, according to traditional astrology, Pisces is the sign most closely aligned with psychic gifts. Known as the "sleeping prophet" because most of the information he gained for the healing of his clients came in dreams, Cayce had delivering the gift of Love built in as the primary purpose for taking an incarnation.

Within the body, Love opens a new chakra point at the base of the brain stem. That is the only point in the body that has no pain receptors and no veils. There is absolutely no judgment in the brain stem and no fear because pain cannot be felt there. All information flows freely between brain and spine. That is a good definition of Love: the free flow of information with no judgment.

Each of the people in our class who wore Love had three things in common. First, they remembered many encounters with angels when they were children. Second, they could recall many times during their lives when they awakened in the night with the profound sense of an energy in the room that was bigger than death, bigger than life, and more comforting than words can describe. And third, each of them had at least one experience in waking reality (usually when they were in a natural setting) during which they had seen (with their physical eyes) the visible interconnection of all things—plant, animal, mineral, human, and man-made.

The students all agreed that Love is a principle that flows through our lives like a river that cannot be dammed or stopped. And yet each of us has the ability to turn from the experience of Love, ignore it, and pretend that it is not the source of our lives.

29 Movement

If someone asks you, 'What is the sign of your father in you?'
say to them, 'It is movement and repose.'

~ GOSPEL OF THOMAS, LOGION 50

In the above quotation, Jesus is saying that the two spiritual principles that bookend all the others are movement and repose. (The angels who transmitted this material to me named "repose" Placement.) According to this statement, the interfacing of movement and repose (Movement and Placement) is the indication that God is in you. The two principles should be contemplated together and if you do not have both of them in your chart, look at Placement anyway for reference.

Movement is actually the other end of Placement. When the zero principle and the twenty-ninth principle come together, the circle becomes whole. It is the marriage of particle and wave.

Movement is the force that keeps one going forward. It keeps one evolving. It constantly pulls one into potential and possibility.

Movement is the aspect of form that magnetizes one toward the realization of highest potential.

Meister Eckhart connects the principles of Love and Movement when he says, "Every movement through which we are moved to love is a movement in which nothing other is moving us than the Holy Spirit" (Fox, 1991, p. 313).

Movement is choreographed by spirit. It is the force that animates the cosmos, and it drives every form toward its destiny.

In another of Eckhart's sermons, he speaks of cosmic movement. "As a result of heaven's movement, everything in the world flourishes and bursts into leaf. The human spirit, however, is never satisfied; it presses on ever further into the vortex (whirlpool) and primary source in which the spirit has its origin" (p. 355). Just as the principle of Movement completes the wholeness of the principles and delivers us back to the beginning principle of Placement, the human spirit is driven to move ever forward in a spiraling return to the beginning—its divine source.

> *Movement resides with the avatar consciousness. People who are contracted with Movement have the potential to be in communion with the avatars. Avatars are beings who have reached spiritual perfection while incarnated as humans. Jesus, for example, became an avatar at the transfiguration. Mohammed and the Buddha also achieved perfection and therefore are also considered to be avatars. Avatar consciousness refers to that potential in any human to reach divine perfection while still in a body.*
>
> *People who are contracted with Movement can sit in the presence of these Beings who have become avatars. They can perceive the intent of evolution and consciously participate in the movement toward the divinity of the future.*

Of course, not everyone who has Movement in their chart has the "spiritual chops" or the vastness of consciousness to sit in the presence of avatars. But those who do have these qualities find themselves in lives that are magical and mystical and profoundly impactful on their human family.

Movement in your pattern does not mean you are always "in the light." You can be dark in expression, but the doorway to light is always present in your incarnational configuration. You may go to a party and offend everyone in the room with a dark mood, but that makes little difference. You have still brought avatar consciousness into the room, because it is woven into your very being.

People who wear Movement may find themselves in very influential positions in life, leaders of movements if you will, whether they are aware of the contact and guidance they receive from avatars and non-embodied beings. Winston Churchill, who is reported by those who knew him to be a highly evolved and highly spiritual person, had a Moon in Movement. Surely, his influence in the free world was profoundly determinant for the direction of both consciousness and political power during the last half of the twentieth century.

Malcolm X also had a Moon in Movement. He stood as a mighty force in the Civil Rights Movement. First, as a leader in the Black Muslim movement, he was influential in the rise of black pride and the education of what was then known as the American Negro. Later in his life, after a mystical awakening in Mecca, Malcolm revised his former separatist position and for the rest of his life preached of the brotherhood of all people. Although his change of philosophy angered his fellow black Muslims, and indeed may have been the reason for his assassination, the message of tolerance and loving kindness that he endorsed at the end of his life has become his legacy.

Another political leader with Moon in Movement has yet to unfold her destiny as a leader: Hillary Clinton. She has certainly cut new pathways for the political life of First Ladies in America, but it remains to be seen how her influence will impact the country in the long run.

British businesswoman, political activist, ecologist, and international web builder Dame Anita Roddick has Movement as her Sun principle. Looking for a way to support her children while her husband was away on an extended journey, Roddick thought back over the traveling she had done as a young woman. She contemplated the body rituals of women in small non-industrialized communities all over the world. She combined the frugality and economy she had learned growing up in war-torn England (Why buy more than you need? Why throw away containers that can be re-used?) with some of the recipes for beauty that she had gathered from around the world, mixed that with her desperate need to support herself, and came up with the Body Shop.

In her first store in England, she merely sold some beauty products in a unique "green" way (i.e., returnable and refillable bottles). But soon, she included in her business plan such values as supporting Third World women by buying their products, and eventually, Body Shop became an international good idea! Her book, *A Revolution in Kindness*, asks the reader to join her passion for an intra-sustaining world through reviving old-fashioned loving kindness as our primary modus operandi. Her dazzling success in business and international relationships stand as an example of Movement's interweaving potential in the world.

Someone who is contracted with Movement is also opening a new chakra point behind the navel. Development of this chakra point— the Point of Radiance—allows a wider range of Movement in the being.

If you have ever watched really masterful dancers, you will remember that they move from their middle. I remember seeing Baryshnikov dancing many years ago. I could almost see the fibers extending out of his navel, pulling him higher and further in those magnificent leaps.

People who have Movement in their charts move from the Point of Radiance. Luminescent fibers sweep the area before them, arriving at the destination just ahead of the body. These fibers stop them from walking into walls—both literal and metaphorical.

Working toward opening this chakra point and becoming highly conscious of its profound gift to the individual is one of your imperatives if you have Movement in your chart.

Julia Butterfly Hill, the beautiful young lady I mentioned earlier who protected a tree in Oregon, has a Sun in Movement. She remembers the early days in the tree when she longed to explore every limb, but she was awkward and afraid to climb, especially on windy days. However, soon enough she learned to hold the tree, balance her weight evenly between her hands, her feet and her torso, and allow Luna to speak to her, guiding her tree journeys.

I feel certain that her fibers intertwined with Luna, giving her not only a physical connection but a profound cross-species communication line. Anyone who has seen the picture of Julia standing on the highest branch of Luna, her arms outstretched seeming to salute the magnificence of life, sees the metaphor of this amazing statement by this courageous, compassionate woman. With Movement as her primary gift to life, a "doingness" that spoke to millions around the world presented itself to her, which called attention to and evoked a movement in ecological accountability.

Movement also controls the inner organs of the human. Those fibers not only shoot out of the navel into the outer world, but they extend into the trunk of the body to control inner movements.

Hildegard of Bingen expressed her understanding of that chakra point, too. She said, "The navel lets the inner organs come into motion" (Fox, 1987, p. 59). She expands that observation by saying, "The navel is in charge of our inner organs because it dominates them gently so that they do not disintegrate. It preserves their alignment and warmth" (p. 71).

To understand Movement better, meditate on the idea that you are here as a part of a soul cluster. There are several other people also embodied right now who are emissaries from the same soul source. Let us say that your responsibility is to be (metaphorically) the dancer/choreographer of the group. You are the one who works with the highest frequency of your particular soul intent. You are trying to bring that frequency into a form that expresses the love of your soul. Movement is a vibration of very high frequency.

In recent years, the newly-developed powerful technologies have allowed scientists to see deeply into the atom's nucleus. At a specific point of magnification of the nucleus of an atom, all matter disappears and there is nothing but vibration. In a very real sense, our world of form is nothing but the vibration of energy. The energy, however, moves so rapidly that it appears to be solid. It moves so consistently that it appears to be solid. That vibration is the principle of Movement.

Our class on the principles came to an ironic end. As we studied the final principle, Movement, each of us had dreams of the beginning principle, Placement. Some of us dreamed of being alone in our rooms, feeling safe and secure. Others dreamed of being transported to a place that felt like "home." Still others dreamed of swimming through a radar-like grid with dolphins who communicated to us about our position (Placement) in each moment. And each dream had a deeply spiritual feeling to it. Here is an example.

> I'm in a room, which apparently is "mine." It feels exceedingly peaceful. The room is very austere, almost monastic—with only a bed, chair, storage place for clothes. It's average bedroom size, though (not tiny like a cell) and has an even more spacious feeling. There is one window, also average size but feels larger. A pleasant white light comes in. The window frame and woodwork is dark brown. I might just add a desk or writing table. I feel so peaceful here, and it feels like home in the sense that it's absolutely the best place in the world to sleep.

These dreams of Movement/Placement made us feel loved, held by the universe, supported by life itself. Movement and Placement truly blended together to give us the feeling that God was in us.

PART III

Wearing Your Invisible Garment

Chapter Six

Your Spiritual Wardrobe: Wearing It Daily

By becoming aware of your own invisible garment, you will experience some important changes in your life. Specifically, seeing each person in your life as a unique thread in a large tapestry changes relationships. One of my students summed up her experience of working with her invisible garment this way:

> "This information has really helped me understand what other people's minds are doing, so I'm not so frustrated any more. In fact, I find that understanding others through their principles helps me support their authentic expression of self. I don't waste time anymore trying to make everyone be like me!"

Recognizing and honoring the spiritual garments of yourself and every person you know can completely transform every relationship in your life.

THE RELATIONSHIP TO SELF

In many years of working with this material, I have given almost 3,000 readings. Only twice has the response been negative, and on both of those occasions, we discovered that we had the wrong birth information. This perspective speaks to very deep truths in people, and the results are quite astounding.

In my own case, studying my spiritual principles lifted a burden I had been carrying all my life. I had always felt that I was not "enough." I had a sense of needing to be more accomplished, needing to be a better housekeeper, needing to be a more involved mom, needing to be a model wife, needing to be a community leader. Then, when I looked up my principles, I saw the truth of my essential self and sighed a big sigh of relief. I learned that my primary reason for incarnating was to live the principle of Humility.

According to the angels, the principle of Humility involves *knowing oneself authentically, and pulling information directly from the light*. Reading that statement hit the mark for me. In fact, this body of information is something I *pulled* directly from the light. I have had several experiences in my lifetime in which the sun (and also light of the dreamtime) seemed to "inform" me, and I "knew" something as a result. When I read my own principles, I knew that I was living my pattern, and the resulting sense of fulfillment was joyous. I do not cook much; I hire someone else to clean for me; I do not give business dinner parties for my husband's associates; and I am not a political activist. But other people are doing that. I am wearing my unique garment; I am living my enduring talents; I have discovered my own spiritual DNA.

Another student, whose Sun is in the principle of Service, experienced a profound transformation when she realized the difference between Service and servitude. The angels transmitted to us that one who is contracted with Service serves life by *being* authentic.

When you as a human live in the consciousness that life is a gift, you are living in Service to life.

She explained her experience this way:

"The principle of Service demands the death of the servant concept I have been enacting for many years. I recognize and grieve the extent to which I have been the servant—the sacrificer. After studying my pattern, I do not demean myself anymore. I no longer take the path of scraping the ego to the bone, crucifying, and purifying. Through understanding the principle of Service, I've transformed the suffering-servant concept into the knowledge that life is the gift, and as I serve life through my beingness, I amplify the gift for everyone."

THE RELATIONSHIP TO ONE'S FAMILY OF ORIGIN

Many of my students and clients have commented that this work "rewrites their personal history." As we learn to see the invisible garments of our parents and siblings, we begin to understand them differently. We are able to see the family dynamic, not through the eyes of the injured child (eyes which most of us carry all our lives), but through the sophisticated eyes of compassion. James Hillman, author of *The Soul's Code: In Search of Character and Calling,* points out that most of us hold a traumatic view of our early years, and that the focus of our personal story carries the toxins of that view (p. 4). However, I have found that by revisiting one's family of origin through examining their principles, people are often successful in transforming those traumas.

My relationship with my sisters certainly was not traumatic. In fact, we "got along" pretty well when we all lived together. However, from my perspective there was not a deep closeness, a real intimacy. There was some kind of undefinable separation or veil between us when we were younger.

When I looked up all of our principles, I saw that my oldest sister's Sun is in the principle of Memory, my middle sister's Sun is in the principle of Focus, and mine is in the principle of Humility. One of us comes from the Ascending group, one from the Containing group, and one from the Descending group. In a sense, we are all "coming from different directions." That in itself explains our lack of intimacy.

It is interesting, though, that both my sisters' Ascendants are in the principle of Generosity, and mine is in the principle of Reciprocity. The Ascendant in this system determines the person's ethical choices. The angels said that Reciprocity was closely akin to Generosity in the sense that both the principles deal with the necessary balance between giving and receiving. Therefore, my sisters and I are are all ethically very similar. That similarity explains our ability to get along so well. My coming to understand these similarities and differences from a spiritual point of view has allowed the veil to lift. I have a much closer relationship to my siblings now than ever before.

My relationship with my mother was more difficult. She and I fought, and we never saw eye to eye on much of anything. Looking at her soul contract helps me understand that. Her Sun is in the principle of Intelligence. This means that she is a very sharp lady. However, due to life circumstances, she never completed her education and she was never really taken seriously as a "smart" woman. I, on the other hand, was not only smart—but "smarty" with her. When seen through this lens, I can understand how my presence must have irritated her and made her long for her own self-actualization.

Meanwhile, I learned that my father's Sun principle was also Intelligence. This explains their relationship. He respected her Intelligence, perhaps as no one else did. The respect that he gave her bonded them for 60 years.

Without fail, clients who have studied their parents' and siblings' soul contracts have had profound "aha's" concerning their family dynamic, and they have been able to solve some of the mysteries around their own childhood memories.

Carol, 40, had been in therapy most of her adult life. Her childhood had permanently confused her. Her parents were abusive (verbally, emotionally) to each other but not to their children. Carol, the youngest of four, had been told repeatedly by her siblings that their parents never fought before she was born. As siblings who grow up in emotionally abusive households tend to do, they were particularly cruel to the youngest, especially in blaming her for the eventual divorce.

All of her life, Carol carried a deep guilt for having brought this pain into her family. Our cultural belief in "original sin" reinforces that kind of self-hatred. All of her life, she tried in vain to make everything nice again. Of course, it had never worked. Her many years in therapy had helped her understand that it was neither her job to make her parent's marriage work nor was it her job to carry the guilt because it had not worked. However, all the years of therapy had not released her from the pain that her childhood had created in her heart. She came to me at the recommendation of a friend.

Fortunately, she had access to her parent's birth certificates, both of which had exact birth times. When we looked at her parent's charts, we realized that they had the same Mid-Heaven principle. Because they were born less than a year apart, this configuration would indicate that they were soul siblings. Two people of the same soul cluster do not necessarily "get along" on an intimate level. They are two individuations (two distinct personalities) delivering a unique aspect of the same soul-gift into form. They love each other, they can support each other, and they can appreciate each other's contribution to life. But their personality differences may simply amplify their individual approaches, which would result in "sparks flying" in mundane, day-to-day reality.

When I saw these charts, I thought of an ex-boyfriend of mine. I loved him deeply, and he, I. We tried many times over the course of about 12 years to commit to marriage, live together, and just agree not to fight over our opposite viewpoints. It never worked. Our love, our admiration for each other, and our total support for each other could not overcome our different social, political, religious, and financial opinions. He and I were born three months apart, and we share the same Mid-Heaven principle.

When I explained this phenomenon to Carol, she literally transformed before my eyes. Her whole childhood had just been rewritten in a way that liberated her from blame, guilt, responsibility, and shame. She was able to see that her parents had made an error in marrying. They had become myopic in their relationship. And through their divorce, they had allowed each other to wear their individual life garments. She has not been in a therapist's office in the ten years since that day.

THE RELATIONSHIP TO ONE'S SPOUSE

Marital bonds and marital difficulties are often explained through comparing the spiritual patterns of two individuals. I have had couples come to me after "giving up" on their relationships in therapy, only to discover, through our work, the reason they are married.

I remember one couple who came to me as they were practically on their way to the divorce attorney. We looked at their charts. Both of them came from traumatic childhoods, and both were insecure as a result. As they articulated the issues, their primary marital problem seemed to be centered around his "addiction" to religious practice. He appeared to be living in extreme escapism, finding no real interest in anything other than his spiritual disciplines. She, meanwhile, carried the burden of being the primary wage earner, as well as the mother and housekeeper and wife and "heart" of the family. When we saw that his Sun principle was Movement, I read aloud the words of the angels:

People who are contracted with Movement can sit in the presence of these Beings who have become avatars. They can perceive the intent of evolution of all life and consciously participate in the movement toward the divinity of the future.

These sentences changed his wife's perspective toward him. She began to contemplate that she had married a very evolved man who is not escaping life but participating in its evolution. Conversely, when he saw that her Sun principle was Love, he also saw her in a new light. He realized that she, too, is highly evolved and is working directly with the angels to bring God's love into form. It suddenly seemed unfair, even to him, that she also had to bear all the burden of keeping the household operating. The two of them left with a new commitment to their marriage, seeing it as a bonding of souls rather than a legal partnership between two psychologically damaged people.

Another couple came with a similar complaint. He was more interested in listening to music and buying art than in making money. She was very career-oriented and ambitious, and resented his trying to "seduce" her into ignoring her responsibilities in order to "play." She was also bearing most of the household chores, as he was "simply too lazy to help out."

Looking at his chart revealed that his Sun was in the principle of Harmony. He likes jazz. He is attracted to the "is-not-ness" of life. He wants to explore the shadows and does not care much about the overt, in-your-face world. Her Sun is in Focus. She wants the facts. She is a bottom-liner. She is nurtured by accomplishment. They decided that their charts bore out their already-in-place decision to divorce and move on. However, this information gave them a new perspective. They left our session no longer blaming each other but rather respecting each other's invisible garments and feeling comfortable with the fact that their paths were neither compatible nor parallel.

My husband and I are contracted with 16 of the 30 principles between us. The ones we share are very powerful bonding principles: Peace, Love, Regeneration, and Reciprocity. When one looks at our two charts together, it is easy to see that we fit like two perfectly aligned cogs in a well-designed machine. And indeed it is true. I have never had another relationship that is so friction-free. Our children even comment that we are "odd" because we do not fight.

A relationship that was not so friction-free, however, was the marriage between Eleanor and Franklin D. Roosevelt. It is quite well known that he was verbally unkind to her. In fact, at one point, they were in a divorce proceeding after she learned of an affair he had with one of his office assistants. No one knows why Eleanor changed her mind and remained in the marriage. A look at her invisible garment pattern, though, reveals some interesting possibilities.

Eleanor Roosevelt's Moon (her mastery) was in the principle of Service in the seventh house (the house of marriage and legal contracts). Shortly after she changed her mind about divorcing him, FDR was diagnosed with polio. Eleanor's principle of Service did become a motivating factor in their marriage after that. While there is nothing in their life story that indicates that she adopted *servant mentality* toward him, it is well-known that without her support and encouragement, he may have dropped out of public life at that time.

His pattern included the principle of Peace in three positions, which most likely drove him to constantly look for ways to create peaceful existence for his depressed, financially beleaguered constituency. The interweaving of their two life's purposes became a powerful force that pulled our nation through one of its darkest hours.

After Franklin died in 1945, Eleanor's career in public life really blossomed. President Truman asked her to be the United States delegate in the United Nations. There she worked extensively to support relief work in Europe as well as many human rights organizations around the world. Another look at her chart reveals that her Sun is in the principle of Focus in the tenth house (the house of career). That principle apparently became the dominant thread in her "invisible garment" in her later years.

One might believe, by looking carefully at her life and her principles, that staying in the marriage was a spiritual choice rather than an emotional or social one. There seemed to be a deep wisdom behind it. Something in her seemed to know that her own life's purpose would be more powerfully accomplished in and through the marriage.

THE RELATIONSHIP TO ONE'S CHILDREN

If more people understood the spiritual fibers that undergird their children, the role of parenting would be revolutionized. When we learn to view our children through using their soul's intention, the kinds of structures we need to create for them become self-evident.

My stepdaughter has always been non-communicative. I could understand her not wanting to talk with me, as she felt that my presence in her father's life was the cause of her parents' divorce. However, she is also not very skilled at communicating with her mother, dad, or siblings. The moment I looked at her Sun principle, I understood: It is Silence. She is not deliberately being stubborn, rude, or rejecting. She is wearing her garment. Someday, in that Silence, she will find the inner peace that will allow her to manifest all her potential. Everyone in the family "eased up" on her after we saw this part of her agreement with life. In fact, she has become much more comfortable with us all.

My biological daughter is dyslexic. I struggled for years wondering how to help her. I have always been a student, reader, writer, comprehender. It has been a deep struggle for me to control some of my own frustration with this child who simply cannot meet the social norms of mental aptitude. After thousands of dollars spent on tutors, brain gyms, healers, and private schools, I read her chart. The mental thread of her pattern (Mercury) is in the principle of Silence. She has to take in data and then process it (sometimes for a very long time) in Silence.

When my husband and I realized that, we changed all our demands and expectations. We told her to forget about college (taking away the stress about grades and SAT scores) and even offered to let her drop out of high school if she liked. She chose to stay in school, and in fact made all A's and B's without a tutor in her junior and senior years. We found ways to allow her time and space to be in mental Silence. What looks like laziness and reclusiveness to most people is actually a spiritually-correct learning environment for her.

My son's emotional principle (Venus) is Randomness. This is an odd principle for him, because in every way, he is an extremely mature, gifted, and talented person. He has a personality that is fetching. Everyone loves him. However, under certain emotional conditions, he becomes rigid and off-putting. He is rude. He is confused. He is indecisive. And then, suddenly, he is easy-going again. For the longest time, my husband and I tried to find ways (through disciplining him, or teasing him, or helping him "work through it") to help him get over this immature behavior.

When I looked at his emotional thread, specific words flashed out to me:

It is in that moment between crystallized patterns that the widest range of possibility presents itself to be manifested.

I realized that under certain emotional circumstances, my son enters the realm of all potential. He is not being immature; he is entering into a sacred space in which he is making profound choices. He is actually developing a mature emotional body. When I explained this to him, he saw that what he does under emotional stress appears to be rude. He has adjusted his behavior so that now he tells us when he needs to be alone for a while. We have adjusted ours by allowing that space and trusting that he will balance the *seen* and the *unseen* realms.

These examples are just a few of my personal experiences with parenting through the use of the principles. Many of my clients have had similar experiences. We find that asking siblings to examine each others' charts is also very helpful, because through their innocent eyes, even more nuances and subtleties of their patterns are exposed. For example, when two siblings who often argue look at the principles they have in common, they see their fights in a new light. It is helpful for opposite-sex siblings to discuss how a woman might express the principle differently from a man. And it is valuable for children to look at their parents' principles to see how they are similar and different. Sometimes this process helps children understand why they chose these parents and these siblings, thus easing the family tension.

One client has a five-year-old son who continually shocks his parents with statements that he claims are quotes from his deceased grandparents.

He never knew these grandparents, but his "quotes" are amazingly accurate statements of facts of their lives. His mother came to me with both a profound curiosity, and a fear that her son is weird.

When we looked at his chart, we saw that his Moon (mastery) principle is Unity, the principle that has to do with genetic consciousness—being aware of oneself as a part of a gene pool or a specific DNA lineage. We spoke at length about the possibility that he is so in touch with his own lineage, that he can actually access information that he "should not" know.

Young children, before they become firmly socialized, before school and community has educated it out of them, are often impressively telepathic and clairvoyant. We also discussed that when one has Unity in one's invisible garment, it is sometimes a life mission to transform and reweave genetic patterns that are no longer useful and should not be passed on. This young mother can actually look at her son in a completely different light now. She can fearlessly respect his abilities, and she can accept the messages from the "other side" as gifts.

THE RELATIONSHIP TO ONE'S CLIENTS OR COLLEAGUES

Many of the people who have studied the principles and the invisible garment information with me are artists, therapists, ministers, rabbis, and spiritual leaders. They have all commented to me that looking up the principles of their clients and colleagues has changed their way of working.

One colleague and student is a transpersonal therapist. She now asks all of her clients to get a soul contract reading within the first few weeks of their therapy. She then structures the next 12 weeks of therapy sessions around discussing the client's life as seen from the perspective of each of his or her principles. She has commented to me that by using this information as an anchor point for the therapy, she and her clients can now accomplish in twelve weeks what used to take two years. They bypass talking about what happened in each client's personal history and move directly into examining the forces that drive the client's life choices.

Another colleague is an educational therapist. She works with children who have difficulty learning according to the old schoolroom paradigm. In her intake session, she asks for the child's birth information so that she can look up his or her principles. By knowing the child's spiritual purpose in life, she can alter they way she tutors the child's learning skills. This, for her, is a very powerful tool. It functions as a shortcut into the minds of her students.

Another friend and student of the work, a therapist and an artist, has made a collage for each of the 30 principles. She uses these pieces of art as meditational tools for herself and for her therapy clients. The visuals take them into much deeper understandings of the energies at work in their lives. In fact, visuals are probably purer ways to study the principles than words. This person, by the way, is using her artwork as her project for her doctor of ministry degree at the University of Creation Spirituality.

Those are a few examples of people who have found the principles to be tools that ease their work and simultaneously deepen it. One of the primary imperatives of creation-centered spirituality is that its practitioners must re-invent their work so that their livelihood and their spirituality are interwoven (Fox, 1994, p. 2). The information transmitted by the angels certainly appears to be aiding many people in that goal.

THE RELATIONSHIP TO ONE'S COMMUNITY

About half the people who have studied with me in the online classes, seminars, and dream circles belong to a spiritual community of one kind or another. They have encouraged people in their communities to also study the principles so that they can work with each other from a new perspective. I have communication with people from different parts of the world who have these soul-based communities. It has been astounding to hear how the principles have helped these people build a collective understanding of their purpose as a spiritual community in these troubled times.

One community in Asia started as a dream circle based on the teachings of my book, *The Woman's Book of Dreams: Dreaming as a Spiritual Practice*. There were 12 women in this circle and as they began to get their soul contracts read one by one, they discovered that they are in many ways a "perfect" circle. Between the 12 of them, they have all 30 of the principles woven into their various patterns. They have begun to study themselves as a "single organism" living the differentiated aspects of spirit. They see themselves as a soul cluster, a unique tapestry.

In my own dream circle, we work directly from our garment charts. As each woman shares her dream, we pull her chart out and look at it. We listen to the images of her dream as if she were giving us lessons on some or all of the principles in her pattern. This practice has created an expansion in the consciousness of every member of the circle, allowing us to hear not only the psychological message of each dream but also the message of Spirit.

Another community in Northern California started as a weekly drumming circle. The facilitator of that circle contacted me after she read my book and asked for my help with suggestions for taking the community into a deeper spiritual context. I suggested that they use the information of each principle as the "message" of the week. They took my suggestion, starting with Placement. At each meeting, one person reads aloud the spiritual definition of a principle. They then meditate on the principle. Then, someone starts the drumming, and they "drum" that principle, and the rest of the week is devoted to the contemplation of that principle. The next time they come together, they share what they have learned, and then they move on to the next principle. They report to me often on the remarkable synchronicities, the amazing "coincidences" (which no one believes are coincidental), and the profound bonding they have experienced through the use of these teachings.

THE RELATIONSHIP TO THE PLANET, TO LIFE, TO GOD

This work changes one's perspective. This information encourages us to walk our life-path with the understanding that our time on this planet is not only a gift and a blessing but that we actually participated in choosing the components of that gift. Knowledge of our spiritual garments opens our consciousness to the inter-woven nature of all beings. It brings us to an understanding that our purpose is pure, rich, and powerful.

In an earlier chapter, I quoted Thomas Merton:

> Then it was as if I suddenly saw the secret beauty of their hearts ...
> the person that each one is in God's eyes. If only they could see
> themselves as they really are. If only we could see each other that way
> all the time, there would be no more war, no more hatred,
> no more cruelty, no more greed. I suppose the big problem would
> be that we would all fall down and worship each other.
>
> *Thomas Merton on Peace*

I end with this quote because it summarizes the profound effect that this information can have on each individual. If we could only see each other as souls dressed in spiritual principles doing our best to live according to our covenant, then we could bypass so many misunderstandings, hurt feelings, and personal pettiness; and we could simply fall down and worship each other.

The "I Am" Meditation

One last treat: the "I Am" meditation. I ask each of my clients and students to use this meditation daily.

Christ is reported to have used the "I Am" phrase often—for example, when he said, "I Am the way, the truth, and the light." Those phrases were quite probably mistranslated. He was not saying that he, as a personality, was the way—he was saying the "I Am" is the way. In other words, those sentences should be translated, "I Am is the way to truth and light." In that context, "I Am" is a way of understanding ourselves as divinity—as a part of the whole. If one understands Who She Is, then she understands the spiritual wholeness of the realm of form.

We are very careless in our society about the use of the sacred phrase "I Am." It is a powerful phrase and when we accompany it with an adjective that is temporal, we diminish ourselves. "I am angry. I am hungry. I am—anything that is not REAL." All those statements are disrespectful to the human spirit. I encourage you to begin doing the "I Am" meditation regularly.

It goes like this: Say "I Am" and then follow it with each of your principles. It can become a chant, a mantra, a monotonous thing you say as you walk or run or drive. For example my mantra goes like this:

I Am Humility
I Am Love

I Am Reciprocity
I Am Silence
I Am Desire
I Am Resistance
I Am Generosity
I Am Regeneration
I Am Love
I Am Ecstasy
I Am Unity
I Am Peace

Try it in all sorts of configurations. For example, try making each syllable exactly the same so that the words lose meaning, but the encoding of the syllables speaks to you. Then try it as you drum—use the heartbeat rhythm, then the monotonous rhythm. Use your imagination with different ways to verbalize the chant. It is a wonderful tool to help eliminate mind chatter.

It quietens the mind and reminds you of who you are.

The "I Am" meditation brings you back to beingness so that the doingness will present itself appropriately. Meister Eckhart says, "People ought to think less about what they should do and more about what they are" (Fox, 1983, p. 97). This is a technique to help you do that.

APPENDICES

Appendix A

The 30 Spiritual Principles that Weave the Fabric of Human Life

The following information has come directly from my own meditation on each principle, as well as from working with clients who have the principles in their invisible garment charts. Most people find it very helpful to reference these short paragraphs that more or less summarize their patterns.

THE ASCENDING PRINCIPLES

~ 0 PLACEMENT ~

Sun in Placement

With your Sun, your primary principle in Placement, we know that you are a stabilizing force for all who know you. You could be called the anchor point for your entire soul cluster, and it is probable that you fill that role for your friends and family, too. You are the centering force around which all vibration can express. This most likely means that on the most superficial levels, where you live, work, and focus your life is very important to you. On the more esoteric levels, it means that you are deeply rooted in your being-ness and that rootedness radiates out of you to the other people around you. Each step that you take on the earth creates a ripple effect, like walking on water, and it actually provides help and motivation for others in your sphere.

Moon in Placement

You are a master of natural order. In other lifetimes and in other dimensions, you have worked very closely with the ever-evolving systems that keep the external manifestation of the cosmos operating predictably and precisely. This may mean that in your life, you need to be rooted—you need permanence; you need to own a home and have a certain level of security in it. As you mature your understanding of your mastery, however, that need for external security will most likely fade, because you will realize that your real security is in the fundamental principle of Placement.

Ascendant in Placement

Because your Ascendant is in Placement, we know that your ethical decisions are well-grounded—rooted in a solid understanding of time and place. You do not make decisions lightly and when you make one, everyone can count on the fact that you will stick with it and follow up. Of course, this can lead to a slightly stubborn or immovable position. But your wisdom as you age will give you the ability to be more flexible. For you, the decision to "do" something or to put your support or energy behind something is a very deep commitment, and your honor depends on following through. This makes you a powerful ally for all who befriend you.

Mercury in Placement

With Mercury in Placement, we know that you use thoughts and ideas to ground yourself. If you do not understand where you are, what is going on, what is being said, you do not feel present. You have developed a mind that is dependable and deep. In cases of profound understanding (perhaps in deep meditation), you have the ability to tune into what might be called "original thought." Your mind can extend itself into the beginnings of form and understand intention and origin!

Venus in Placement

With Venus in Placement, you have a little bit of an emotional challenge in life. You need/want things to be clean and clear emotionally and when they are not, it makes you very uncomfortable. In your more immature days, you may have gotten caught in the snares of people's emotional traps. But as you mature, you will find yourself less and less attracted to drama created by lies. As you evolve in this principle, you will find that to yours, and everyone else's surprise, you become the emotional stabilizer for your community of friends.

Mars in Placement

With your physical vehicle in the principle of Placement, we know that your body is very sensitive to earth energies. WHERE you are at any given point is very important to you. Your body is so sensitive to the frequencies around you that you have learned that when you are uncomfortable, it is imperative to MOVE. Your body is your stabilizing factor in life. If you are comfortable in your position (and this can mean literal physical position, or it can mean your life placement—career, relationships, and so forth), then you are in mastery of your life. If you are uncomfortable, nothing matters until you find the right place.

Jupiter in Placement

With Jupiter in the principle of Placement, we know that you get those moments of being tapped on the shoulder by the god of good fortune when you are in the right place at the right time. Every once in a while, you just feel it. It is a major "ahhhh" for you, and the universe says, "Atta girl." These moments may come on spontaneously, or they may come at the price of a struggle. Perhaps you have found yourself in a really wrong place, but society makes it hard to leave—a marriage, a university, a job. When you finally make the move and go to your right place, the feeling of universal support is almost overwhelming. As you mature spiritually, those moves will not be so difficult.

Saturn in Placement

You are closely aligned with the micro universes of this planet. Your view of form is directly linked to the highly sophisticated organizational patterns on which natural laws rest. You are part of the consensus reality that keeps cycles moving, keeps natural laws consistent, keeps movement from becoming chaotic. On the very deepest levels, you participate in projecting order into the external world.

Uranus in Placement

Your experiences of authentic self-knowing come when you are rooted. You have this sense of being "in the right place at the right time" and suddenly you remember who you are and why you incarnated. It is a magical experience, because it is connected to the Earth and to the natural laws of Earth. It most likely happens in nature—by a stream, in a forest, in a cave, on a walk by the ocean. Your connection to the micro universes of the planet is profound.

Neptune in Placement

Neptune moves slowly and appears to go retrograde often. Because of this erratic and slow movement, several birth groups come in over a period of many years representing the same sign. Neptune has represented Placement in Cancer, Leo, Virgo, Libra, Scorpio, Sagittarius, Capricorn, and now Aquarius in this century. Many of these periods were in war times and immediate post-war when there was not much stability to the societies of the world. That would be a good time to infuse human collective consciousness with a sense of Placement. For example, in 1943, we were preparing for the explosion of the bomb (although very few people knew it) and therefore an explosion in consciousness that would change our lives forever. That birth group was a grounding force during that highly chaotic time.

Pluto in Placement

Your journeys into the underworld serve as profound anchoring experiences for you. When you move down into the depths of yourself, what you actually find is a great underground or invisible realm grid work on which the whole world resides. Like Persephone, you understand in the most elemental way that for anything to grow in height, it must also grow in depth. Your self-discovery work, therefore, becomes a gift to the species, for as you liberate yourself from the fears and errors that may reside in the unconscious systems, so you liberate us all.

Mid-Heaven in Placement

Placement is the principle you contemplate to point you toward your soul's intent. You are sourced in the philosophical understanding that the first stage of manifestation is to establish a position. In other words, one must locate oneself in time and space before any living is possible. You participate in the part of consensus reality that glues form together by holding the basic grid work of the time/space continuum in your consciousness. Your most holy experiences come when you have moments of seeing the wholeness of what appears to be separated, because you understand the unified nature of Placement.

~ 1 INNOCENCE ~

Sun in Innocence

You are a natural teacher because you never stop learning. With your Sun in the principle of Innocence, we know that your primary reason for taking an incarnation is to learn. You are here, not to "learn lessons" in that negative sense that the New Agers use, but to explore all the possibilities of form. You do not gather critical or cynical evidence against people or the world; you simply face each new experience and each new circumstance as if it were totally new. You hold a freshness of attitude not only for yourself but also for your family, associates, and soul cluster. When you get criticized for this, remember that the person who is criticizing does not understand the value of innocence or the profound gift you are giving by being Innocence.

Moon in Innocence

With your Mastery in the principle of Innocence, we know that you simultaneously never quit learning, and you never quit teaching. Teaching how to learn is probably your most reliable gift. You remain acutely aware of the metaphors that parallel your experience, and you are able to use those metaphors to give meaning to your life and to the lives of those around you. You are profoundly loyal as a friend, and as a result of that, people count on your presence—and your innocence—to be stabilizing factors in their lives.

Ascendant in Innocence

With your Ascendant in Innocence, we know that when you make a decision about behavior, the opportunity to learn is always present. You will make choices that give you chances to learn new things, and you will always learn from your choices. In addition, you have a young attitude—not childish, but childlike. There is an open-eyed availability to life that keeps you regenerated—always ready for the next challenge or opportunity.

Mercury in Innocence

Innocence is the perfect mental principle. It means that you stay ready to learn, eager to explore in an unbiased and a fresh way. Although you will certainly develop opinions and discernment as you mature your Innocence, you will never develop cynicism and pessimism. It means that you can rely on your mind. There is a mental stability to an innocent mental body—it does not confuse itself with the facts.

Venus in Innocence

You are not an emotional scorekeeper. With Venus in Innocence, we know that you let things go. You experience them, feel them, learn from them, and then you release them. Innocence keeps you emotionally clean, pure, ready to move on. However, it does not mean that you do not learn from emotional situations. You are a fast study—if something hurts emotionally, you do not repeat it. This is good. It keeps you from falling into non-beneficial patterns in relationship and career. It keeps you willing to try something new and unknown, whereas most people will opt for the familiar even if it is unpleasant and painful.

Mars in Innocence

With Mars in Innocence, your physical experience of the world is very pure. In other words, you are usually ready to learn and to be fully present to whatever is happening. You love to try new things. You are like a child in that you experience many physical things in a new way every time even though you have already done them. You learn through your body as well as through your mind. In fact, you probably learn more about life through your physical experience! Life stays fresh and new for you because your body is always ready to experience it in that way.

Jupiter in Innocence

You have the profound experience of remembering that the universe supports you when you learn something new and exciting, especially when that something opens your heart. Innocence demands an open and pure heart. When you are available to receive new information—or even old information in a totally new way—Jupiter taps you on the shoulder, and you remember how totally loved you are.

Saturn in Innocence

You learn from the world of form. By placing your Saturn in the principle of Innocence, you guaranteed that the world would be your classroom. You find form to be amazing, inspiring, uplifting. Going out into nature or going to see an incredible structure of man both thrill you. Because we forget that we are spirit embodied, sometimes we also forget that the realm of form is only one of the many dimensions on which we reside. But there is some level of your mind that always knows that. You are in awe of the realm of form, and you simultaneously know you are just a visitor here—a traveler—a voyager. That is why it holds such curiosity for you!

Uranus in Innocence

You love to learn and when you learn something new, like an innocent child, you are in wonderment. You have the most authentic sense of yourself when you discover something new—or when you rediscover something as if for the first time. The capacity to mature and maintain an ability to be in awe, an ability to be innocent, is a fundamental sign that you are a mystic!

Neptune in Innocence

Your birth group brought a big dose of teachability to the planet. When you were born, it was essential that the consciousness of the human species begin to expand. We needed to be enabled to learn quickly, efficiently, and without blockage from old "wiring" systems. By reintroducing Innocence to the collective mind, your birth group brought a fresh and healthy curiosity. Because of you, the whole species began to learn again—in new ways. Of course, some of the old systems—specifically the educational system— have to adjust to this new influx of radical learning/thinking every time a new birth group brings Innocence as its gift. That has been a challenge especially in the last few decades, because teaching systems and learning patterns are not necessarily in sync.

Pluto in Innocence

With Pluto in the principle of Innocence, your underworld journeys are more like fact-finding missions than they are depressions or "downers." Innocence keeps you teachable, and the self-investigation that Plutonian energy demands is an opportunity to learn more about the self. Pluto's information is always there but remains unconscious until we plunge into the depths of ourselves and bring it to the light, so to speak. Like the "win-win" Persephone, your journey into the darkness is more out of curiosity than out of dramatic life experiences. That does not mean that you are able to avoid the life experiences of betrayal, and so forth, that would send you "down." It simply means that when you go down, you go with an openness and willingness to learn—you go as an act of power.

Mid-Heaven in Innocence

Your connection to the level of consciousness that we call "soul" operates on a frequency that keeps yourself, and our species, teachable. It vibrates with curiosity and can always see the fresh and the new in any circumstance. As a being, you are very committed to a life that is altruistic, philanthropic, and self-forgetful. You pour love lavishly on the object of your devotion—people, pets, plants, and rocks. Your entire soul cluster is working to bring Innocence to the consciousness of the people with whom you come into contact.

~ 2 Purity ~

Sun in Purity

Your Sun in Purity tells us that this lifetime is about correcting error. You have taken the responsibility to bring the gift of Purity from the level of your soul into the level of human consciousness. You are here to perceive error, track it back to its origin—which IS divine, because all things come from divine blessing—and then correct the error. This is a contract of BEINGNESS, however. You are not required to run for Senate and rewrite the laws. You are simply to perceive the error and perceive its purification. This error may be on the densest levels, and it may be on the most subtle levels of consciousness. Your communication with the devas (the earth angels) will be your primary guide in life.

Moon in Purity

With your Moon in Purity, we know that you have spent many of your incarnations learning to see and speak with the nature spirits. You have reached a comparative level of mastery in devic communication, and you brought that mastery with you into this incarnation in order to enrich your ability to deliver your soul's gift to the planet. While it may have taken you many years to accept the talent, after you have finally integrated it, you will be able to speak freely with the devic worlds and bring their messages into form. It is your imperative and your safety net. Ironically, even though society may try to tell you are "crazy," the devas are your most solid supporters in this incarnation.

Ascendant in Purity

Your Ascendant in Purity tells us that action must come from pure intent for you. Your behavioral decisions are rooted in the highest and truest possible ethic. You are much more interested in intent and impeccable action than you are in result. You are strict with yourself about measuring your actions against the blueprint of morality and kindness. People may comment to you that your behavior is unusually kind or thoughtful, but to you, that is absolutely the only way to be! In fact, you are the opposite—you are stunned when people behave badly.

Mercury in Purity

With your mental body in the principle of Purity, we know that you have a very special way of thinking and processing information. First, you do not like error. Flawed thinking is an annoyance to you. You are particularly interested in always going to the source or the original intent behind an idea. You can see the basic reason for an idea coming forth —and you like to work from that. So, it becomes very complex. You are not a ruthless logical thinker, and yet if there is a flaw in the logic that was woven in somewhere between conception and product, you are ruthless about eliminating the error. There is a sweetness to the way you think that endears everyone around you, because your commitment is to the purity of the idea.

Venus in Purity

With your emotional body in the principle of Purity, we know that your emotions take you to an essential place in consciousness. Through emotion, you are able to understand the divine plan and go to a plane of consciousness that is similar to that of the Devic Worlds—the level of consciousness that tends to the blueprint of form. This may be hard for you to understand, because it is so much a part of your nature that you think everybody does this. But that is not the case. Emotional experiences whip many people around, leaving them confused and disoriented. You, on the other hand, become more deeply engrained in an experience through your emotional response to it, and you come to deep understandings of the meaning or metaphor around the experience through your emotions.

Mars in Purity

To have Mars, your physical body, in Purity is a little bit of a paradox. Because the nature of Purity is pre-form, being physically contracted with the principle takes you constantly back to a level of consciousness that does not include matter. As a result, you may be a little annoyed by the constant attention the body needs. You may tend to ignore it until it demands your attention. You are more interested in the IDEA of a body than in the body itself. On the other hand, your pull toward Purity also makes you want to experiment with using the body to express your gifts in the world in the most efficient and impeccable way.

Jupiter in Purity

When you are able to shift your consciousness out of the appearance of any circumstance and into the intent of that circumstance, Jupiter pats you on the back, and you feel totally supported by the universe. For you, a Jupiter experience simply reminds you that everything that appears to exist ultimately sprang forth as an idea from the unseen and every visible form is rooted in the invisible. This experience brings inner peace, because the sense of being so inextricably interconnected with all that IS opens your heart.

Saturn in Purity

What does it mean to have Saturn in the principle of Purity? It means that when you are able to release yourself from the density of form, you can see its essential nature. Now, of course, eventually the essential nature of all forms is NOTHING. But on the way to nothing, the plan or design of the form gets purer and purer. You can see that. I expect that it is easiest for you to see it in nature. It is easiest to see the pure essence of a tree, for example, no matter how gnarled and weather battered it may be. However, with Saturn in Purity, you also have the ability to see essence in any form.

Uranus in Purity

Your experiences of deep self knowing come when you are in nature and the devic kingdom has your ear, so to speak. When you are in the purest states of consciousness and the purest locations of nature, you will experience lightning-bolts of clarity. You remember Who you Are, and why you took this incarnation. Those moments may not come everyday—or even every week or every month. But they come often enough that you never forget that you are a child of this earth, and that her blueprint is deeply imprinted in your being. For this reason, you long to be in natural environments as often as possible. Do not confuse this drive to go to nature with thinking you "should" live there. Your work may very well be in urban areas. It is just the experiences of nature that you need from time to time.

Neptune in Purity

Your birth group came onto the planet with the intention of bringing a freshness, newness, cleanness to consciousness. You infused the planetary consciousness with a deep knowledge of the blueprint behind all the forms and belief structures in which we operate. Because of that infusion, the political and social systems of all the major countries in the world have restructured themselves and purified themselves in the last few years!

Pluto in Purity

With Pluto in Purity, we can know that your underworld journeys take you into a place of deeply understanding the blueprint behind life. You are like one of those devas who can see the "isness" behind whatever you are examining. You are like the pre-patriarchal Persephone who went into the underworld because she was fascinated with the root system of the plants. Your depressions and/or deep personal investigations take you to an understanding of form and of life and death that is very clear. Your ultimate victory over life and over death is sourced in your ability to see the pure intention behind any form.

Mid-Heaven in Purity

The principle that points you most directly to the root of your being is Purity. Your most direct access to the soul's intent for your incarnation is to simplify everything in the moment to the most basic, most pure, and most foundational intent of the moment. At anytime, if you learn to look through the eyes of the devic kingdom—or through the eyes of the "isness" of any event—the level of soul will shine forth for you. As a soul, you participate in manifesting the blueprint of form. This means that as a being, you are one of the carpenters of life. If you begin to look at you actions and decisions from that perspective, your tendency to personalize everything will dissolve and you will remember Who You Are.

~ 3 MEMORY ~

Sun in Memory

With your Sun in the principle of Memory, we know that your primary reason for incarnation is to remember—re-member. You have a unique ability to access the most ancient records, and you hold an anchor point in human consciousness that allows evolution to include all that has come before and surpass it. Your special gift is that you can communicate with Earth's angels—nature spirits—the devas—"kontumble," as Malidoma Some calls them. You are most deeply connected to the spirits that speak through the stones. You have a tremendous access to the history of Life by communicating with the stones; therefore, your life is a contributing editor to the New Creation Story! Whether you are conscious of this ability to remember, it is still there in the energy field around you!

Moon in Memory

With your mastery in the principle of Memory, you are carrying a very deep spiritual continuum for your soul cluster. You have in your bones the records of the soul's journeys through consciousness. You can access that memory, if you like, by meditating, working with the stone people, and clearing your mind of fear and beliefs that you cannot. Do not be concerned if you do not remember mundane things well. Most people who are contracted with Memory comment, "But I do not have a good memory!" The truth is that this kind of memory is Spiritual Memory. It is encoded in your cells. It is bone deep!

Ascendant in Memory

With your behavioral body in the principle of Memory, you may often have a deep sense of deja vu as you make personal decisions. More than most people, you have access to the DNA imprints that remember the evolution of life. That means that on some level, you understand tribal thinking, group mind, ancient behaviors, as well as modern, self-conscious thinking. Your personal decision making process may be more complex than that of many of your peers, because you often take all of life into consideration as you make decisions. You are a natural ecologist—you know, bone deep, the interconnectedness of all living beings.

Mercury in Memory

Mercury in Memory means that your mind thinks along the continuum of life. You have access to what might be called the "Hall of Records" of the cosmos. Everything that has ever happened is recorded in cosmic memory. Everything that resides in the realm of potential is also recorded. Your mind has the possibility of accessing those records. In order for this to happen, you must learn to relax your personal mind, suspend all judgment and opinion, and allow the mind to follow the track of Memory to the collective mind. You are always interested in balance and healing, so any thought that leads to separatist or fundamentalist thinking will be rejected by your mind.

Venus in Memory

With Venus in Memory, we know that you are working toward perfecting your spiritual ability to use emotions. "E-motion"—energy motion—drives and colors the human experience. It is through our ability to nuance emotion into so many different experiences that we become unique contributors to the whole of consciousness. Memory is a principle that creates continuum, and it creates a collective repertoire of experiences. Your work in the emotional body in this lifetime is very serious and very important. You must work to make the emotional experience part of the collective evolving system. The lower frequency tendency in this principle may be to become ensnared and invested in emotional experience. Your higher goal is to release the density of feeling so that it is free to flow gracefully through your life and the lives of those you touch!

Mars in Memory

You physical body is a walking encyclopedia of evolution. You have an uncanny ability to resonate with other species and other sentient forms physically. You can learn from your body more readily than most people, because it carries the open Book of Life—sometimes known as the "Akashic Records." Because of the unique relationship of the mineral kingdom and the principle of Memory, you are especially attuned to the Earth, her pains, her joys, her needs. They may even manifest in your body as personal pains, joys, and needs. It is a blessing to have Mars in Memory, because it gives you the opportunity to embody evolution.

Jupiter in Memory

With Jupiter in Memory, we know that those experiences of being supported by the universe come when you have a sense of yourself as a part of a continuum of time-space. They may come when you are in the presence of your family and you get that sense of being a part of a tribe. Or they may come when you touch a stone and you feel the ancient and ageless quality of the bones of Mother Earth. When the stones of the sweat lodge are singing to you, you may have such an experience. Whenever those moments come, you "remember" that we are ancient beings here to update and call forth the future. There is a real peace in that experience for you.

Saturn in Memory

Your relationship to the realm of form is very matter-of-fact. You know the natural laws and you expect matter to obey those laws. You are one of the people whose "vote" in the consensus of form is quite precise. You are not emotional or subjective about form. It is what it is. For you, the laws of form are carved in stone. Solid is solid, liquid is fluid. This is not to say you are rigid or unbending or even conservative. You can, for example, speak with the earth angels whom most people do not even "believe in," much less talk to. However, you are precise in your opinions about the realm of form, and you expect precision in return.

Uranus in Memory

Your experiences of knowing exactly who you are and having authentic understanding of yourself most often come when you are in nature—or at least when you are working with the mineral devas in some way. You have a close kinship with the earth angels, and when they speak to you in whatever way they communicate with you, your most ancient Memory is stirred. Who you are, why you are here, where you are going all become clear—for that moment anyway. There is a certain lightness to your being, because you are related to these very light beings!

Neptune in Memory

When a birth group brings Memory, it is because the species is about to make an evolutionary shift and the coding of where we have been and where we have potential of going needs to be reinforced. For example, Neptune was in Memory in the sign of Libra in the early part of 1944. Ironically, during that time, we were making plans, via the atomic bomb, to change the karmic patterning for all times. The day that bomb went off, we irrevocably changed directions. We had been reinforced with Memory a year and a half earlier.

Pluto in Memory

Your journeys into the underworld are fact-finding missions. When you go into a "depression" or a particularly contemplative time, you are actually exploring the deepest knowing of Mother Earth. You are entering the hall of records as kept in the mineral kingdom. Caves are a natural space for you and a place where you receive very important information. Your life challenge may be not to become addicted to those inner journeys. Your talent at reading the ancient records may become such an obsession for you that you will resist "normalcy." You are here to give form to what you know/remember! Do not forget that.

Mid-Heaven in Memory

Your Mid-Heaven in Memory points to the idea that on the soul level, you participate in the great continuum that strings life together. When your egoic mind is quiet and your personal mind is surrendered to your divine purpose, you will have full memory. We are star fire in a configuration of form called "human being." We have the potential in our cells to recall the initial moment of creation. Your soul holds the records of the beginning of time/space/matter. Your soul sent you here to bring the gift of memory to the human species and to the planet.

~ 4 BEAUTY ~

Sun in Beauty

Your primary reason for incarnating is to walk the Beauty Way. This means that physical beauty is very important to you and in your young days, it may have been all-important. However, as you mature, you will discover that Beauty is a spiritual power, not a physical asset. One of your most important "jobs" as a human is to literally see Beauty. Your eyes grant beauty to all they behold. Again, this may be an ability that you had to develop and mature, for often we cannot see the beauty around us because we are too damaged psychologically to see the mirrors clearly. The ability to bring spiritual Beauty into form is truly a profound blessing and a mighty challenge, and you are one of the beings who have agreed to make that your life commitment. You have a very special relationship with the gemstones of our planet, and in fact, you are one. Gems are stones that have perfected themselves so thoroughly that they become transparent. They are solid, but they let the light shine through. That is your personal life goal—to be seen—to let the light shine through you.

Moon in Beauty

You have a natural radiance that makes people stop and notice you. Whether it is a physical beauty as defined by social trends or a spiritual beauty that is defined by your level of evolution, you cause heads to turn when you walk into a room. This relationship to the principle of Beauty is one that is earned by many lifetimes of work in this field. You have purified your errors so that, like the gemstone, light can shine through you and catch the eye of the beholder. Hopefully, you have also matured your own understanding of this principle so that you know it is the light and not you that is attractive. And hopefully, you know how to allow that light to mirror Beauty back into the world.

Ascendant in Beauty

With your behavioral body in the principle of Beauty, we know that you are practicing the great spiritual path known as the "Beauty Way." In our Native American traditions, this is a path of great peace and great honor. One walks recognizing Beauty before them, behind them, and all around them. Every spiritual tradition describes this path differently, but all honor it. The goal when one has placed one's ethical body on this path is to always make decisions that beautify the planet, the being, and the perception of all sentient beings. In our Western culture, that path has become distorted into an obsession with appearance. Of course, this path is about discovering, nourishing, and acting out the REAL essence of Beauty. Understanding the real essence of Beauty involves deep contemplation! Your daily spiritual practice is, therefore, of utmost importance in this lifetime.

Mercury in Beauty

Your mental body has a natural bent toward seeing the divine perfection in all ideas. You know how to recognize Beauty, and you know how to amplify it through your thought processes. In other words, if left to your own devices, your mental process will always consider, magnetize, and focus on the natural unfolding of the Beauty Way. This may be hard for you, because people may accuse you of a naiveté in your thinking. Standing strong in the face of cynicism is not easy. However, you must rest in the truth that your mind is one that sees simplicity and grace. In truth, simplicity can also see complexity—whereas complexity can often not see simplicity. So, your mental position is one of expanded consciousness!

Venus in Beauty

Emotionally, you are dedicated to truth. For you, an emotion is a wave of feeling that washes over you so that you can see the awesome qualities of a situation. Even if the emotion is one that society might label as negative—anger, jealousy, greed—if you let it wash through you without taking hold and possessing you, the result is one of Beauty. You feel purged, cleaned, and translucent as a result of emotional experience. As you mature your emotional body, you will also learn how to help others use emotion as a purifying and deepening process.

Mars in Beauty

With your physical body in the principle of Beauty, you have set an interesting challenge for yourself—especially if you live in twenty-first century North America. Our culture has some very skewed ideas of what is physically beautiful, and anyone who truly subscribes to the social trends also subscribes to a life of disappointment. The beauty goals are impossible to reach—and even more impossible to maintain. Your real goal is to learn to allow yourself to shine like a gemstone! No matter what your physique looks like, you have a very strong relationship to inner beauty—and whether you are drop dead gorgeous or relatively plain, it is the inner beauty and the inner potential for extending light into the world that will attract the eyes of the world to you! Use your Beauty wisely, and you will have given your greatest gift to the species.

Jupiter in Beauty

Jupiter in Beauty means that your experiences of feeling totally supported by the universe come when you are awestruck by nature or something that strikes you as particularly beautiful. You are stopped in your tracks, and in that moment, you know that the universe is actually and literally supporting your incarnation. You know that you have unique gifts to give and a unique vision of the world, and you are inspired to move forward. Beauty is connected to the stones and minerals of our planet, so your work with or appreciation of stones may also be a source of your Jupiter experiences.

Saturn in Beauty

Because your Saturn is in Beauty, we know that you perceive form through the eyes of Beauty. In other words, when you see a tree, you do not see the gnarls and rips and tears; you see the wholeness and the harmonic of the tree in its environment. You do not see flaws in form; you see the intended pattern that holds a specific beauty for every form. You do not see the danger or ickyness of a bug or a spider or a snake; you see the beauty of the form. This is one of the imperatives in your pattern—to see the intended structure of form and to recognize its innate beauty.

Uranus in Beauty

Your moments of most authentic self-knowing come in nature. Most specifically, the mineral kingdom speaks to you. You understand a gemstone as form that has purified itself so that the light can be seen through it. In many ways, that is who you are. You are a diamond. You are a being who allows the light to shine through you; therefore, you allow people who really see you to experience Beauty in themselves. You intuitively know when those moments have occurred, and they give you a sense of self that is profound.

Neptune in Beauty

Your birth group came to infuse the planet with Beauty consciousness. Millennia ago, one of the sacred names for God was Divine Beauty. That has slipped from our Western mind vocabulary. Your birth group tried to reinstate that memory. In fact, the contemplation of Beauty is one of the sacred jobs of the human species—the true understanding and appreciation of Beauty is our birthright and our imperative. Through the thousands of babies born during your Neptune phase, that reminder is installed into our morphic field!

Pluto in Beauty

Your journeys into the underworld are especially empowering for you because they show you the roots and depths of Beauty. When you go into a deep self-investigation, you learn more about the truth behind all appearances. This knowledge gives you a strength and an understanding about the essential nature of life. From that knowledge, you become a beacon of

Beauty. In the two stories that most represent the underworld journey—Persephone and Inanna—both the women returned from their underworld journey more Beautiful because of the ordeals they went through in the core of their beings. Beauty that is only skin deep fades, but inner beauty radiates from the core of itself eternally.

Mid-Heaven in Beauty

The one undeniable fact about our universe is that it is magnificently beautiful. Our Mother Earth is the source of awe for any who truly behold her. Think of a time when the Beauty of this planet forced you to catch your breath. You are one of the beings who radiates out of the principle of Beauty—and who returns to the level of soul riding on the principle of Beauty. Your connection to Creator is simple, elegant, uncomplicated. You return to the level of soul every time you experience Beauty.

~ 5 EXTENSION ~

Sun in Extension

You are in profound partnership with the earth angels. That is your life's primary focus. How you have chosen to express this will probably be the most interesting aspect of your invisible garment. If you work with the plant devas in some direct way, you probably find enormous peace and happiness in your daily activities. You may be a gardener, florist, cook, herbalist, or healer who works with plant essences. If you have chosen a career that does not put you into constant contact with the plant world, then you surely have other ways of being in touch with this very essential part of your life. Your hands are gifted, and your talent is in them.

Moon in Extension

In many lifetimes and on many dimensions, you have practiced and developed the gift of working with the earth angels. This relationship to the plant kingdom may cause a little confusion for you, because on the one hand you are one of the most grounded and fully incarnated people on the planet (by virtue of having such a profound connection with the angels of the earth) and on the other hand, most cultures think it is a little "wacky" to be able to see and talk to the plant devas. But never mind—you are one of them, cleverly disguised as a human, and that is the truth of who you are. The devas of the plant kingdom will never fail you—they are your primary support system—so honor them as such.

Ascendant in Extension

Your behavioral decisions always center around how to maintain your personal space without disconnecting from the wholeness. You are like a wild plant that wants to reach into the depths of the soil and the heights of the sky, while simultaneously participating in the grandeur of the forest. Each time you are required to make a decision that involves your personal ethic, your first measurement is, "What will this do to simultaneously distinguish me and connect me?" In some cases, this makes you vulnerable to other peoples' opinions about your choices, so one of your plumb lines will be to establish very clear boundary definitions for yourself, and act from that position of power. Of course, your decisions will also be eco-centric (as opposed to ego-centric) in nature, as your heart-mind beats to the rhythm of the environment around you.

Mercury in Extension

With your mental body in the principle of Extension, we know that you always think along the lines of wholeness and healing. You probably have an uncanny ability to "read" plants and know how they are most useful to humans. In addition to that, you have a mind that is never at rest. Like the root and stem system of a plant, your mind is always reaching into the unseen as well as into the obvious and seen realms to find more truth. You will never stop growing mentally, because curiosity is in your nature. When you become confused, the best place to go is to the garden or to the flower mart. The smell of the earth and the fragrance of flowers will clear your mental confusion faster than anything else.

Venus in Extension

Your emotional body is an amazing agent for growth for you. You always want to feel all that is possible to feel. You deepen with your emotional body like a plant system deepens when it looks for nourishment. You also grow with your emotional experiences, just like a plant's stems and leaves always turn toward and grow toward the light. Emotions are not fearful for you, but are instead a source of nourishment.

Mars in Extension

With Mars in Extension, we know that your physical hands are very important parts of your incarnation. You have healing power in your hands. Also, we know that your sense of personal space is important. You are more aware than most people of the auric field around your body, and you can learn tremendous amounts of information through the energy around you. It is also important, therefore, for you to have plenty of solitude space so that you can stay healed. Your physical body is your primary teacher of compassion. Through your own physical experience of life, you know how to extend compassion into the lives of others. When you feel ill, constricted, or dispassionate, your best technique is a walk in the woods. Be awake and alert and very conscious, and simultaneously give yourself to the woods! That will restore physical balance quickly and efficiently. If woods are not available, find a garden, a nursery that grows herbs, or a labyrinth.

Jupiter in Extension

Your moments of knowing that the universe supports you totally most often come in nature—especially in the garden. Your connection to the devas of the earth is what evokes this sense of cosmic support and protection. Whether you are working in the flower garden, picking vegetables for dinner, or simply walking in a particularly beautiful area, you will from time to time be washed with that delicious and all encompassing feeling of being fully supported by the universe. These moments string together like a strand of pearls for you, and they keep you going forward!

Saturn in Extension

You are truly blessed with a view of life and an understanding of form that is quite sophisticated, and simultaneously quite simple. You have an innate understanding of the interconnectedness of nature—and specifically of the plant kingdom. Botany is an easy subject for you, because the basic structure of the plant kingdom is obvious to you. You tend, therefore, to see the realm of form as clusters of intercommunicating cells. Life is not as blindly mysterious for you as it is for some people, because you understand that light is the primary carrier of energy, and that through our relationship to light, we all interconnect.

Uranus in Extension

With Uranus in Extension, we know that your experiences of authentic seeing of the self most likely come in the garden. This could be literal—that when you are tending to your own garden, you have these experiences—or it could be that it is when you are in Mother's garden (in nature) that they come. Your hands begin to buzz, and you suddenly have a strong image of knowing exactly who you are and what your power is. You feel your roots deepen and your branches sprout new leaves! These experiences are probably very "high" for you, and you may attribute it to too much sunlight or to a fragrance. Your relationship with the plants is very important—when you cook, when you touch anything or anyone, when you take herbs—anytime you work with the plant kingdom—your authentic self is more available to you.

Neptune in Extension

Your birth group infused the planetary consciousness with the energy of life extending itself. In many ways, you brought a healing, plant deva awareness to form. You can probably gain a great deal of understanding about the principle of Extension by simply meditating on the state of human consciousness at the time of your birth and imagining how bringing this kind of awareness into focus at that time was a great gift to all beings—especially human beings.

Pluto in Extension

With Pluto in the principle of Extension, we know that your underworld journeys are similar to a plant's rooting. Each time you go into a phase of deep investigation (each time you take an Inanna or Persephone-like journey), you are really just deepening your root understanding of yourself/life so that your branches and leaves, or your overt self, can reach higher and be healthier. There is a certain delight about these kinds of journeys. Even though they may not be easy or pleasant, you know they always result in a stronger self. Your ability to heal others (through your hands) also increases each time you take a journey into depression! Your relationship to the plant kingdom is profound.

Mid-Heaven in Extension

Millions of years ago, a bacterium (a single-celled organism) discovered how to eat light and transform it into usable energy to sustain life. At that moment, a new level of soul began expressing itself in form. It is by surfing the wave of Extension that your consciousness is returned to the level of Soul. When you come into alignment with the deep understanding of life as an expression of Extension, you are automatically sitting in the lap of God. Through you, life extends itself. Through Extension, you return to the source of Life.

~ 6 REGENERATION ~

Sun in Regeneration

Your primary reason for incarnating is to give livingness to the principle of Regeneration. It is important for you to understand that this cosmos is a self-generating—and RE-generating—event. While on the one hand we can say that 15 billion years ago a great flaring forth began the universe as we know it, we can also say that several times per second, this entire universe disappears into the great unknown and then flickers back into perceptual reality. Each time the cosmos returns to perception, it returns fully regenerated. Your job in this lifetime is to hold that consciousness. See yourself and the world around you as fully new in every moment.

Moon in Regeneration

For millions of years, the consciousness that is now "you" has studied, mastered, and participated in the principle of Regeneration. On the deepest levels of knowing, you are aware of the constant rebuilding and replenishing aspect of life. You are a master of recreating yourself and your world. In a very real way, your gift to life is the gift of hope and awe. You never tire of watching life recreate itself in multiple forms and multiple expressions. You have a very deep bond with the Great Mother—she who constantly gives birth and nurtures newness.

Ascendant in Regeneration

With your behavioral body in the principle of Regeneration, we know that your every decision is based on your awareness of life's ability to recreate itself. You know that everything that lives is programmed through DNA to reproduce itself exactly. You make behavioral and ethical decisions from that frame of reference. In other words, when you plant your garden, you take the regenerative potential of the plants into consideration. You plan for the plants to not only recreate themselves, but you allow for how they spread, how they nurture the soil and other neighboring plants, and so forth. Similarly, in your metaphorical garden of ideas and philosophies, you only nurture those thoughts that say "yes" to life. You are by nature a highly ethical person and that ethic shows in all your choices. You make choices that create the greatest benefit for the greatest number of beings.

Mercury in Regeneration

With your mental body in the principle of Regeneration, we know that you are consistently replenishing both your own mind and the collective mind with clarity—clean thoughts. You are most likely a student of life, and your learning always helps replenish your mental system in healthy ways. Like skin that regenerates itself, you tend to slough off old thoughts that are "dead" and develop new thought cells often. Of course, also like the human body, you do not develop an entirely new paradigm. You stay within the original flow of the riverbed of your mind—but you never let the water of your thoughts become stagnant.

Venus in Regeneration

With Venus in the principle of Regeneration, we know that emotional experiences are enlivening and healthy for you. In your youth, you may have had to learn to appreciate the power of emotions. But as you mature, you will find that they are more and more empowering for you. The emotional body is designed to be the part of life that gives it richness and value and meaning. In your case, it does all that and simultaneously reminds you of the blessing of life. Your emotions can be compared to the emotions of a tree, for example, because Regeneration is connected to the plant world. Trees feel deeply and express themselves in beauty, but they do not allow emotion to overwhelm them or to stop their growth.

Mars in Regeneration

With your physical body in the principle of Regeneration, we know that the process of having the body heal itself and recreate itself is an important part of your life. This may mean that you live a very healthy and robust life, or it may mean that you experience the paradox of having many physical struggles throughout life. Your challenge with this placement is that you must remember to see the process of life as one that is constantly new, constantly recreating itself, and constantly holding the potential for perfection. If you take your physical health for granted, or if you get into the pattern of "being unhealthy," you may end up fighting against that which is most innate in you!

Jupiter in Regeneration

Your relationship to plants is an important part of your understanding that the universe supports your life unconditionally. These moments in which Jupiter puts his arm around you and lets you remember how divinely loved you are may come when you are in the garden, you are cooking, or you are working with aroma therapy or plant essences. Whatever your momentary relationship to the Plant Beings, they are a defining part of your Jupiter experience!

Saturn in Regeneration

You have the uncanny ability to watch the forms of life recreating themselves. Your natural tendency is to see the recreating more than the destruction in life. You do not see a snake shedding its skin; you see a snake birthing a new skin. You do not see death; you see transformation and rebirth. It is not that you are in denial or naive, it is that your natural focus is on Regeneration. As the cosmos flickers in and out of perceptual reality, you are able to sense the darkness as periods of reconstruction, and that attitude spills over into your daily life. You are a constant source of inspiration for Regenerating the best of what life has to offer.

Uranus in Regeneration

You have that lightning bolt experience of remembering yourself authentically when something happens that truly regenerates and refuels you. It can come after a good nap, a great dip in a pool or spa, the taste of a fresh peach! Suddenly, your cells begin to sparkle, and you totally remember yourself as the Child of the Creator—the result of the love affair between heaven and earth. In those moments, your sense of freedom is almost overwhelming.

Neptune in Regeneration

With Neptune in Regeneration, we can imagine that your birth group brought a sense of renewal to the planet. It was time for humanity to have a renewed sense of hope and growth and movement when your birth group came. You injected the consciousness with the idea of rebirth and newness.

Pluto in Regeneration

Your "down" times—your journeys into the underworld—may come as a result of exhaustion and depletion. However, they result in a renewal and a rebirthing that is quite remarkable. You know how to descend into silence and hear the tones of your own vibration there. You know how to metaphorically go into the cave and allow the womb of Mother Earth to reconstruct you. Your challenge may be to remember to do that—to close down, go on sabbatical, hangout the "no vacancy" sign—BEFORE your body demands that you do so.

Mid-Heaven in Regeneration

With your Mid-Heaven in Regeneration, we know that you are intimately connected to the fact that the cosmos is constantly recreating itself—that it is new in every instant. When you are able to move your attention out of the consensus reality and into the concept that we are really just quanta of energy flashing on and off millions of time per second—each time being as new as the first time 15 billion years ago—in that instant, you are in direct communication with your soul. Your relationship with nature, specifically with the plant kingdom, is a very important part of this lifetime for you. They keep you in constant communication with the soul level.

~ 7 GENEROSITY ~

Sun in Generosity

You are the representative of your soul—here to be generous. This means that not only are you a giver but that you have made a sacred commitment to understand the balance of giving and receiving. You are here to learn and express the great give away, which means that you are here not only to serve life but to live life fully. In a very real sense, you are not burdened with life the way many people are, because your innate understanding that life is a gift sets you free of feeling pressured to "understand."

Moon in Generosity

You are a master at giving and receiving. In your most innate self, you know the absolute necessity of balancing the two—not only in your daily life but in your very being. As you give, you receive. Consciousness of both the giving and receiving is important to assure a stability in your mental, physical, and emotional bodies. Some people are so blinded by what they do not have that they absolutely miss acknowledging what they do have. This will only be the case for you if you get out overly stressed and lose your perspective. You brought Generosity with you into this incarnation as a safety net—as a guide or plumb line to help you keep accurate measurement of your growth. Generosity is such second nature to you that you may not have given it much thought!

Ascendant in Generosity

With your Ascendant in Generosity, we know that you base your decisions on the giving and receiving principle. When you make a conscious behavioral decision, you always consider the effect that doing is going to have outside you and what it is going to bring back inside you. Ultimately, your goal is to only do things that are beneficial to both you and the other beings involved. The danger in this position is that you may burn yourself out. Too often, people—women especially—do not pay enough attention to "receiving." We give, taking care of other people's needs first, and we often forget to slow down and let ourselves receive and be replenished.

Mercury in Generosity

With your mental body in the principle of Generosity, we know that you are almost always thinking about balance and equality. It is hard for you, in fact, to "take sides" on almost any issue, because taking the best of both arguments and creating your own "side" is so much more natural. You like to use your mind to create results, and you do not particularly relish results that are lopsided or ill-founded. You think with your instinctual brain, as well as your logical brain—allowing all levels of information to penetrate the system. You are animal-like in that way.

Venus in Generosity

Venus in Generosity indicates that when you have an emotional experience, you are reminded of the reciprocal nature of energy. When you truly feel, you have a cathartic, cleansing experience. Your emotions are strong and can be overwhelming, but they are also very powerful in teaching you the truth about energy. Your emotions force you to self-reflect and see life more clearly.

Mars in Generosity

With Mars in Generosity, we know that your body processes food, energy, and information by seeing the relationship to the greater whole. In other words, like an animal's body, your body understands on an involuntary level the value of nutrition, water, exercise, and rest. You have a strong body, and it is very sensitive to the environment in which it lives and thrives. You take in environmental information (and we all do this through our pores, hairs, and invisible antennae), and your body perceives the world through its senses.

Jupiter in Generosity

You feel most supported and validated by the universal forces in moments of pure, raw, unflawed generosity. These moments may take the form of giving money to a homeless person—an obvious expression of generosity—but they most likely happen when you give something (time, energy, advice, love) so freely that it does not even seem like giving. In those moments when there is a free exchange—when you have experienced the highest vibration of the principle of Generosity—you feel a warmth in your body. That is the heat of Jupiter's arm as it embraces you!

Saturn in Generosity

The principle of Generosity in association with Saturn means that you put boundaries around form by seeing a form's relationship to other forms. When you see a tree, you see it as an individuation of a forest. When you see a sunset, you see it as a magnificent light shed on the world that says good-night. You do not isolate and dissect. You integrate and include. The perceptual world for you constantly shows wholeness and connection. The reflective world mirrors unity and oneness.

Uranus in Generosity

With Uranus in Generosity, we know that you have those "aha" moments when something happens that demonstrates the principle of giving and receiving to you. If you make a sacrifice of some sort and then you receive a new job or a check in the mail, it all of a sudden makes sense to you and you remember yourself fully and honestly. These moments erase doubt and fear around whether you will be "okay" in this material world and allow you to remember your holiness.

Neptune in Generosity

Your birth group came in bearing a great big dose of Generosity to give to the people of this planet. You brought with you a natural bent toward balance and a natural urge toward reciprocal thinking and behavior. If we are to ever evolve into a peaceful species, this kind of energy and this way of thinking need to penetrate our consciousness more and more thoroughly. Your task is enormous!

Pluto in Generosity

Pluto in Generosity tells us something about your underworld journeys. They come as teachers of the giving and receiving principle. If you get greedy or fall into scarcity mentality, you are signing up for a trip into the underworld. And even more surprising, if you give too much and do not take time to receive and restore, you are on your way down. Nothing like a good old-fashioned depression reminds you that you must not burn out and over give. Women are especially talented at giving too much without receiving in equal measure.

Mid-Heaven in Generosity

With your Mid-Heaven in Generosity, we can imagine that you come from a soul source that is connected to the qualities of giving and receiving. On a soul level, you know that there must be a balance in that apparent duality.

You have come into an incarnation both to give the gift of your wisdom and to receive the benefits of having been in form. At the soul level, you are in joyous union with all human souls, and you see the interconnectedness of all humans. Your challenge is to live in the polarized world while remembering that connectedness.

~ 8 GOODNESS ~

Sun in Goodness

With your Sun in the principle of Goodness, we know that your life is a very specific walk with God. Your every step is intentional, just like an animal's. You do not meander. You always keep your senses alert for the signals so that your next step can be equally intentional. Any error on your life journey is perceived immediately and corrected. Your primary motivation for life is to be a walking prayer. You are more interested in your walk than in results!

Moon in Goodness

With your Moon in Goodness, we know that in some other lifetime or in some other dimension, you have mastered the concept that life is about "being" rather than about "doing." Your primary safety net in this life is that on the deepest levels of yourself, you know that you can always fall back into your core—your beingness. Like the mammals that operate mostly out of their instinctual self, you have a self-confidence and a profound understanding of who you are which always provides a foundation for you.

Ascendant in Goodness

Your behavioral ethic—in the principle of Goodness—indicates first that you are not a judgmental person. Your priority is more toward understanding, or "as is-ing" a situation rather than judging or even assessing it. Before you make a behavioral decision, you intuitively check out the energy of the circumstances. And after making a decision, you measure the consequences of it and track the effects of your action. It is animal-like, and yet it is highly sophisticated and it serves you and all around you well.

Mercury in Goodness

Placing your mental body in the principle of Goodness did not insure that you would always see the "good" side or that you would be one of those "love and light" New Agers. It really meant that you are more interested in the purity of the mental process than you are in the results or structure (belief systems) of the mind. You are not necessarily logical or reasonable, because you are more attracted to truth than to facts, and you are more galvanized by inspiration than by argument. Your mind is akin to the animal mind—you sense what is right, true, and has mental value, and then you go for the proof!

Venus in Goodness

Your emotions are animal-like. Just like an animal, you feel very strongly, very passionately in the moment, and then you move on. They color and give dimension to the moment, but they do not stay with you and taint your experience of the future—except, of course, in cases of serious and long term abuse in which not only your emotional body but your physical chemistry has been altered. You use emotion, for the most part, to return you to a clean, wholesome, fresh outlook on situations. This placement is very healthy and very stable. If this is not the case for you, then you are most likely an emotional abuse victim, and a good therapist can help you sort it out very quickly.

Mars in Goodness

With your physical body in the principle of Goodness, we know that your body is dependable and strong—like an animal body. You probably have a strong sense of intuitive and instinctive truth. With any luck, that has not been programmed out of you and you have grown up with a strong trust in the physical. The strength and reliability of your body has most likely enabled you to be active and healthy most of your life. This is a great blessing. It may be hard for you to actually understand people who do not have that same kind of body strength!

Jupiter in Goodness

Your Jupiter moments most likely come when you are in nature and more likely when you encounter a wild animal. Jupiter is present in the peace that you experience when swimming with the dolphins, or coming eye to eye with a deer on the trail—or even when a wild bunny hops out from under one of your garden plants. Your innate sense of Goodness is evoked by these experiences. You realize that no matter how things look in the outside world, the universe is fundamentally good. Life is good. Even people are basically good. All is right with the world.

Saturn in Goodness

You perceive form much the way animals do. You do not project judgment or opinion. It simply is what it is. You do not get involved with what "should" be—you simply observe the facts and work with them. Your instincts are strong and if you have not overridden them with too much logic, they are trustworthy. You walk in a good world because you see it that way. Even danger is not frightening to you—it is just a part of the life we live when we take human form.

Uranus in Goodness

You are sometimes temporarily stunned by the goodness of all things and all beings. When something happens—whether it is an encounter in the wild with an animal being or just a simply act of kindness that you witness—you experience a lightning bolt of clarity. In that moment, you remember Who You Are and you remember why you are here. You may not have more than one or two of these experiences in a year, but when they come they feed you for a long time. Your faith in life is restored.

Neptune in Goodness

Your birth group brought deep memory of the basic goodness of all beings and all forms. In almost any situation, you, and anyone in your birth group, can sway the mood and attitude and opinion of people by calling on Goodness. Either through your words or your own attitude, you can remind humanity of the basic goodness in life. By infusing the consciousness with Goodness, you help to augment its presence in the world.

Pluto in Goodness

Your Pluto in Goodness indicates that when you take your underworld journeys, you go into the instinctive—animal—part of yourself. From there, you are able to ascertain deeper truths and apply them to your middle world reality. In that sense, we would call your underworld journeys shamanic journeys. They really are about closing down your daily, mundane consciousness in order to plunge into the levels of consciousness that are either unconscious or what scientists might call "involuntary." In making that sort of journey, you reach a level of self-inventory that is beyond judgment. It is an "as-is-ing" place where you simple see the "isness" of yourself. With your roots firmly planted in "isness," you can return to ordinary human consciousness with great gifts to give.

Mid-Heaven in Goodness

If your soul's essence is in the principle of Goodness, you are a being who stays close to God. You are always aware of the power of life, the gift of life. When you become fully embodied—when your soul is fully in charge of your life—you will be a walking prayer. Your primary attention as an emissary of Goodness is to the profound peacefulness of a life well-lived. Your longing is to always be in the consciousness of yourself as an aspect of God.

~ 9 AWARENESS ~

Sun in Awareness

With your Sun in the principle of Awareness, we know that your primary "job" in this incarnation is to expand your consciousness. As you do this, you, of course, expand the consciousness of all your soul cluster and that impacts the consciousness of the whole species. At first, depending on the wisdom of your parents and teachers, it may be very confusing for you. Yours is a life full of paradox! Your challenge is to keep growing spiritually so that you can encompass those paradoxes rather than be paralyzed or tossed around by them. However, that very growth may feel diffusing and disorienting. As you mature, however, you will find your stability. Like the sunbeam that makes every leaf "more green" when it strikes it, you are the kind of being who makes everything you encounter more clear and encourages everyone you meet to be more authentic.

Moon in Awareness

You have an innate ability to sense a wide spectrum of possibilities in any situation. With a Moon in Awareness, we know that you are naturally able to see a fuller spectrum of emotions, energies, and dynamics at play in any circumstance. You can embrace the paradoxes and ironies of life, because you know them to be the "stuff" of life. This most likely gives you a level of patience and acceptance that most people do not have.

Ascendant in Awareness

With your behavioral body in the principle of Awareness, we know that more than most people, you are alert to the consequences of your decisions. The classic definition of an ethical decision is a choice that benefits the greatest number of dynamics. When you make a decision, you are aware of the impact it has not only on yourself but also on family, friends, clients, colleagues—and on more subtle levels the plants, animals, air, water, earth—and even on more subtle levels the angels, stars, and gods! Of course, you may not consciously stop and consider the stars when deciding what to have for lunch, but there is some antenna-like part of you that is always scanning to make sure you are helping rather than hindering. Earlier in your life, you may have learned the hard way that your decisions are important—but as you have matured physically and spiritually, you have learned to be account-able for the ramifications of your choices.

Mercury in Awareness

With your mental body in Awareness, there is good news and there is bad news. The good news is that you have the innate ability to expand your consciousness and consider a wide spectrum of possibilities. Your mind extends further than most people's, and you can therefore easily embrace both ends of a polarity. The bad news is that you may develop the habit of diffusing your thoughts and becoming inarticulate with them. Of course, this tendency can be tempered by your other personal pillars. Cer-tainly, as you mature spiritually, your desire to think clearly and precisely will emerge. Awareness in the mental realm gives you great breadth of thought and a wide mental option.

Venus in Awareness

With your Venus in the principle of Awareness, we can know that the primary function of your emotional body is to awaken you to the more sub-tle levels of any given experience. Some people simply react or respond through the emotional body. You, however, discover and investigate through it. If something is perfectly "normal" in every way but you have a little bit of a weird feeling about it, you will pay closer attention to the feeling than the appearance. Your emotions serve as your constant wake up call, bring-ing your attention to the nuances and metaphors around life.

Mars in Awareness

Your body serves as an antenna, constantly scanning the horizon for the deeper meanings and unseen dynamics! It is through your body that you process much of the information around you. Your body awareness, which some call "intuition" but others simply call "wisdom," is potentially highly developed. Tai Chi, yoga, or any of the energy studying martial arts is the perfect disciplines for you to develop!

Jupiter in Awareness

In those moments when you have to expand your consciousness to include both ends of a polarity, your mind suddenly becomes clear and you feel the arm of Jupiter around your shoulders. You know that your life is totally supported by the universe. You remember that your "job" is to continue to expand your understanding of life so that nothing is excluded from your awareness. It is a very clean and clear and expanded feeling!

Saturn in Awareness

Saturn in Awareness is an interesting paradox. The principle of Awareness, by definition, expands your consciousness. The energy of Saturn, by definition, restricts. However, the process of creating boundary can also be an expanding experience, because by learning to put all of your attention in one spot, one learns more about the whole. Quantum physicists, for example, have learned that the realm of form is 99.9 percent vibration—probability. And they have learned that by studying the interior of the nucleus of the atom. You have the unique ability to gain deeper understanding of the whole by studying the parts!

Uranus in Awareness

You have those moments of absolute divine self-recognition when your consciousness is involuntarily expanded, and you realize the interconnectedness of all things—yourself to all things, and all things back to yourself. You simultaneously become the ever-regenerating center of the universe and the No Thing from which the universe continually reproduces itself. You become No Thing and Every Thing all at once. You remember who you are and that all is right—nothing needs to be fixed! What an amazing experience it is.

Neptune in Awareness

Your birth group brought a big dose of consciousness-expanding potential to the planet. You infuse the planet with an ability to widen the mind so that polarity need not be seen as a lock down or a battleground but as a mirroring process that creates openness and newness. It is a big task, because you are trying to infuse a system that has perpetuated warrior mentality for thousands of years.

Pluto in Awareness

With your Pluto principle's being Awareness, we know you have a certain telephone line to the underworld that is never really turned off. By that, I mean that you are always vaguely aware of the deepest implications of any action or thought. This may have bothered you early in your life—as if there were always a depression lurking just under the surface waiting to grab you. However, as you have matured, you have come to value that ability to go to the depths of yourself at any moment. In almost every myth that involves descending into the underworld, there is an imperative not to eat of the fruits there. In other words, do not indulge yourself in the underworld. It can be addictive to be myopic constantly—constantly examining only the self. However, your Awareness principle has taught you to come and go at will, never withdrawing your awareness from the darkness but controlling your focus and attention at all times.

Mid-Heaven in Awareness

With your Mid-Heaven pointing to the principle of Awareness, we know that your primary connection with the level of soul is through a deep awakening. Your spiritual journey is mostly designed toward broadening your understanding of the deeper implications of life. You have a never-severed phone line to the highest planes of existence, and it is your imperative to try to listen deeply to the intuitional wisdom that the communications on that line provide for you. It is not easy to learn, but you must practice keeping your attention open on several levels at once.

THE CONTAINING PRINCIPLES

~ 10 RECIPROCITY ~

Sun in Reciprocity

With your Sun in Reciprocity, you are a natural peacemaker because you understand the laws of karma. You know that while nothing is innately "good" or "bad," every thought, word, and deed creates its own balancing counterpoint. When one makes choices based on a thorough knowledge of the Great Force of Equilibrium (Reciprocity), then healing, wholeness, balance, and harmony are the inevitable results. Relationship is important to you, and creating balance within relationship is your "career." You will be a great arbitrator or a diplomat.

Moon in Reciprocity

With your Moon in Reciprocity, we know that you are never outside the very basic awareness that what goes around comes around. You have within your consciousness a very deep understanding of the laws of balance—the laws of karma. Making sure that your actions are in integrity with your deepest self comes as naturally to you as breathing. You could no more intentionally harm another person, or the planet, than you could intentionally stop breathing. You are one of the beings who holds the balance of our world and of life on the planet as sacred and you feel an accountability to life—more than most. In fact, you are rather shocked when you encounter people who do not have that same level of wholeness in their belief system.

Ascendant in Reciprocity

A rising sign in Reciprocity indicates that you are always looking for the balancing, healing, appropriate choice of action. Your behavioral decisions will always factor in other people's feelings and responses to what you say and do. It is very important to you not to "rock the boat," because anything that you do to create turmoil is deeply painful to you. Your life is karmic in that you have promised to create balance. You may be balancing karmic traces from former lives, or you may simply be here to help balance the karmic energy of our present times.

Your best technique for meditation is a moving meditation. Your body needs to be involved in the movement of energy so that it is balanced. Walking the labyrinth, Tai Chi or one of the other martial arts which involves energy techniques, or certain meditational sports (skiing or tennis) will do more for clearing your mind than sitting or yoga.

Mercury in Reciprocity

Your Mercury in Reciprocity makes you very interested in balance, harmony, and peace. You never accept ideas until you measure their fullness. In other words, you are also interested in the balancing energy of an idea. It is important to you that the ideas you put forth always contribute not only to your own inner peace but to that of the collective. Thoughts are bridges for you. They connect the dots. They make life make sense. Although you have a brilliant mind, you are not particularly academic. You do not like to argue for argument's sake. You like to connect and flow through proper use of ideas, thoughts, and words.

Venus in Reciprocity

Emotions are balancing agents for you. This gives you a highly unique emotional body—because most people use emotions as polarizing agents. You cannot do that. You have to feel the wholeness sides of an experience, not just one side. Even when you feel a polarizing type emotion (anger, for example), you then continue the feeling all the way through itself until anger releases into appropriate action. If you are an immature person, the action may not always be appropriate—and learning appropriate emotional behavior may be one of your tasks—but the point is that the emotional experience does not stop with polarization. You complete the experience with resolution.

Mars in Reciprocity

You have the kind of physical body that makes sense. It operates according to the basic cause and effect laws. If you eat too much, you gain weight, for example. Believe it or not, some people do not have bodies like that. It is important for you to do two things in relation to this body. First, be thankful for it and take very good care of it. It is your most reliable personal pillar. Second, learn through the body to have deep compassion for all beings. Realize that physical struggle is a burden for many people. Be gentle with yourself and gentle with others!

Jupiter in Reciprocity

You feel most gratified, most supported by the universe, and most "in the right place at the right time" when there is a sense of equanimity in a circumstance. You long for equal rights for all people, you crave justice, and you feel most comfortable in the world when you see signs of that kind of balance. You are a pro-active person who loves to participate in justice-making. When that happens, you feel the arms of Jupiter wrap around you and you feel divinely protected.

Saturn in Reciprocity

The world of form for you is "fair." You can see the cause and effect laws as they weave the world together. This makes you a naturalist. You know the importance, for example, of the rain forests. You can literally track the benefit that we all receive from the breathing of the trees. You may have trouble understanding people who do not see those connections and create external chaos by over-cutting the forests. Your Saturn principle is very important in your chart and will drive you into social justice-making activities.

Uranus in Reciprocity

With Uranus in Reciprocity, we know that your moments of real authentic self-knowing come when you have an experience of balance and equanimity. Harmony and well-being are important to you. You also have a keen sense of the ebb and flow of energy. You know the cosmic laws that govern the flow of energy on a very deep level, so when you see the "what goes around comes around" principle in action, you have a Uranian experience. There is a spiritual poise in your most authentic self that you may sometimes forget in your mundane life. But when Uranus strikes, you have deep repose and an elegant sense of all is right with the world.

Neptune in Reciprocity

Your birth group came in to infuse the consciousness with the principle of "what goes around comes around." It is not that difficult to understand why. When you were born, society had slipped into a very myopic and anthropomorphic state of mind. We had forgotten our responsibility to take care of all the species and all the babies. We had come to believe that the world is here to serve us, not the other way around. Your birth group came blasting in with a deep reminder of the profound accountability we have to our own reality. Neptune is the big dreamer planet. Many of its attributes are dreamy and film-like. (Neptune was discovered by astronomers the same year film was invented.) Neptune's principle represents the big dream. Your birth group came in to transform the dream and to remind humanity that we have created a world in which all the species are required to live our dream.

Pluto in Reciprocity

When you take your journeys into the underworld, your gift is greater balance. From time to time, when you shut down and go inside, you find that the principle of "what goes around comes around" is operational and healthy. For you, inner journeys are as essential as inhaling. For that reason, solitude and long periods of silence are absolutely essential. Your relationship to the death and rebirth process—to deconstruct and reconstruct philosophy—is what keeps you forever young!

Mid-Heaven in Reciprocity

The most direct access you have to the soul's intent is through the principle of Reciprocity. When you feel the breath of life running through you, you are in direct alignment with the level of consciousness that we call "soul." Breath, breathing techniques, and meditation on the breath—these are all personal tools for you that keep you always walking your path with integrity. The soul speaks to you through the breath.

~ 11 FLOWERING ~

Sun in Flowering

With your Sun in the principle of Flowering, we know that the main purpose of your incarnation is evolution. You took this incarnation in order to evolve yourself and the species. What does it mean to evolve yourself? It means that you will never stop looking for more efficient ways to use and express energy. You will never stop weeding your own garden of separatist thoughts and ideas. You will never stop seeking more complex and simultaneously more direct ways to communicate and create. Your energy is dedicated not only to survival but also to wisdom and success.

Moon in Flowering

If your Moon is in Flowering, you have probably come into human form several times when evolution was moving us as it is now. We seem to evolve in spurts, and we are definitely in one right now. You know in your deepest/highest self how to assist that process—you have mastered it—and that is part of your job this time. Evolve yourself in the most graceful possible way, and you will always be on track. Moon in Flowering also indicates that you are particularly talented in the area of reading the Akashic Records and that your lifetime is dedicated to assistance in the evolutionary process—not only for yourself but for your personal family and the greater family of man.

Ascendant in Flowering

A part of your job in this incarnation is to evolve the ethical field of the human. Of course, first, you must do that for and within yourself. We no longer can afford to live in an "eye for an eye" mentality, nor can our species survive if we continue to live in separatist mentality. You are here to work toward understanding the unity of all things. You must learn to examine the consequences of each of your actions—indeed each of your thoughts. And you must realize that those consequences affect not only you, but all the other dynamics as well: your family, your friends, your community, the planet, the animals and plants, the ecology—indeed the universe. It is an enormous honor to be one of the beings creating the morphic field of high ethical standards on which future societies will live. It is also difficult, because you are treading new territory.

Mercury in Flowering

With Mercury in Flowering, we know that you took this lifetime to help evolve the way humans process mental information. Of course, in this approaching New Age, it will become more and more necessary to filter the information through the heart chakra and blend information with compassion so that it can become wisdom. Your mental thread is about doing that—first in your own life and later to make that contribution to the wider arena.

Venus in Flowering

Emotionality is your primary route to evolving/maturing. When you have an experience that calls an emotional response from you, it becomes a growing experience for you. You learn and deepen from your emotions. Sometimes, this may feel a little overwhelming. But usually, these experiences bring you to such profound understandings that they do not sweep you away. Your natural attraction and desire are to understand life more fully, and the expression of emotion is your primary tool for doing just that.

Mars in Flowering

Your body is an evolving body. You are one of the "lab rats"—a part of the cosmic experiment that is constantly revising the human body so that it more perfectly functions as a vessel of spirit. You have probably spent most of your life noticing that your body is different from others and wondering why. Whether this difference is what society calls a "handicap" or simply that your body seems to operate and respond differently, you still have most likely been aware of it all your life. This is why: Your thymus gland has remained more awake than most, and you have been participating in the evolution of the physical form.

Jupiter in Flowering

With Jupiter in Flowering, we know that you have your Jupiter experiences when something occurs in your life that you can see yourself or your loved ones evolving. You have a natural feeling for the empowering experience of moving toward a being more sophisticated and more loving and compassionate version of yourself. When something actually happens and you realize that you have matured or developed in that way, Jupiter taps you on your shoulder and you feel that familiar "aha."

Saturn in Flowering

With Saturn in Flowering, we know that your view of the realm of form is quite unusual. You see form as fluid—evolving—trans-forming, so to speak. Most people are interested in seeing the world as a static, completely "finished" product. You see development. You see construct and deconstruct simultaneously. For example, when you look at the Grand Canyon, you see the millions of years that it took to carve it just as clearly as you see the present beauty—and your imagination takes you a million years hence with all the possibilities of its future. When you see a mountain, you also see the forming of that mountain, and you see the fact that pebble-by-pebble, it is breaking down and returning to the sea. Your picture of the realm of form is more complete than most people's.

Uranus in Flowering

From time to time during your life, you will be struck with the realization that you are participating in a great movement of sentience—an unfolding of consciousness. These moments may be the result of something that happens in nature that reminds you of the never-ending growth and change that happens on this planet, or it may simply be an "aha" that you experience when ideas suddenly crystallize and make sense. In those moments, you remember yourself authentically. You know that you are at once all and nothing. You know the importance of your individual self, and you know the vast impersonal nature of your deepest self.

Neptune in Flowering

Your birth group brought an evolutionary spurt to the human collective. Physics shows us that evolution does not occur like the steady growth of a tree. Evolutionary change comes in jolts—starts and stops—spurts. Your birth group infused the collective consciousness with a reminder that we must evolve, we must change, we must be willing to move to new levels of life experience in order to fulfill our destiny.

Pluto in Flowering

Your underworld journeys are very beneficial to you. When it is time to evolve a little more, you tend to go inward, get very quiet for a while, and then spring forth with new aspects of yourself ready to bloom. You are plant-like in this sense. You go "dormant" from time to time, and then with the energy gathered during your repose, you are ready to perfume the air with the new fragrance of yourself. Now, during these times of repose, you may actually "go dark" (meaning you do not do much of anything except vegetate) or you may find yourself very active in an internal investigation of your personal patterns. It may be a dormant time, or an internal housekeeping time. But either way, it is very helpful and very necessary in your process.

Mid-Heaven in Flowering

To have one's Mid-Heaven in Flowering is to come from the aspect of

God that governs evolution. You are a prototype, a lab rat so to speak, always trying to push forward in consciousness toward the ultimate potential that the species holds. You are an emissary from the plane of evolutionary law to the human species. The other aspects of your contract determine the specifics of how you express that drive to evolve.

~ 12 CREATIVITY ~

Sun in Creativity

With your Sun in the principle of Creativity, we know that your primary reason for incarnating is to "work" the creative principle. In other words, you are constantly looking for ways to put ideas, actions, and people together in ways that have not been tried before. You are fascinated with the choreography of energy, and you love to try to make things work in new, delightful, unusual ways—ways that have completely unique results. You are driven to find the most beneficial ways to express your life force. You work with Creativity for your own sake, but you also are anchoring this principle for an unknown circle of people—your soul cluster. You have a vague sense that when you come up with a truly original idea or plan, it ripples out and affects a large number of people!

Moon in Creativity

You are a master of developing new ideas, thought patterns, and designs. This may take many manifestations in your life. You may be an artist or a designer, you may be a revolutionary politician or personal guidance worker, or you may simply be eccentric. The thing you need to know about yourself and remember about yourself is that your most trustworthy quality is your unique ability to reinvent yourself and the world around you. Until you have a real grasp of this aspect of yourself, you may be very lonely, because you think differently from most people. You are much more interested in new ways and new ideas than you are in status quo. That makes school and standard ways of learning boring for you! However, when you do find teachers (whether academic or life teachers) who recognize Creativity as a positive quality, you will shine!

Ascendant in Creativity

With your behavioral body in the principle of Creativity, we know that when you are making a decision about doing something, you take all kinds of unusual factors into consideration. More than most people, you consider the consequences of your actions before you make the choice. You also look for effect of choice as well as results in your decisions. You may opt for the eccentric when something much more mainstream would "do" just because the effect of the behavior will evoke a response that is new, fresh, and alive! The creative drive runs through your personality like a river. Other people or society may have tried to damn it or block it, but you have never allowed that because it is too much fun like it is.

Mercury in Creativity

With your mental body in the principle of Creativity, we know that you do not think along linear, predictable, and patriarchal lines. This could have presented some challenges when you were trying to fit into the schooling mode, but it should serve you well in life. When you process information, you may put it together more like a jigsaw puzzle than like building blocks. And your conclusions and results, while solid and useful, are rarely "obvious." Your ability to use ideas to create is refreshing, and people are attracted to you because of it.

Venus in Creativity

Your emotions are your choreographers! These then guide you toward the new and interesting. When you feel excited, happy, and inspired, you know it is because you have stumbled onto a new way of experiencing life force. When you are sad, or depressed, or grumpy, you know that you are living life too mundanely. Your emotions will always tell you when it is time to break out into a new dance and live a little more wildly. Creativity craves freedom. For you, anything less than emotional freedom is stifling!

Mars in Creativity

Putting your physical body in the principle of Creativity is an interesting choice. It means that your physical body is unusual. You may have had some struggles with health—not because you are unhealthy, but because your body works in ways that doctors and healers may not recognize. However, it is an intelligent body and knows what is best and healthiest for it. Your personal challenge is to learn your body's encoding and participate and cooperate with it rather than try to force it to be "normal." This physical uniqueness also blends into the way you walk in the world. You are an extremely creative person. You juxtapose ideas, circumstances, and objects in totally new ways. This is part of your charm!

Jupiter in Creativity

With Jupiter in Creativity, we know that you have those magical experiences of knowing that you are totally supported by the universe when you have just succeeded in putting something together in a totally unique way. Ideas, words, objects, symbols, or colors—the medium does not matter. What matters is that from time to time, some energy flows through you and you create a unique experience. Jupiter then pats you on the back and says "attagirl." These moments are important to you, not only because you love the process of creating, but because the Jupiter moments are what relieve you from a sometimes nagging questioning about whether you are living the life you agreed to live. In the Jupiter moments, you are self-assured and not lonely!

Saturn in Creativity

With Saturn in Creativity, we know that while you are willing to obey the rules of form and limitation, you do not particularly care to. When a wall is placed in front of you (literally or metaphorically), you immediately begin to figure out how to see through it, get around it, and/or decorate it so that it is really an opening! You are never still in your mind, because your natural tendency is to blend ideas and objects together in ways that no one else has seen! An obstacle is inspiration for you. An apparent limitation is a springboard!

Uranus in Creativity

Uranus in the principle of Creativity indicates that you have those moments of truly remembering Who You Are when you have just put something together in a way that makes it greater than itself—whether they are two or more ideas that you have juxtaposed into a new way of seeing something, or whether they are objects or colors or abstract symbols that have come together to become a thought-provoking piece of art. It can even happen in the way you design a garden, decorate a room, or put on your clothes. Whenever you are the vehicle for some new perspective, Uranus shoots you with a bolt of lightning, and in that moment you remember yourself authentically.

Neptune in Creativity

Your birth group came into life with the imperative to infuse the world with newness. Thousands and thousands of babies were born with the moon at 12 degrees, in the few months around your birthday, and each of those people carries the same kind of urge that you do: to break out of the mold and find absolutely new ways to live and express life. It is your "job" to inspire and encourage everyone constantly around you to use his or her own creative drive!

Pluto in Creativity

Pluto in Creativity tells us that when you make your underworld journeys—when you go into depression or other levels of deep self-investigation—the result is creative. You are able to see the unseen by going into the realm of darkness, and you are able to blend the unseen with the seen in a unique way. This may not be an easy task, but it is a productive one. This is the Plutonian journey of the artist. This is why so many artists and musicians seem tortured: because their creative process involves a visit to the god of the underworld. We must always remind the artist, however, that the journey results in victory over life and death.

Mid-Heaven in Creativity

Creativity is the essence of your soul source. You feel closest to the level of soul when you are in a wildly creative process, and you have the deepest memories of your spiritual nature when you allow yourself to walk the Via Creativa. This does not mean you "should" be an artist. It simply means that what is most natural to you is putting things together in unusual ways—whether your medium is ideas, objects, people, or words. On the soul level, you participate in creating new structures through which life can express itself. When you go too long mired in the mundane activities of daily life, you begin to lose confidence and the memory of Who You Are begins to slip. It is important for you to always have creative projects in process!

~ 13 Intelligence ~

Sun in Intelligence

Your Sun in Intelligence tells us that you are an agent of change. You are very interested in interfacing all kinds of energies so that a beneficial transformation takes place. This transformation can be in terms of developing your own potential as a being, or it can be in establishing a balance in the community, or it can be in the arrangement of objects in your home. You are a natural choreographer of energy—an architect of the design of form. You love to see things come together so that they are right! One warning: You may stand in the way of your own Higher Self by being sure you know what is right without consulting higher source.

Moon in Intelligence

Your Moon in Intelligence tells us that you have a very sophisticated central nervous system. Your body is a free agent of information, and your nervous system is sensitive to the slightest and most subtle physical changes. This most likely spills over into all your personal pillars. Also, you are a natural at gathering and processing energy and information of all kinds. This may make life a little difficult, because you probably have a very low pain tolerance level and you are able to feel collective pain or feel the emotions of other people. However, it is also your greatest asset, because it gives you the advantage of deep personal compassion and the profound ability to "know" on a larger spectrum than most people.

Ascendant in Intelligence

With your behavioral body in the principle of Intelligence, we know that you factor in a wide spectrum of data before you make any of your ethical decisions. This data is not all empirical. In other words, you also consider your body "hunches." In fact, even unconscious and involuntary information has a "vote" in your process. It might have been hard for you when you were young to trust this, because you do depend heavily on intuition, a practice that is not strongly endorsed in Western society. However, as you have matured, you have most likely become comfortable with your accuracy, innate goodness, and ethical trustworthiness!

Mercury in Intelligence

This Placement could be a paradox. It seems like it should indicate genius. However, it indicates that you think uniquely and that you process information more in your nervous system than in your brain. You are smart, no question. You know how to take data in and process it. You know how to juxtapose thoughts and ideas more quickly than most people. And you know how to calculate the results of your thinking. This ability may not register as making good grades in school or receiving high scores on standardized tests, because it may mean that you think so differently from most people that you cannot relate to the ordinary learning processes. On the other hand, it may mean that you are very good in school but not very good in other aspects of life (say athletics or relationships) because your mental dominance prevents you from mastering physical and/or emotional skills. However, with your mental body in the principle of Intelligence, we know that in this lifetime, you are developing amazing mental skills and that they will hopefully serve you and your community beneficially.

Venus in Intelligence

This placement is a bit of a paradox, as Venus represents the emotional body and Intelligence is typically considered to be a mental principle. However, if you deeply understand it, you find that intelligent love—intelligent emotion—is actually the goal, not only of your life, but of the species. You are here to mature your emotional body so that love is not a sentimental attachment to and investment in someone, but it is instead an empowering and liberating force that runs through you. Intelligent emotions, running through your body on your nerve lines, is a large part of your power. The goddess of love, Venus, works with you in the most sophisticated way—through the free flowing information of the Intelligence principle.

Mars in Intelligence

Your Mars in Intelligence tells us that your body is a beacon for information. You perceive truth through your body. The cells of your body exchange information freely and without judgment or hesitation. The nervous system of your body is probably one of the more sophisticated of our species. Your brain and spinal cord are working together to keep information flowing instantaneously. You probably are physically telepathic—meaning you could learn to pick up information from objects. There is another word for that: psycho-kinetic or something like that. You could hold an object and tell us something about its owner because your body naturally grabs information and puts it together in an understandable order.

Jupiter in Intelligence

With Jupiter in Intelligence, we know that when you access some body of information not reachable by you before (perhaps not reachable by humanity before), you have that Jupiterian experience! You know you are in the right place doing the right thing. Connecting the dots and putting the puzzle pieces together is a gift of yours, and when you do it well, your sense of blessing far outweighs your sense of accomplishment.

Saturn in Intelligence

For you, the realm of form is a perfectly rational, logical place. You are one of the people who holds form in predictability. In other words, you "know" that the purpose of a wall is to provide privacy and boundary. You, therefore, participate in the consensus reality by projecting that walls are solid. You do not see through walls (yes, some people do) because they are solid to you. You do not walk through walls (yes, some people do) because they are concrete boundaries for you. This makes you somewhat rigid in relationship to form, and perhaps a little afraid to try outrageous and daring things. However, it also makes you an important "vote" in the consensus because you are part of the glue that holds the world in place.

Uranus in Intelligence

When you learn something new and when that something is the result of juxtaposing data in a new way, you have an epiphany of self, knowing that is simply marvelous. It is important for you to never stop learning. You will always be pulled to study new ideas and research new topics, because that learning sparks the Intelligence that is such an essential part of your nature.

Neptune in Intelligence

Your birth group brought in a shot of Intelligence in order to help the species integrate all the new information of the decade before your birth. Massive changes in consciousness had occurred just prior to your birth, and massive changes in society were preparing themselves to come forth. You brought in this reminder that we must pull that information together in new and creative ways in order to use it for beneficial reasons. Metaphorically, your birth group is functioning as the central nervous system of the species!

Pluto in Intelligence

Your underworld journeys are fact-finding missions. We do not call your dark times—your downtimes—depressions at all. Instead, when you go into the underworld, you go with questions, looking for information, much like Persephone who went to observe the plants growing deeper. In fact, we can say that you do that—you grow deeper each time you take a dive into the land of Pluto. Your access to information is almost limitless when you are still, quiet, and in your personal cave.

Mid-Heaven in Intelligence

You are in closest communion with the level of soul when information is flowing freely. This is true inside your body, when the nervous system and brain are in sync, and it is true in the outer world when you are in honest and authentic communication with your friends, family, and colleagues. Lies that sometimes wend their way into any communication system are more shocking and disruptive to you than they are to most people. You are not a "born" politician. You need to be in closer touch with truth than that. As long as information is flowing, you are ensouled!

~ 14 ECSTASY ~

Sun in Ecstasy

With your Sun in the principle of Ecstasy, you carry a very deep knowing that 15 billion years ago when consciousness first expressed itself as light, all the energy that has run the universe sense then was created. We are 15 billion-year-old energy being recycled. And each of us has the opportunity to become that first expression of light anew with every second of life. We are the cosmo-genesis in the sense that each time we take a breath, take a step, and make a decision, we create the reality in which life expresses. Your main reason for incarnating in this lifetime is to be mindful of that profound truth.

Moon in Ecstasy

In addition to knowing that we are constantly restructuring the cosmos by living our lives, your Moon in Ecstasy tells us that you are aware of what I call "the stardust factor." All the elements that make up our planet—indeed our bodies—were created when a star became a supernova and burned itself out. In the last two weeks of a star's life, it burns so brightly and becomes so hot that it melts the hydrogen and helium atoms together to create all the other elements in the universe. It then spews them out into space, and they eventually, through the principle of Attraction, find each other and create planets and other bodies. We are made of stardust. You realize that in the cells of your being. You are a master of that level of consciousness. You can almost remember the light of the brilliant star from which you came. Your Moon is your mastery—your safety net. When life almost swallows you up, you remember that you are old, old, old energy reconstituting itself again in order to participate with the great plan. That soothes your immediate discomfort!

Ascendant in Ecstasy

You are one happy camper with your Ascendant in Ecstasy! You are very interested in making behavioral and ethical decisions that bring out the awe you feel for life. Remembering wonder, experiencing awe, being amazed—those are your favorite activities. In fact, you are really a mystic. Wonder, awe, and amazement are so deeply embedded in your life that you constantly inspire others to remember that life is nothing short of a miracle. Of course, you also run the constant risk of being so addicted to wonder and amazement that you will stop at nothing to experience it. Mind-altering experiences are so attractive to you that you must learn very early to monitor your alcohol and drug intake, and you must even monitor your addiction to fantasy!

Mercury in Ecstasy

It is through your mental body that you achieve full body wholeness. Your mind processes information in a way that allows for the entire evolutionary process of life to "factor" in. You, in other words, are not a linear, logical, rational thinker like most people. School may have been difficult for you because you could not train your mind to eliminate unseen or unprovable information. While this Placement may have made it harder for you to live in the cultural world, you have unique access to sensations of being at one with the entire universe, because your mind knows that it is aligned with a Oneness that is much vaster than the rational mind can comprehend.

Venus in Ecstasy

With your emotional body in the principle of Ecstasy, we know that you have quite a complex emotional system. At its most, mature, emotional experience actually gives you a sense of profound well-being. You are able, through the movement of emotions in your body, to keep yourself balanced, nourished, and pure. At its least, mature, emotional experience can swing you around like a yo-yo, and a tendency to become addicted to pleasant emotions is inevitable. The good news is that eventually you learn that you can put yourself in balance—and indeed share that balance with others. Then you will find that Ecstasy is one of the gifts you have to give!

Mars in Ecstasy

Your physical body is in the principle of body wholeness. This tells us that you are only comfortable in your physical body when all your other bodies (emotional, mental, spiritual, astral) are in alignment, too. You need to be fully attuned in order for everything to work. Yoga or Tai Chi or some form of movement/meditation is probably extremely important to you, because you need to involve all of yourself in your daily practice. When you are fully aligned, you experience a divine sense of rightness in the world. When you are out of "whack," the whole world distorts for you. It is a blessing to have this sort of body, because it will not let you stray too far off your spiritual track. It is too uncomfortable.

Jupiter in Ecstasy

Periodically, you have moments of divine wholeness. You know that you are in the right place, it is the right timing, and you are doing the right thing. You feel totally surrounded by the arms of the universe and completely supported by Mother Earth. Those are your Jupiter moments—and they are moments of Ecstasy. In those moments, every system of your body is realigned to the song of the spheres, and you are healed, whole, and organically tuned to the vibration of life. These moments feed you. They keep you alive. They string themselves like a strand of pearls for your neck, and when you are in the midst of one of them, you remember Who You Are.

Saturn in Ecstasy

With Saturn in Ecstasy, we know that your experience of the realm of form is like the mystic's. A mystic sees the interconnectedness of all things. All his or her bodies are in alignment with the all-nourishing abyss out of which everything erupts (those are Brian Swimme's words, by the way); therefore, all forms are interdependent on, interrelated to, and interconnected with all other forms. When you are in a forest, you are not just walking in a single forest, but in forest-ness! You may have trouble holding mental awareness of this expansive sense, because it is a supramental experience. But when you do have those magical moments and shift your attention to the divine and mystical aspect of form, you have an experience of ecstasy.

Uranus in Ecstasy

With Uranus in the principle of Ecstasy, we know that your moments of authentic knowingness are quite alive and interesting. Ecstasy occurs when all the bodies—behavioral, mental, emotional, physical, and spiritual—align with each other. You experience a moment of absolute wholeness. You feel as if you were a series of concentric circles expanding out into the edges of the universe. In those moments, you have an absolute experience of remembering Who You Are and how you are connected to the All and the Everything. The feeling of ecstasy in those moments may be highly energized, or they may be simple and quietly profound.

Neptune in Ecstasy

With Neptune in Ecstasy, we know that your birth group came bursting into life to bring new ideas, possibilities, and creativity as a gift to consciousness. The principle of Ecstasy is like a volcano spewing forth energy ready to be configured in new ways in form. You and your birth group bring hope for the New Age. You have infused the consciousness of the human realm with a wholeness that carries us forth.

Pluto in Ecstasy

With Pluto in Ecstasy, we can assume that your ultimate victory over life and death will be the result of a completion of your deepest Inanna journeys. When life circumstances and life energies take you all the way into the underworld, you are able to transform them and yourself and come spewing back to the light like the phoenix rising. You know how to let the ashes (the stardust of which you are made) reconstitute themselves and become life anew. Each time you take your underworld journey, even though it is not easy and you may have to be stripped and left to die just like Inanna, you also participate in the genesis of life—the rebirth of consciousness. This part of your pattern is what has kept you moving forward even in times when it seems like "they" have succeeded in bringing you down.

Mid-Heaven in Ecstasy

What does it mean, then, to say your soul is sourced in Ecstasy? It means that your soul resides in the mind of God at the exact point of creation. When that supernova exploded and spewed all those elements into the cosmos, your consciousness was born. Your life is a mission from that point of divine creation. All the other clauses in your chart construct a pattern through which an ecstatic soul can express.

~ 15 RESISTANCE ~

Sun in Resistance

People who have their Sun in the principle of Resistance are great manifesters. You have an innate knowing of what needs to be done to transform the energy of thought, for example, into the form. You have a natural knack for creating exactly what you need. In addition, you are a good group person because you know how to put the energy of a group on the right track and make things flow well between people. It is a good metaphor for you to look at yourself as the transition point of a circuit of energy.

Moon in Resistance

Moon in the principle of Resistance indicates that you have spent other lifetimes working to transform energy into its appropriate form. It is the challenge of any life form to grab energy—in the form of light, air, and food—and transform it so that it is beneficial for the body. However, you have gone further than that. You have learned to transform energy so that it becomes beneficial for others. You can bring "information" (not necessarily verbal information—chemical or energetic information applies, too) into your own system and change it into its most useful form. Resistance is a difficult principle. It requires dedication, focus, and a nonjudgmental mind to master!

Ascendant in Resistance

Your ethical and behavioral decisions will always lean toward transforming the present energy. This may have been misunderstood in the past by a society that likes everyone to "be nice and get along." You may have felt like a misfit because when you see that something is not working, you name it. As you mature with the principle of Resistance, you will learn that transforming energy through your well-chosen words and appropriate behavior is a great gift. You are here to interfere! But you can interfere with great compassion, humor, and joy. Your choices in life will lead you toward more joy with your authenticity.

Mercury in Resistance

You use your mind as an energetic transformer. Energy (thoughts) comes into your mind, and they get translated or transformed into ideas that can be used by yourself or by your circle of influence. The collective field of thought is rife with misunderstanding, error, flaw, and lies. Part of your contract with life in this incarnation is to investigate each idea that comes to you and eliminate the errors. This not only puts your life on a truth track, but it creates a cleaner collective system of thought. It is not easy to think differently from the collective. It is the path of MOST resistance, but it is a rewarding path and an important one.

Venus in Resistance

You are an emotional transformer! You made a pledge to use this lifetime to really study the emotional system of the human and learn how to use the energy beneficially. It is not an easy job you set for yourself. It requires dedication, discipline, and deep awareness. If you let emotional energy come in unawares, it can flatten you! Each emotional experience, on the other hand, becomes a transformation experience for you—one through which you grow, learn, develop, and evolve.

Mars in Resistance

With your physical body in the principle of Resistance, you may have set up a challenging situation for yourself. The physical body takes information or energy directly into the cells—through breath, through light, through food. The body itself serves as the resistor, and translates that energy into appropriate forms. This may mean that you get "hit" from time to time with a greater jolt or voltage than your body can handle. Bizarre symptoms and strange body shutdowns could be the result. However, you could also have learned very early, or in some other lifetime, how to modify the energy you take in so that it does not blast your body. However it works for you, your physical being is a source of important information, both for your own incarnation, and for those in your sphere of influence.

Jupiter in Resistance

With Jupiter in Resistance, we know that when you have had an experience of transforming energy, you have a sense of being supported by the whole universe. This may be something very simple like your resolving an argument or a simple problem-solving situation. Or it may take a more dramatic turn when you handle the energy of a crisis or an emergency. Whether large or small in scope, the effect is the same. You have a sudden sense of being in the right place at the right time, doing exactly what you came here to do. Jupiter, the god of good fortune, pats you on the back, and you feel whole.

Saturn in Resistance

You are one of the beings who holds form to its contract. You expect a wall to be solid and to provide boundary and privacy. You expect a tree to be rooted and to stay in place. Believe it or not, there are some people who see through walls from time to time, and it does not bother them. There are instances in which people walk through trees, and it does not affect them. But you are one of the people who gives the gift of solidity to form. We need people like you. You help anchor the world so that we can count on it. You are a part of the glue that holds this universe in its patterns.

Uranus in Resistance

With Uranus in Resistance, we know that when you have literally transformed the energy flow—either in your own body, or in your community—you have that electrical charge of authenticity. For example, if you see a community or group operating with a lie—weaving it into their reality, you will most likely be the one to name it. Suddenly, the energy of that group will be transformed (sometimes shattered, sometimes strengthened), but the personal impact on you is profound. You glimpse who you are on a deep level, and your commitment to living the authentic life is renewed.

Neptune in Resistance

Your birth group brought the principle of Resistance to the collective consciousness. One of the most recent birth groups born with Neptune under the principle of Resistance came in 1964. That is very interesting. In late 1963, we were stunned in the United States and worldwide by the assassination of President Kennedy. Suddenly, the American myth began to shatter. We began to question and object openly to everything inauthentic—every lie. Your birth group came along and helped turn what could have been chaotic mob-mindedness into a relatively structured, ordered "resistance" to society's ailing structures. Of course, that resistance had its harshness and deep pain. However, it resulted in a nation-wide soul searching that is still unfolding in the early twenty-first century.

Pluto in Resistance

Your journeys into the underworld are probably quite painful. They require a deep look at the errors, not only of your own belief systems, but (depending on the sign and house placement of your Pluto) possibly the errors of collective consciousness. It is always hard to learn that one has been "wrong." However, these journeys into the deepest part of your psyche are really opportunities to correct, recapitulate, and emerge with a level of clarity that was never available to you before. As you mature your understanding of your relationship to the principle of Resistance, you will come to welcome the "downtimes." They are like a spring cleaning—opportunities to look into those closets and behind those well-placed pieces of mental furniture and clean out that which is outdated and no longer needs to be held.

Mid-Heaven in Resistance

The principle of Resistance points you to your soul. This means that as you learn more and more about transforming energy into its proper form, you learn more and more about your soul. As you mature in your ability to receive energy and information from the most subtle realms and translate that information into what can be used and understood in the denser realms, you also get more in touch with who you are at the essential core. Resistance is in the middle of the 30 principles. Your soul is one of the aspects of humanity that is pivotal. You are one of the balance keepers—one of the beings that help hold the species in unity.

~ 16 UNITY ~

Sun in Unity

Your primary reason for incarnating is to develop and evolve the human understanding of the principle of Unity. First, you must understand it thoroughly yourself. Your primary job, on behalf of your soul cluster, is to grasp the New Creation Story mentally, emotionally, and physically so that you can operate in your every-day life with a deep commitment to weaving the fabric of the universe. Your first assignment is, of course, your family of origin. Whether you "like" your family is not the issue. It is important only that you see that you ARE like your family, and that certain family patterns need to be perpetuated through you, and others need to be shattered by you. Yours is a powerful contract, because it demands very high levels of evolution, awareness, and conscious action.

Moon in Unity

With your mastery in the principle of Unity, it is reasonable for us to believe that you have taken many incarnations with difficult genetic issues. This particular lifetime may or may not be one of those. Either way, you have an innate understanding of the idea that we are all One—that the universe is a seamless whole—a cosmic fabric—and that anyone who walks without that knowledge seriously diminishes his or her own potential. You feel a kinship with all beings, human or not, organic or not, alive or not. You have natural talent for expanding your consciousness and a natural freedom from restrictive lifestyles, mindsets, and emotional boxes.

Ascendant in Unity

With your Ascendant in Unity, we know several things about you. First, we know that you have a very strong contractual commitment to your family—your genetic line. You may have even come in with a pre-birth agreement to make some decisions that will break family patterns and change the heritage/traditions of your family. We also know that you are very interested in the concept of Unity—that we are all one family. Your ethics will be based on creating community. When you make personal decisions, you consider how your actions will impact the greater whole. You are primarily interested in creating a sense of family across genetic, cultural, and political barriers.

Mercury in Unity

Because Unity is in the genetic line, it is possible that you contracted with the mental body of your gene pool. In other words, you chose this gene pool because the way they think was a necessary part of your life. This may be because the way your ancestors processed information is strong and helpful for you—or it may be that the way they processed information needs purification and/or transformation. Either way, this is a very strong part of your life. Unity is the principle most needed in the world today. Our technological burst of the last century has simultaneously connected us in one big web and divided us into little tiny pieces. Unity at work in the world will bring us into a synthesis that allows us all to evolve. To learn to use our minds to unite is a beautiful goal.

Venus in Unity

With your emotional body in the principle of Unity, we know that you have "inherited" your way of processing emotions. It is possible that you chose the family that you did because some aspect of the way, your gene pool has traditionally processed emotions needed to be purified, and you agreed to do that. Conversely, it may be that your gene pool is particularly healthy, and you knew you will need that tool in this lifetime. Either way, your emotional body is very tied to your family line. Through your emotions, you are able to pull yourself out of a self-centered and self-conscious way of operating in the world. Emotional energy brings you to unity consciousness.

Mars in Unity

With Mars in Unity, it is quite possible that part of your life agreement is about purifying the physical aspects of your gene pool. As we move toward more evolved beings, it becomes necessary to eliminate any part of ourselves that is no longer serving life. You most likely chose your parents because of the potential body they could build for you by combining their genes, and your life's work is partly centered around perfecting that body so that it can serve you and life in profound ways. If there is a history of disease or some sort of genetic problem in your ancestral line, it stopped with you.

Jupiter in Unity

Your sense of being divinely supported comes when you have an experience of union. This experience may be as grand as a dream or a vision in which you actually see the fibers that interconnect all beings—or it may be as small as a simple self-recognition in the eyes of a stranger. But when it comes, a deep calm washes over you. You have the sense that "all is right with the world." And you feel the benevolent arms of Jupiter around your shoulder. Your burdens are momentarily lifted, and gratitude fills your entire being.

Saturn in Unity

Often, when we contract with Unity, we are making a pledge to purify our gene pool in some way. Saturn in Unity indicates that you have taken on the challenge of seeing the world through the eyes of your ancestors, making conscious choices about whether that is an appropriate perspective. If it is, you will help solidify the view of your lineage into the future New Being. If it is not, you will change the way you see the world in order to pass on a new lineage that is closer to truth. This is literal—in the sense that you may actually begin to see things in four dimensions rather than three (including the dimension of connection to all other things). It is also metaphorical in that you may begin to change old tapes about the solidity of form, since you know that form is really vibration appearing to be solid.

Uranus in Unity

There are two messages we receive from a Uranus in Unity placement. First, it is through your family lineage that you come to know yourself authentically. You are deeply connected to your family (if not your family of origin, then at least your genetic heritage). You will do well to study the indigenous spiritual systems of your lineage, as well as the mystical and occult traditions of your people. Second, we know that the principle of Unity—the feeling of deep interconnection with all beings—is who you are on the deepest level. Your ability to transcend differences and create wholeness is what keeps you constantly remembering your own authentic nature.

Neptune in Unity

Your birth group came into incarnation with the imperative to teach Unity. You are an initiatory part of the great wave of consciousness that swept the planet in the last 50 years of the twentieth century. You are tearing down old systems that perpetuate separation: organized religions, racism, sexism and genderism, governments that override the will of the people, corporations that become top heavy. While at times it may not seem as though your message is being heard, because there are so many of you, the message continues to echo through the ears of people of good heart, and Unity will eventually win the hearts and minds of us all.

Pluto in Unity

With Pluto in the principle of Unity, we know that your underworld journeys are orchestrated and evoked by your family—your genetic line. One of the ways in which we know ourselves is as members of a gene pool. We are "like" or in unity with our genetic lineage. And yet a part of our individuation and evolutionary imperative is to explore the uniquenesses and diversifications that we also carry. Pluto in Unity often sends you into a self-investigation based on family. Perhaps an even more important myth for us is the Inanna and Erishkegal story in which Inanna, queen of the world, goes into the underworld to check on her sister, queen of the underworld. If you do not know this story, read it—memorize it. It is important for you to integrate it into your understanding of your own life's purpose.

Mid-Heaven in Unity

Your soul resides in the mind of God in that aspect that holds all things in continuity. Everything that is "alike" is that way because the principle of Unity holds a continuum of consciousness. You come from a soul vibration that is healing and wholing in intent. Your entire soul cluster came into incarnation to bring a message that encourages us to see our likenesses more than our differences and to see the differences as places in which we amplify and clarify each other rather than separation points. You came here as an emissary of Unity.

~ 17 ATTRACTION ~

Sun in Attraction

You have a talent for magnetizing exactly what you need in life. Whether it is money, relationships, jobs, or toys, you know how to manifest them. If you really trust this, and if you do not abuse it, this will be your greatest life gift. You need not worry about anything, because the universe is looking out for your well-being. However, of course, if you misuse the power of attraction, you will pull energies to you that may be tough to handle. This is the gift you chose as your main gift to life!

Moon in Attraction

Your Moon in Attraction tells us that you have already learned the principles of magnetizing what you need when you need it. It gives you great freedom in life (if you remember and trust this principle), for you do not have to put much energy into worrying about the basics. This means you are free to develop and grow and give your gifts to life. Other people with Moon in Attraction might inspire you: John Kennedy, Wolfgang Mozart, Clara Barton, Rudolph Steiner, John Muir, and Werner Erhard. They all were at liberty to express life creatively because they were not tied to worrying about how to get food, clothing, shelter, and partnership.

Ascendant in Attraction

With your behavioral/ethical body in the principle of Attraction, we know that you have a personality that is magnetic. You are probably a popular person—or at least an unusually interesting and charismatic person—fun, inspiring, and influential. You know how to use that magnetic part of yourself to bring things, people, jobs, and situations into your life that you think you want or need. Your challenge, of course, will be to understand that what you think you need may not be what you really need. Learning to allow personal will to rest and trust that what comes into your path is of more value to you than you may know is your spiritual imperative.

Mercury in Attraction

Your mind has a wide range of ability. It can connect with the collective mind and understand the bottom line of almost any idea. You have a cohesive mind—you can grab a concept and stick to it with passion. We would call it an enormous, insurmountable intensity of mind when you want to really examine a subject or a topic. Of course, this kind of intensity can lead to fundamentalism of thinking, too, so it is necessary to make sure that you let yourself mentally expand from time to time. Consider the outrageous as well as the legitimate! People with Mercury in Attraction tell me that they almost never hit a mental dead end. They hit roadblocks, but their minds immediately begin to magnetize new ideas, data, and ways to move.

Venus in Attraction

Venus in Attraction indicates that your emotions are extremely important and tell you who and what you like. Not all people are like that. Some people use the mind and "just the facts." You, however, are fiercely loyal to your feelings and your gut responses, because they serve you well. You are emotionally stable, unless you are betrayed, because betrayal means that your gut instincts were wrong—you placed yourself in a vulnerable emotional position to someone else, and if they betray you, it makes you not trust your own instincts. You like to be mutually supported and respected in a relationship. The danger is that you can get addicted to your emotional responses, and then the emotional body dominates your experience.

Mars in Attraction

With your physical body in the principle of Attraction, we know that your body magnetically draws you toward saying "yes" to life. Your body is reliable in that way. Your body tells you when you are in the wrong place, when you are doing something out of integrity with your deepest self, and when you are inauthentic. Conversely, when you are in the right space, time, and doingness, your body tells you. You do not belong to a specific race, culture, religion, or club (although you may be a card-carrying member of any or all of these). You are, rather, a planetary citizen and a cosmic doer.

Jupiter in Attraction

With Jupiter in Attraction, we know that you receive those pats on the back from the god of good fortune when you have magnetized something into your life that you needed. Sometimes those things are obvious—a new job, a mate, a perfect house. Sometimes they are more veiled, and it may take years for you to understand that the moment was particularly poignant. An illness, a teacher, a relationship with someone—all kinds of things can be Jupiter moments. Becoming aware when you have pulled something to you will empower you and help you see the magnificence of life force. Depending on the house and sign of your Jupiter, you may find that you magnetize things first in the dream. You must learn to watch your dreams to see what "comes true" in your waking reality. These dreams, by the way, will most likely awaken you to a very happy day!

Saturn in Attraction

Your way of perceiving reality is unique. You can "see" the principle of Attraction at work. You intuitively understand gravity (a principle that even the most advanced scientists are still trying to "prove"). You intuitively understand the power of the magnetic bond. Your view of the world is one of cohesiveness and unity. You see nature and all its magic as visible proof of God's covenant to creation.

Uranus in Attraction

You have the sense of knowing yourself authentically when you have magnetized something that you need. It may be a job, a relationship, a place to live—but it may also be a parking spot, a lucky penny, a book that falls off the shelf and hits you on the foot that says exactly what you needed to hear. The point is that your awareness of the connectedness of all things and all beings will bring what you need into your path—and when that happens, you have a lightning flash of recognition that you participate with the universe in very profound yet subtle ways. That reminds you of Who You Are.

Neptune in Attraction

Your birth group came in with a particularly acute talent for magnetizing what is needed in certain situations. In a way, you are the social teachers about the principle of Attraction. You show the world, both in a positive and in a negative way, that what you attract to yourself determines the way in which you experience life. There is a level of accountability— "I'll take responsibility for my life, thankyouverymuch"—with your birth group that does not exist in the wider consciousness. Most people are better at being victims to life, while your birth group wants to take life by the horns, so to speak.

Pluto in Attraction

With Pluto in Attraction, we know that your trips into the underworld, or your journeys into your deepest self-investigation result in your being able to magnetize what you need in the world. You do not indulge in long depressions. But when you feel called to do your inner work, you go deep. Because Attraction is a gravitational principle, you do not "fall apart" but rather you come together as a result of these journeys into your soul space.

Mid-Heaven in Attraction

With your Mid-Heaven pointing toward the principle of Attraction, we know that your primary spiritual work is in the realm of cross-cultural awareness. In other words, you are here to help eliminate the "isms"—racism, sexism, ageism, religionism. Any philosophy that separates us from each other as human beings or from the wholeness of the universe in general is your spiritual enemy! Your imperative is toward unity consciousness—toward the understanding of all life as interdependent and interconnected. Your most direct contact with the level of soul is through that kind of connectedness with all beings.

~ 18 Focus ~

Sun in Focus

With your Sun in Focus, we know that your primary reason for incarnating this time is to play with perception. You came here to bring the gift of perception to form, and yet you are challenged to remember to change perception often so that you will not get stuck in a groove of simply seeing things according to a socially agreed norm. You have the marvelous skill that metaphysics calls "one pointedness." This means that you can eliminate all interference in order to give full attention to one detail. As a result, you are a great manifester. This lifetime is about learning to mature the ability to focus so that you can give the species the gift of perspective.

Moon in Focus

With your Moon in Focus, we know that you have spent many lifetimes and much of your between-life work studying the value of one pointedness. The human mind is unparalleled in its ability to give attention and to make the object of attention real. You are masterful in using attention. Many times, people with Moon in Focus feel that they should be able to concentrate more intensely than others. This may not be the case, especially if you are trying to force concentration (like on a school subject). The ability to use Focus masterfully on a spiritual level means that you are able to use your mind to help create the fields of resonance around ideas, plans, thought forms, and make them manifest. Because you are a master of Focus, this ability may be unconscious. We often take our mastery for granted.

Ascendant in Focus

When you make a decision, it has the power of your ethic behind it. Focus in the Ascendant means that your decisions are not lightly made. When you decide what you are going to do about something, there is clarity and power behind that decision. You carefully evaluate the consequences of a decision before you make it, and then, pow! People know to get out of your way.

Mercury in Focus

With your mental body in the principle of Focus, we know that you have an uncanny ability to eliminate all incoming data except that to which you have given your attention. Unfortunately, this does not guarantee that you are a "good" student. Indeed, you can only focus on that which interests you—and school may not have fallen into that category. In this incarnation, you are training your mind to perceive deeply. You are learning the power that the human mind has to determine what is to be perceived. And you are studying the realm of form with a scientific eye.

Venus in Focus

Your emotions are very strong and quite influential in your life, albeit not the central driving point of your life. Believe it or not, that is unusual. Many people either discount emotions or amplify them. Not so for you. Emotional experiences DEMAND that you use Focus. You are required "by law" (by the law of your incarnational contract) to examine the cause, ramifications, and implications of an emotional experience. If you learn to use Focus well by becoming intimately accountable to emotions (but not governed by them), you will develop skills in communication, compassion, and concentration. This principle is truly a gift, and if you give it to others, you will be helping to deliver the gift of Soul to the realm of form.

Mars in Focus

Mars in the principle of Focus means that your physical body is very intelligent. You can give all your attention—mental and physical—to one topic. You can put the power of your physical form behind the concentration of choice. I imagine that many scientists and artists have Mars in the principle of Focus. Those are the people who can become so absorbed in their work that they lose track of time and space.

Jupiter in Focus

Jupiter in Focus tells us that you have these profound experiences to remember that you are connected and supported by the cosmos during times of limited attention. In other words, if you are limiting your vision to contemplate a flower or a butterfly, Jupiter will most likely tap you on the shoulder and you will have a moment of feeling particularly blessed. Your ability to eliminate extraneous sound and visual input, so that you can place your laser-like attention in a desired arena, is a great gift.

Saturn in Focus

You are a natural scientist. You understand the qualities of form, and you have the mind that can put your attention to the study of form. However, this principle also gives you permission and capability to expand your understanding of form into a cosmology of form-ness. You can give unbendable attention to the smallest nuances of a form; you can also expand what you learn from that close attention into a full-blown theory of Wholeness. You have the gift of being able to break things down into parts in order to understand the whole.

Uranus in Focus

Uranus in the principle of Focus indicates that when you have these "aha" experiences, they are very sharp, clear, and defined. You do not get a vague sense of your authentic self—but rather a very specific picture of who you are, where you came from, and where you are going. I expect that you can also remember these experiences and call them up as often as you need to keep yourself on track.

Neptune in Focus

Your birth group brought the principle of Focus to the collective as an infusion of the ability to eliminate all but that which is being studied. The collective consciousness had been shattered and scattered a few years before by the explosion of the atomic bomb, and it became necessary for each individual to pull his or her attention back to the most trivial of circumstances in order to move forward. We became a society of "students"—public education and scientific emphasis became the central focus. The principle of Focus balances the principle of Awareness so that the collective can maintain a perspective that encourages personal growth as well as national growth.

Pluto in Focus

Your underworld journeys are third-eye opening experiences for you. When you take the time to deepen, your intuitive abilities amplify significantly, and your ability to see the unseen dominates your consciousness. Hopefully, you learned this early enough in life that you developed a pattern of going within often and fearlessly. Sometimes what we see on the inner planes is frightening or too mysterious for us to understand, so we avoid acknowledging it. It is very important for you to accept it, love it, and work with it—because that intuitive seeing is your victory over life and death.

Mid-Heaven in Focus

With your Mid-Heaven in Focus, we know that you have to eliminate all external noise and all internal dialogue in order to have a true soul experience. You are able to commune with your soul by narrowing your mind's eye to a pinpoint. You are like a subatomic physicist who goes deeper and deeper into the center of the atom and eventually finds nothing but vibration. When you are truly communing with your soul, you have looked through the microscope of yourself and burst through all matter and all form into the universe of vibration.

~ 19 SERVICE ~

Sun in Service

With your Sun in Service, you have a deep understanding that life is a gift and that you are here to bring focus and form to the gift. You can DO a lot (become Mother Teresa, if you so desire) or you can BE. Either way, you are serving life by being alive. Train your mind to remember that each time you enter a room or a circumstance, you alter it. You bring a very sacred energy into that room by being life's most dedicated servant. If you do this, you will continue to fall more and more in love with life everyday, and the benefits will be unspeakable.

Moon in Service

In other lifetimes or in other dimensions, you have mastered the understanding that life is a gift and to fully appreciate the gift, we must become servants to life. You are truly that. On the most essential levels of yourself, you know that you are here to serve—to serve others, to serve the planet, to serve life itself. This may have been a frustration for you early in your life, because it is hard to find the place, job, and opportunity to fulfill the longing to serve. However, as you have matured, you have most likely become clearer about how you, as a unique individuation of God, can serve most effectively.

Ascendant in Service

All your ethical and behavioral decisions require that you consider all of humanity! You do not really see yourself as an independent ethical unit! Most likely, even as a child, you were a sharing, giving, including playmate. Most people have to be taught that they are not the center of the universe. It never occurred to you! This principle's location in your chart indicates that you are an evolved being, and in fact, I do not know what the numerological/astrological odds are that one would have a 19° rising. But in my experience of doing these readings, this one is rare.

Mercury in Service

With your mental body in Service, we can say that you do not think like other people think. You do not even process information the way other people do. You are more impersonal and less selfish than other people. Most people apply information to themselves first and then move outward from there. You start integrating information by seeing how it applies to the whole, and eventually you may apply it to yourself. It is more like inductive than deductive thinking. Your primary concern in your mind is to serve the greatest number of dynamics with the information that you bring in. Now, that may or may not ever reach "doingness." You may just sit and think about how this information could serve others. It depends on your other personal pillars how you act on it.

Venus in Service

Venus, or the emotional body, in the principle of Service can be very tricky. You may confuse your training to take care of everyone else before you take care of yourself with service. You may tend to burn out emotionally and not really understand why. The best possible relationship between Venus as service comes when the being understands that her feelings and emotions are her give away. How you feel is your gift to life. By living in integrity with your soul, your feelings become the most authentic gift you have. You need not be afraid that your feelings are selfish little narcissistic acts of a bratty ego. No, your feelings are your service. Learning to trust your feelings and to act appropriately according to your feelings is a big part of your life commitment.

Mars in Service

Your Mars in Service means that your body—your physical presence— is in service to the soul consciousness of life. As a physical being, you radiate a higher frequency than most. You bring people to a resonance with you and with themselves just by being present in a room. This is a special relationship: physical body and service. For you, the only reason to be incarnated is to serve life. It is beautiful and touching that you chose this!

Your knees are chakra points, and you must tend to that very carefully. Learn to make sure that energy runs all the way down your legs into your feet and out into the earth. Many people who are contracted with Service tend to leak energy through their knees. Their feet never get warm and never get the empowerment they need to walk an impeccable path. Also, be careful with your exercise so that you do not damage your knees. Do not do too much (English) riding, do not do martial arts like karate that require kicking, and so forth. I rarely say "do not." But in this case, I have seen too many people contracted with Service in the hospital having knee surgery, so I warn.

Jupiter in Service

With Jupiter in the principle of Service, we know that you get those moments of feeling totally supported by the universe when you have just done something to be of service. This can be a little tricky, because we cannot fool ourselves into thinking we are being of service and therefore get our cosmic noogies. In other words, the service has to be given with no self-consciousness, and it has to be given with no expectation of recognition. This is rare. Most of us are charitable but very aware of the act of charity as we perform it. True service to life involves an awe of life that eliminates the consciousness of self. When that happens, you feel Jupiter's arm around your shoulder, you get a goose bumpy feeling, and you know the universe is looking out for you!

Saturn in Service

With Saturn in Service, we know that your response to form and your understanding to form is very sweet. You have a sense of yourself as a servant to life, and you consider all form of life as sacred and powerful. When you see a form, you are more likely to understand its "soul" than its physical presentation. This can mean anything from seeing a tree, to a building, to a form of worship. The chakra points in your knees are like little headlights that allow you to bring enlightening consciousness to any form you see. Your knees' response to forms gives you information as to the validity of the form. Your understanding of servitude is a part of what keeps your life moving ever forward.

Uranus in Service

You have those sweet moments of remembering the authenticity of your deepest self when you have been of true service to life. In your more immature years, this may have gotten confused with doing things for people that you did not necessarily want to do—the doormat syndrome. However, as you mature, you will understand that TRUE service means taking an action that serves the greatest number of dynamics—self (first), family, community, animals/plants, planet, and all sentient beings. Any action that depletes your sense of self is not an act of Service. When you truly understand that, then you are blessed with many, many experiences of ecstatic self-regenerative giving! In those moments, you remember all of Who You Are.

Neptune in Service

Your birth group came in to remind all of humanity of their soul's connection to form. You infuse the collective consciousness with a deep spiritual commitment, and you influence the collective morphic fields toward compassionate action. Your birth group has a profusion of evolved beings in it. Your goal is to raise the spiritual consciousness of the human species.

Pluto in Service

Your underground journeys—whether they be actual depressions or simply deep self-investigations—come as a result of some profound act of loving kindness on your part. You intuitively know that you are a servant to life, and it is when you stumble into those moments when life needs you to perform some service for others that you realize your own power. Ironically, this service may have to do with death. You understand death as a transition, a journey of an unfamiliar nature; therefore, you are of enormous service to those family members and loved ones who suffer loss at death. You are, like Persephone, fundamentally aware of the richness of the underworld—in the power of "growing down" and rooting oneself!

Mid-Heaven in Service

With your Mid-Heaven in the principle of Service, we know that when you align yourself with the true purpose of life—to bring the gifts of your soul into form—you are in complete understanding of your soul's purpose. You are here as a servant to life. As you mature, your understanding of your contract, your life's work and life decisions will reflect that more and more perfectly. Soon enough, you will be uncomfortable with the slightest deed, thought, or decision that takes you away from that purpose. Service, and thereby the contemplation of the meaning of service, is the principle that points you directly to your essence. It is the mirror through which you see your clearest reflection.

THE DESCENDING PRINCIPLES

~ 20 GRATITUDE ~

Sun in Gratitude

With your Sun in the principle of Gratitude, we know that you are primarily here to offer Eckhart's most sacred prayer: "Thank You." You live your life constantly aware that life is a gift. You never forget that the gift must be used well—or it will use you. You can see the connections in all aspects of life, and this makes you take a deeper level of responsibility or accountability than most people. You know the law or cause and effect on a bone-deep level; therefore, you are always alert to what effect you may be causing. You have a deep respect for all beings—human, plant, mineral, animal, and atomic. Your commitment to life makes you easy to live with and lovely to have as a friend.

Moon in Gratitude

With your Moon in the principle of Gratitude, we know that you are deeply aware that life is a gift, you are a servant to life, and staying in an attitude of gratitude is the source of your sanity. When you are in sync with yourself, you are constantly offering the most sacred of prayers: "Thank You." You have a mastery of the understanding of sentience, and you know that all intelligence throughout the universe is interconnected in a way that makes all sentient beings a part of each other. Because of that deep knowing, you are able to stay in contact with your life's purpose. Many people see themselves as disconnected, solitary figures. However, you know yourself to be deeply intertwined with all life, and that knowing keeps your mind and emotions clear of clutter.

Ascendant in Gratitude

Each time you make a behavioral decision, the awareness that life is a gift is in the back of your mind. You have a deep understanding of the dynamics that each of your choices affects (self, family, humanity as a whole, the planet, consciousness, sentient, and Creator). With your Ascendant in Gratitude, you are obliged to consider and accept the consequences of every action, more so than most people. You are conscious of your actions, and accountable to them on a conscious level. It is a beautiful way to walk your talk.

Mercury in Gratitude

With Mercury in Gratitude, you have a rare mind that holds the uncanny ability to connect with the sentience of all forms. It is neither a scientist's mind nor an analyst's mind. Yours is a poet's mind. You can hear the messages of the inanimate, you can perceive the memory of the stone, and you can contemplate the wisdom of beauty. While this mind may or may not receive social validation (depending on your family, schooling, and culture), it is certainly one that serves your incarnation well. One of your primary purposes is to understand sentience. You are not particularly interested in creating a mental cognitive database. You are ravenously hungry for the knowing-ness of form.

Venus in Gratitude

Venus in the principle of Gratitude means that your emotional body WORKS BEST when you understand each experience as a part of life's gift; therefore, you are thankful for any experience that makes you feel life more deeply. Part of every individual's life is to mature the emotions. We are all born with childlike neediness and demands, but as we mature physically, it is necessary to mature emotionally. It is not easy to be thankful for hurt feelings or betrayal, but the truly mature emotional being understands that every experience strengthens and empowers us if we learn to respond with life endorsing behavior and attitude. Demonstrating Gratitude in the emotional body marks a truly evolved being.

Mars in Gratitude

Your physical body is constantly aware of the blessing of life. You are a walking body prayer. That may mean that you do a lot of physical type workouts, or it may mean that your body itself is highly sentient. Or both. You have feelers—sensors—antennae. Your body is like a giant database that takes in information constantly and processes it easily. Walking meditations are most likely very powerful for you, and they could be your primary way of working out problems.

Jupiter in Gratitude

Jupiter in Gratitude tells us that when you have those wonderful moments that make you remember that you are supported by the universe, you are filled with gratitude. You remember that life is a gift, and you rededicate yourself to living that gift fully and with passion. Your breath changes, and your walk becomes a moving prayer. These moments are very sacred to you.

Saturn in Gratitude

With Saturn in Gratitude, we know that you are particularly aware of the sentient nature of form. You know, perhaps on a very deep level—a level beyond typical consciousness—that all forms are simply energy configured in a unique way. You know that energy has a certain self-knowing or sentience. Therefore, when you look at a tree—yes—you see a plant being, but you also see intelligent energy. Your attitude and awareness of the real spiritual nature of forms is unusual. You may have learned not to speak of it, because it sounds a little "crazy" in a world where most "things" are supposed to be solid and inert. However, you give a great service to the realm of form by remembering the true nature of energetic design!

Uranus in Gratitude

You have your most authentic self-knowing moments when something happens that brings you to your knees in Gratitude. As you walk through the busy-ness of life, from time to time, you are hit with a bold of spiritual lightning. You realize just what a gift life is, just how fortunate you are, and just how amazing it is to be a part of the unfolding process on this Earth. Those are the moments in which you remember exactly Who You Are!

Neptune in Gratitude

Your birth group came with the gift of Gratitude for the planet. You remind us all that we are to be thankful for living at this powerful and exciting time. We need to dream a new dream now, because we must create a world that is safe and nurturing for all species, not just our own. Living the Gratitude principle is the only way to do that. Your birth group, the last of the baby boomers, brought that principle in to permeate our imaginations so that we can move toward life rather than extinction. All baby boomers came in on a volunteer mission to try to turn the tides toward transformation!

Pluto in Gratitude

Pluto in Gratitude tells us that the way you experience the ultimate victory over life and death is to be thankful. It is that simple. When you get depressed or you go into a phase of deepening yourself, just remember to give thanks for everything in life and for the gift of life. Each journey into the underworld will be rich and full of power.

Mid-Heaven in Gratitude

Your soul is anchored in the deep understanding that life is a gift. With your Mid-Heaven in Gratitude, we know that the most efficient and direct way for you as a human being to be in communication with your own divinity is to pray Eckhart's prayer: "Thank you." When you are truly humbled by life, when you are in total gratitude for its gifts and possibilities, you open a pipeline that allows spirit to speak to and through you. It is a tender and beautiful soul—one that simply longs for you to acknowledge the gifts that you came into life to deliver.

~ 21-HARMONY ~

Sun in Harmony

With your Sun in the principle of Harmony, we know that your primary reason for taking this incarnation is to work with multiple dimensions of consciousness. You took a vow to see the unseen, be the spokesperson for the unspeakable, and bring attention to the invisible energies from which all form erupts. Life may have seemed very strange to you in your formative years, because you were not "normal." Like the jazz musician who hears the not-tune, you never quite "got" the norm. Unless you were born with full memory, it may have taken you a while—30 or 40 years—to realize that your life imperative is to be something other than the norm. Hopefully, by now you are comfortable with your beingness. You probably are or you would never have asked for this reading.

Moon in Harmony

Your mastery enables you to see the unseen. When you observe the actions of others, you can see the intent behind the action, the shadow of the action, and the harmonic dynamic around the action. This gives you a real leg up in terms of knowing the whole picture. You can help heal any situation, because you have a perspective that allows access to a wide spectrum of information. Your power in this arena is profound, and it requires impeccable attention.

Ascendant in Harmony

With your behavioral ethic in the principle of Harmony, we know that you are concerned about the "shadow" effect of all your actions. You stay acutely aware that every action has an equal reaction, and you like to take full responsibility for the effect you have on people and events. You might compare yourself to a conscious tree that realizes that by casting a shadow, you limit the light to some of the plants that grow in your immediate vicinity. This does not really require that you DO anything other than maintain an awareness!

Mercury in Harmony

Your mind works in a most unusual way. You operate mentally more from the unseen, unspoken, and unknown than from the obvious and overt. You have a strong sense of intention. When you communicate with others, you hear what they mean more than what they say. When you draw conclusions, they are not typically based on Aristotelian logic but more on intuitive knowing. In your early years, it may have been a challenge for you, because you do not think like most people. But as you matured, you began to see the value of factoring in consequences and implications as equal partners with facts and data!

Venus in Harmony

With your emotional body in the principle of Harmony, we know that you work with the unseen energies through your emotions. This is a slightly difficult Placement, because it means that you "feel" what cannot be seen or quantified. Society does not give much help there, because according to our social standards, if you cannot see, it does not exist. Even psychology as it is typically practiced will not give you the support you may need (support in believing that you are NOT crazy) because a therapist will guide you toward examining your own shadow side, which can be a never-ending maze of inconclusive investigations. This principle indicates you have a shaman's emotional body. The shaman sees, knows, feels, and experiences that which cannot be seen, known, or felt.

Mars in Harmony

With your physical body in the principle of Harmony, we know that you may sometimes process "negative" or "shadow" experiences in your body. It means that you have some physical psychic abilities—you can literally feel the repercussions of actions. Unless you have come to a deep understanding of this gift, it may have been a burden for you. Society does not generally endorse psychic ability, feeling what cannot be seen, sensing the "is-not" of a situation. However, it is a wonderful gift, because it gives you the advantage of knowing the consequences of the physical world in ways that other people cannot.

Jupiter in Harmony

When you have an experience of Harmony—when you see the multiple dimensions of an experience and know the metaphor of that—then Jupiter has tapped you on the shoulder and reminded you of how safe, protected, loved, and sponsored you are in this life.

Saturn in Harmony

With Saturn in Harmony, we know that in many ways, you are more interested in the shadow the tree casts than in the tree itself. That is to say—your eye and your interest are drawn in directions that other people usually do not see. You are, in fact, able to see the unseen side of form—if you let yourself. In art, you like the negative spaces. In nature, you like the shadows, the holes, and the unnoticed. You have a very deep understanding of dimension, definition, and subtle differences. This may be something you keep to yourself because other people might call it "weird." It may be something you do not even notice about yourself because it is so deeply engrained that you do not separate it out as a uniqueness. It is unique, and it is important. As your contribution to the realm of form, you notice the "not-isness" of form.

Uranus in Harmony

With Uranus in Harmony, your experiences of authenticity come when you can see the shadows. That does not mean the negative or non-benevolent side of things. It does mean that your ability to see the "not yet" is what resonates with you as a being. Periodically, you are struck with a lightning bolt of understanding, and you see all the dynamics and dimensions around your life. At that moment, you understand Who You Are as a being. Just as quickly, it goes away. But that moment of insight was enough to change your perspective and give a new intention to your walk.

Neptune in Harmony

Your birth group infused consciousness with a memory of the need to understand all the dynamics of energy/action. When you were born, most of the people on this planet were living in a sort of amnesia—walking around asleep to the greater dimensions of life force. Your birth group came in to awaken people to the multiple dynamics of consciousness. The responsibility of keeping the collective awake has been a part of your life journey.

Pluto in Harmony

When you go into your underworld journeys, you experience a wide variety of feelings, sensations, emotions, and reactions. You sometimes have to "stop the world" and go into the depths of yourself because there are so many parts of your life that never reach expression otherwise. You are very complex, and that complexity requires periodic radical investigation. You have the temperament of the jazz musician. Your ability to "play" all the not-ness (the aspects of your life that remain in the shadows) is sophisticated, but it requires constant and conscious attention on your part. If you do not stop periodically, be silent, and search your depths, you will be pulled down by them.

Mid-Heaven in Harmony

As a soul, you are one of the "musicians" of the universe. The principle that takes you most directly to the soul's imperative for your incarnation is the principle that includes the shadow, unseen realms, and portion of life that is both not apparent and yet gives life dimension and texture.

~ 22 Dreaming ~

Sun in Dreaming

Your Sun in Dreaming tells us that you have come to this lifetime to help create a new world. It is the job of the dreamers to reach into the realm of potential—the dimension of truth—and magnetize into form that which is ready to manifest. You came into this incarnation as an emissary for your soul as a dreamer. You take responsibility for all your realities, because you know the multidimensional nature of your being. You must read my book, *The Woman's Book of Dreams*! It will be very helpful and a source of support for you.

Moon in Dreaming

Now, do not get upset if you cannot remember your dreams. That does not mean that you are not living your soul pattern. With your

Moon in the principle of Dreaming, it is possible that your "dreams" come more in the form of the visionary. Whether you have night dreams that teach, inform, instruct, heal, and "grow" you, or whether you have visions for the planet and the human family—you are a master dreamer. Your work in this incarnation is to bring the magic of the dreamtime into form. Live in such a way that nothing is impossible, everything is potential, and all is well.

Ascendant in Dreaming

With your behavioral ethic in the principle of Dreaming, we know that you make your decisions from a much wider span of consciousness than most people. You have the ability to see a broader spectrum of the consequences and effects of your actions. When you make an ethical or behavioral decision, you take a larger degree of responsibility for it than most people. If you truly understand this, then it is a blessing, but if you do not understand it, it becomes a curse. You may either be blessed to see yourself as a visionary, or you are cursed to see yourself as a victim, or as a caretaker who receives no gratitude.

Mercury in Dreaming

With your mind in Dreaming, you probably have spent your entire lifetime frustrated with the fact that you think so differently from other people. Your imagination (read that as ability to image) is so much more sophisticated than most people that you almost never think linearly and along the same lines as other people. You think in circles, which is actually much more natural (close to nature). You create a reality for yourself that is interesting, rich, and full of potential—but somewhat lonely because you are the only one who can really access it. Your challenge will be to learn to love and appreciate your mind in spite of pressure to "normalize."

Venus in Dreaming

This may be a difficult placement for you. Indeed, it is a rare configuration. I have read very few people with Venus in Dreaming. It probably means that your emotional body has a tendency to magnify experiences, see the "unseen" in the experience, and possibly react more strongly to emotional experiences than most. In fact, because Dreaming involves the human ability to create metaphorical images, your imagination may paint an emotional experience in ways that other people simply do not understand. It is important for you to know that when you "feel"—when your emotional body is at work—it is moving outside the typical band of human consciousness. In your emotional body, you experience potential as well as reality.

Mars in Dreaming

Your Mars in Dreaming tells us that you have a little trouble staying in the physical body. Your dream body is more active, and perhaps even more familiar to you than the dense, gravity bound, slow physical body. You may have been made to feel badly about that, because we do not have many dreamers in our society. There is nothing wrong with it as long as you understand the dangers of not being present in the physical body—especially when you are doing dangerous things like driving, and so forth. Part of your life challenge is to create a communication and working relationship between the physical and the dreaming bodies.

Jupiter in Dreaming

With Jupiter in Dreaming, we know that the moments when you feel most supported by the universe are outside the typical band of human consciousness. You may feel it in your sleeping dreams. You may feel it in your daydreams. You may feel it in meditation. But the point is that you feel it in your dreaming. It may have been difficult for you at first to realize that these "atta girl's" are real, because you were able to dismiss them as "just a dream." However, as your dreaming talents have matured, you have (will?) become more comfortable with a deep knowing that the universe is supporting your incarnation unconditionally and that you receive proof of that in your dreamtime.

Saturn in Dreaming

Your relationship to the realm of form is not "solid." You see waking reality as a dream, just as you do dreaming reality. The realm of form just does not hold the density and guaranteed safety for you that most people demand of it. You may have been accused of living in your own world—or of daydreaming—or of escaping and not ever really "being here." But that is all social projection. In fact, it is your JOB to remember for all of us that none of this is "real" in the way most people make it real. It is all the result of our minds playing the "what if" game. You are doing your work by NOT buying the density. Thank you.

Uranus in Dreaming

With Uranus in Dreaming, we know that you have the most authentic experiences of yourself when you have released the personal mind and the personal will into an expansive space outside the typical band of human consciousness. This kind of dreaming does not necessarily require your being asleep. This relationship with the principle of Dreaming simply indicates that you have the ability to transcend collective consciousness or at least to loosen the boundaries that consensus reality puts on you. And when you do that, you go to a mind space that reminds you of Who You Are and why you came into being at this time.

Neptune in Dreaming

Your birth group is highly attuned to the Great Dreamer. You are all dreamers who have come in to infuse the species with memories of the Plan. You all probably tend to be idealistic and materialistic (in the sense that you want to see the Plan manifested here and now). By "the Plan," I simply mean that you and your birth group have the ability to discern the organizing force of the universe and you have a deep commitment to seeing that force put into form on this planet. You long for peace, you strive for justice, and you constantly work toward developing a family of humanity on this earth who can live in harmony with each other and with the planet.

Pluto in Dreaming

Pluto in Dreaming indicates that your ultimate victory over life comes in your ability to dream—to enter the deepest parts of yourself, access divine potential, and be fully integrated with the truth. Your underworld journeys are empowering for you because they give you a sense of life after death or victory over death. They also help you understand that we are multidimensional beings and that our consciousness must not be limited to the mundane world.

Mid-Heaven in Dreaming

With the Mid-Heaven in Dreaming, we go a step further than what Dreaming means to the incarnated personality. On the level of souls, while there is not the kind of dualism and separation that we experience in form, there is a hierarchy of responsibility. It is like the cells in the brain: The brain is one organism made of many cells, each with certain responsibility to the whole organism. The cells interface with each other through electrical synapses. Souls are cells in the mind of god. The Dreaming souls are beings who nurture the Void. As a Dreaming soul, your contact with your most essential self comes through moving outside your typical band of consciousness into the dimension of truth!

~ 23 RANDOMNESS ~

Sun in Randomness

Your primary purpose in life is to learn to work with the chaos theory in a healthy way. You are one who knows how to allow change to occur—not for change's sake but for the sake of evolution. You are involved in a spiritual principle that is difficult for many to understand, because most people want to feel that they are in control. Your life's work has to do with realizing that "control" is not the issue at all. Accountability and responsibility (the ability to respond) to what appear to be random occurrences are what make the human truly interdependent with life. As you mature and develop the ability to allow deconstruction, your talent at reconstruction will also develop and mature.

Moon in Randomness

Your Moon in Randomness indicates that you have a certain proficiency in coming out of the chaos of life with the right decision! You know how to trust chaos—let it work its magic, present its options, and eventually weave the right thread. "Trust" is the keyword here. Most people who are not familiar with the power of Randomness panic when the path becomes foggy, and they often make decisions and take willful action in the wrong timing. You, on the other hand, have an innate ability to wait, trust, watch intently, and leap when the timing is right.

Ascendant in Randomness

Placing your Ascendant in Randomness signals that this may be your area of challenge. If there is challenge in our lives, it is often found in the egoic/behavioral part of ourselves. Actually, though, Randomness in your Ascendant may simply be a challenge for others around you, not for you. It indicates that when you find yourself in chaos, or when everything around seems to be shattering or in crisis, you pop into action. Out of the chaos, you are able to pull the best possibility and move toward actualizing it. The downside is that you may get addicted to creating the chaos so that you can operate in your most powerful stance. When you learn this about yourself, however, it is enormous! You are capable of greatness because you do not lose yourself—indeed you find yourself and your deepest creativity—when stress, pressure, disaster, failure, and change are present.

Mercury in Randomness

With your mind in Randomness, you may have had some trouble earlier in your life—perhaps with school or with socialization—because you periodically go into chaotic thought patterns. To other people, this seems disturbing. However, for you it is perfectly normal. When you are trying to "figure something out," your mind expands massively while it takes all possibility into consideration and then eventually narrows and crystallizes onto one thought. The one thought on which you land is the "right" answer—but the process for getting to that answer is not linear, logical, rational, and according to the rules of Western thinking. Believe it or not, you are making a contribution to collective thought by doing this. Your mind is one of the human minds that keeps the consensus reality in which we live from being rigid and stifling.

Venus in Randomness

With Venus in Randomness, we can surmise that you run the whole gamut of emotion. An experience of emotion for you is one that takes you into chaos and all potential. You move into chaos, but you come out with the most empowering choice. In other words, when you experience something in your emotional body, you almost overdo it. You run the spectrum from overwhelm to being cold and calculating. Then you eventually crystallize the best emotional path for yourself and take it. Emotions seem to rule your life at times. They are powerful. Yet you glean enormous wisdom from having true emotional experience.

Mars in Randomness

With your physical body in the principle of Randomness, you have probably spent your whole life being accused of inefficiency. In truth, you work better in chaos, because it is only when you can see all the options and all the possibilities that you make the best choice. You have a natural talent for magnetizing toward the "right" physical action and/or activity. So, rest assured that this practice is part of your spiritual contract!

Jupiter in Randomness

When the kaleidoscope turns and everything starts shifting, you have a Jupiter experience. When all the pieces of the puzzle seem to fly up in the air, you always catch the one that is exactly right. The universe continues to demonstrate to you that control is not really possible and certainly not desirable. If you try to control the outcome, you will always mess up the plan.

But if you flow with the random presentation of energy, you will always have good fortune.

Saturn in Randomness

Saturn in Randomness is very interesting. It means that you participate in the consensus, but you do not necessarily "buy" it. You are able to see other possibilities and other aspects of form all the time. Your perception of form is not "stable." You are not the type of person who freaks out if you could see through walls—or even walk through them for that matter. Sometimes walls open for you, and that is okay. Other people need form to be more solid in order to give them the security to operate. You are wild and untamed in your perspective.

Uranus in Randomness

With Uranus in Randomness, we know that you have highly unusual experiences of your authentic self. They occur when everything seems to fall apart. Suddenly, in the midst of chaos, the kaleidoscope of your life turns, and a new pattern forms. You realize that no matter what configuration the energy that is uniquely you take, it is always essentially the same. You "recognize" yourself when forms shatter around you. You are probably GREAT to have around during a crisis or emergency, because that is when you most profoundly recognize the never changing nature, yet ever changing circumstances of your authentic being.

Neptune in Randomness

Neptune in Randomness tells us that your birth group infused the collective consciousness with divine potential. You came in to remind us that we are capable as a group of dreaming a new dream—writing a new script for the evolution of our planet. Neptune was discovered by astronomers the same year film was invented. They have similar qualities—the sort of dreamy, mystical, magical way they play with our imaginations. When your birth group came in, the world and especially our country were in a great chaos. We were falling apart and destroying any systems and social structures that did not work. We were in that part of the kaleidoscope experience when the rocks are all going chunk-a-chunk-a-chunk on their way to a new pattern. Your birth group reminded us of the unlimited potential of the new patterns!

Pluto in Randomness

With Pluto in Randomness, we can see that your underworld journeys are quite chaotic but result in marvelous benefits. Whether you call those journeys depressions, or whether they come at the insistence of something other than your psychology (for example disease or accidents may have thrown you into your personal investigations), they are really journeys into the realm of potential for you. Like the kaleidoscope, you may feel that all your rocks are being rattled during those times, but eventually a new pattern forms and it is more beautiful than you could have imagined if it had all been directed by your personal will. Truly, your underworld journeys are some of the most important times of your life because they force you to open your options and expand your perspective.

Mid-Heaven in Randomness

As a soul, you are a part of the temple of manifestation. You bring things to fruition. You help others do the same. You have the ability to strengthen and liberate others from their limitations. You can direct the power of the will of others. Used correctly, this gives you the ability to help the world transform.

You are unparalleled in your ability to shatter old beliefs, thus liberating yourself and others from bondage (mental, emotional, and physical). When your soul is fully incarnated (meaning that your soul is more in charge of your life than your will), selflessness is your primary hallmark. You have the ability to see ALL of the divine plan (from its original blueprint all the way through its manifestation, its ultimate destruction, and finally its resurrection).

~ 24 HUMILITY ~

Sun in Humility

It is not an easy Placement to have your Sun in Humility. It means that you must constantly be on the alert for either arrogant or self-defacing thoughts and actions. You must be in continual self-investigation. You must ruthlessly eliminate lies and projections from your reality. In short, you must walk your talk, stay in your own reality, and never get caught in someone else's dream. Deep authentic self-knowing is the ONLY path that is right and comfortable for you. There is no room for whining, victimization, or self-importance. You must never stop checking for self-importance!

Moon in Humility

With your Moon in Humility, we know that in some other lifetime and/or in some other dimension, you have mastered the ability to know yourself authentically. This ability to always pull back from the stresses of "reality" and remember Who You Are is your big safety net in this lifetime. You are constantly on alert for arrogance or self-deprecation; you are on a constant mission of self-investigation. However, one's mastery is often so integrated into a being that he or she forgets to pay special attention to it—it may be something you take for granted and do not honor in yourself. It may be also something that you automatically expect from other people because since it is so much a part of your being, you think it is "normal." Believe me: Humility is not widespread!

Ascendant in Humility

With your Ascendant in Humility, we know that you make your decisions from a very earthy, grounded place in your mind. You find your own authenticity in a situation and make your decisions from that position. You are concerned about the effect of your decisions on all the other beings and dynamics involved. You are reliable and trustworthy. You do not lie or manipulate to get your way. Your strength is in your self-knowing. People will follow some who knows himself or herself because they long to do the same!

Mercury in Humility

When you placed your Mercury in Humility, you accepted a very deep responsibility. Your mind must align itself with your own authentic self in order to work well. If you ever try to work outside that deep self-knowing, you get mentally confused. This is a challenge because you can get myopic if you allow yourself. However, as you mature spiritually, you will find that this is a true gift. You have the unique mental ability to see the outer world more clearly by measuring it against an inner authority. You have the ability to know what is authentic within yourself. Therefore, you have a measuring stick or plumb line to see what is authentic in the collective mind. Humility in the mental body requires ruthlessness of thinking—cutting away all that is untrue without hesitation.

Venus in Humility

Venus in Humility tells us that through your emotional experiences, you come into deep contact with your authentic self. Sometimes, this could mean that your emotions bring you down out of a grandiosity. Other times, it means that your emotions elevate you out of a self-imposed head trip into the pity pot. Either way, when you experience the emotionality of life, you find it balances you and brings you into an authentic knowing of yourself. As you have matured the ability to use emotion as your ally, you have become an emotionally stable person—not that you do not still experience the whole spectrum but that you do not let either end of an emotional pendulum swing frighten you.

Mars in Humility

With your physical body in the principle of Humility, we know first and foremost that your relationship with nature is the key to your physical well-being. Humility—humus—demands that you stay in touch with the earth. You must TOUCH the earth with your bare skin. Gardening is one good way—farming an even bigger way—walking barefooted on the grasses and sands also works. As a physical being, the way you stay grounded, healthy, clear, detoxed, and solidly embodied is to work with the earth. Also, because Humility involves integrating the energy of the light, it is important for you to receive sunlight. Wear plenty of sunscreen, of course, but be aware that absorbing the sun's rays is part of your most personal path. Your personal physical pillar demands that you receive and integrate not only the esoteric light, but the sun as well.

Jupiter in Humility

Jupiter in Humility is an incredibly appropriate and powerful Placement, albeit rare. You get your pats on the back from the universe when you experience a moment of deep, authentic self-knowing. These experiences may often come in nature. Humility comes from the word *humus* meaning "of the earth." We must constantly remember that the elements that made this planet did not originate here. They were spewed into the cosmos when a star died and burned so brightly and reached such outrageous temperatures that it melted simple atoms together to create complex ones. The elements that make our earth are stardust. The elements that make our body are stardust. When you truly remember that we are star people made of particles of light, Jupiter puts his arm around you and blesses your incarnation.

Saturn in Humility

You have a special relationship with the realm of form. By observing form, you come to know yourself more authentically. You bridge inner and outer realities more gracefully than most people. It may come so naturally to you that you do not realize that you are "different." You see external reality as a mirror for what is going on inside. Conversely, you experience your internal reality as a reflection of the outer world. Most people separate them—thinking that their inner is private and separated from the outer world. Through nature and human relationships, you learn more about the divine nature of your own incarnation.

Uranus in Humility

Periodically, you have an amazing moment, usually in nature or in some peak experience, which illumines who you are in the most profound ways. "Uranus in Humility" is almost redundant. The Uranus clause is about self-knowing, and Humility is the principle of self-knowing. Combined, they are a double whammy. When you have an experience with Humility, it is very powerful, life changing, and the memory of it is long lasting.

Neptune in Humility

Your birth group brought the principle of Humility and infused the species with that longing to know the self. Neptune is the planet of the collective dream, and your birth group planted the seed of the theme for generations to come: the theme of knowing the self authentically and from that knowingness creating a dream of peace and harmony on the planet.

Pluto in Humility

Pluto in Humility tells us that your underworld journeys and your depressions usually bring you closer in touch with your authentic self. When you take the time to go deep and probe far beneath the surface, you find a reality that is rich, true, and validating. You remember that on the deepest levels, you are a being of wisdom and profound knowingness. Pluto becomes not your kidnapper and rapist, but your partner and mentor. Your dominion in his realm gives you a sense of authentic beingness.

Mid-Heaven in Humility

With your Mid-Heaven in Humility, we know that you will always eventually return to your own authenticity. You are rooted in a soul that demands truthful knowing of who you are. You may, in various lifetimes, try to fit the mold of society and meet the expectations of people, but you will always eventually return to the truth of yourself. The humble soul is one who serves life. The humble soul is one who is nurtured by earthiness. The humble soul is one who knows Who She Is, and therefore has no needs beyond that.

~ 25 Desire ~

Sun in Desire

Your primary purpose in this lifetime—or perhaps it would be more accurate to say your primary motivation for life—is to really come to the understanding that while you appear to be separated, you are really One with the whole universe. You appear to be living a life that is unique (and you are), and yet there is a bond between you and the Great Plan and the Great Dream and God that is totally unbreakable. It was your intent when you took this incarnation to live fully and yet to remember fully your Divine Nature. It is not an accident that you chose to live in a capitalistic, commerce-oriented society. It would be easier if you lived in poverty in India, so that the possibility of getting wrapped up in buying, owning, and possessing just would not be there. Your job is to buy, own, possess and yet know that all of it represents your passion to be fully embodied as a divine emissary for your soul.

Moon in Desire

Your mastery is in the ability to connect continually to Divine Source. Your eyes continually give you information that shows you that all things are One, interconnected, and interdependent! Your longing to reunite with your own soul, and therefore with the Wholeness of the universe, is sometimes overwhelming. It is lonely here! And yet because you have been trained in the ancient temples, there is a memory that flows in the marrow of your bones. This memory reminds you that there is no greater honor than to be a human, for it is only in this form that we can choose wholeness, love, and divine perspective.

Ascendant in Desire

Your Ascendant in Desire tells us that each decision you make is based on your belief that you are connected to Divine Source. Every choice you make is controlled by your awareness of that connection. Your longing to be united with that source is sometimes overwhelming, and it causes your behavior to seem erratic at times—until you truly grasp the meaning behind your desires. In other words, you could be tempted to be an addictive shopper or an insatiable collector until you realize that you ARE connected to Source and all you need to is let Source work through you. Suddenly, all your behaviors will become easy without grasping, holding, or needing.

Mercury in Desire

Your mind is passionate about creating a "perfect" world. You are an idea shopper. You never stop looking for and collecting ideas that when put into action will create a world of wholeness and connection. In your youth, you may have been (or may be if you are still very young) an insufferable debater. This principle brings passion with it, and so your passion about ideas is sometimes overwhelming. You have probably had to learn how to rein your passion, keep from overwhelming and/or judging others who do not share your passion, and express yourself in ways that can be heard by others. What we know for sure, though, is that you will not stop until you have found truth—which means you will be reading and gobbling information until the day you die!

Venus in Desire

Venus in the principle of Desire indicates that your emotional body is very deeply connected to your soul. You long to be at "home" with your highest self. When you have highly emotional experiences, they either remind you of "home" (which would make them comfortable and nourishing experiences), or they remind you of the pain of being away from "home" (which would make them painful and separating experiences). This could be the biggest challenge of your incarnation—to remember that you are connected to home and that you can access that connection at any point.

Mars in Desire

You live inside a paradox. Desire in your physical body makes you simultaneously want to be fully in life and appreciate all its gifts, while longing to go "home." This may be a challenging area for you when you are young, because the principle of Desire can translate as an insatiable appetite to collect "things" or to be healthy or beautiful or socially prominent. Before you realized the true spiritual definition of Desire, it may have thrown you around. However, it is truly a blessing to have your physical body so connected to your soul! Your roots are in heaven, as they say in Kabbalah; therefore, you will likely not lose yourself in materialism.

Jupiter in Desire

You have those amazing moments of feeling that all is right with the world and in your life when you realize that you are the object of your own Desire. Whether in nature or in the middle of a city on a shopping spree, you realize that your deepest longing is to be yourself. You understand that it is not necessary to own anything, because you have life—you have everything. In those moments of profound integration, Jupiter, the god of good fortune, puts his arm around your shoulder and fills you with the comfortable feeling of having come home!

Saturn in Desire

Saturn in the principle of Desire is what keeps you connected to form. Each of us has to limit ourselves in some way—we have to agree to be "without" something—in order to stay in form. If we had everything, there would be no longing, and without longing, there is no reason to stay embodied. Your "without" is the realization that even though you "have" everything you could possibly want, there is no thing more important than your connection to soul. You have a paradox because your longing is to go home, but your contract requires you to be in form. The Saturn clause gives you clues about how you can do both.

Uranus in Desire

Uranus in the principle of Desire tells us that when you have those "aha" moments—when you truly remember your contract, your reason for being, your soul connection, you know that you are at home. You remember that you already possess everything, and that acquisition and ownership are not necessary. These moments, which are probably visions, because your eyes perceive the light in some truthful way, remind you of your divine nature. You remember that you represent a highly subtle soul, and that your imperative in life is to create a form through which that soul can express. These are very sacred moments for you personally.

Neptune in Desire

Your birth group came to infuse the planet with the consciousness that only when the inner and the outer are the same do we truly understand the power of life force. When we get stuck in separation, polarization, and duality, we ramble—lost—unable to find a true sense of home. Your birth group brought "home" to the consciousness of the human species to remind us all that life is a gift; life is a sacred journey. It is not an exile but a walk around the block!

Pluto in Desire

Your deep internal journeys—your times of self-investigations—are times when you see things about yourself that have never been brought to the light of your attention before. These periods are very enlightening to you, because they help you understand what you think you lack in your ordinary life. In fact, when you achieve something or acquire something that you thought you wanted in your life, you may spontaneously go into a sinking period. During that time, you realize that nothing in the external world really satisfies your need to be in touch with yourself, be in touch with the intention of the soul, and be touched by God. You emerge from these inner journeys victorious, because you achieve self-understanding.

Mid-Heaven in Desire

Your longing to go "home" is what drives you toward communication with soul. You are never far from that ache to return to Unity. There is a natural, built-in loneliness as a result. Earlier in life, you probably tried to satisfy that loneliness and longing with human relationships. It is not possible. Only a relationship with the soul—only a deep and penetrating understanding of the nature of human life—only a resonance with the tone that has created your form will fill the need.

~ 26 SILENCE ~

Sun in Silence

Is it not ironic that your primary purpose for taking this incarnation is to listen? You are not only to listen to the world around you, but you are to listen to the music of the spheres—you are to listen to the vibration of the cosmos! All your "doingness" will be directed by your Silence if you surrender to this great purpose in life. This is probably not an easy role given that we live in a fast lane, noisy, information highway, move, move, move society. This pattern asks that you follow your inner guidance—go against the flow—and learn to be very still, very quiet, very centered in the midst of external chaos.

Moon in Silence

This rare thread in your garment is very powerful. You have the unique ability to "stop the world" and listen to the sound of truth. This ability is second nature to you. Therefore, you may not realize that it is unique. It is, however, a very important part of the gift that you have come to deliver to form in this lifetime. You know how to align with the intention of God—to allow God to speak to and through you. It is a holy aspect of your being and one that you must honor from the depths of your being. Do not let the noise of the external world distract you!

Ascendant in Silence

With your behavioral body in the principle of Silence, we know that before you make any sort of decision, you have to go to the realms of silence. Your mind must be very quiet, and you must attune yourself with the music of the spheres—the tones of the cosmos. If you make decisions in the midst of internal noise, you make errors. It is important to your personal ethic that you sit still before making a big choice. Even little choices are more "right" when you take a moment to breathe. Your meditations are very important. As you mature into understanding silence, a daily practice of sitting in meditation will become more comfortable to you. Bells and gongs are necessary for you. When you are struggling with noise, the tone of the right gong will clear all the static for you.

Mercury in Silence

What an amazing mind you must have! Most people spend their lives in eternal internal chatter. Your mind, when it works best, is quiet. In order for you to think clearly, you must first go into solitude, and you must do some sort of "magic" to trick your mind into being quiet so that it can resonate with Great Mind. This is an amazing promise that you made to your soul— to learn to work with Silent Mind.

Venus in Silence

Your emotional body requires a great deal of solitude and repose in order to stay healthy. As long as you give yourself plenty of room and time to process emotions quietly, you will stay healthy. If you demand too much of yourself, demand that your feelings be expressed without proper time to feel them, or spend too much time in the "noise" of other people's emotional expressions, you will suffer. You have taken an extremely mature emotional contract, and it is probably an aspect of your personality that continually grows and evolves as you mature. Your emotional strength and wisdom are a big part of your gift to the world.

Mars in Silence

Your most important healing tool is solitude. When you are ill, emotionally disturbed, or are experiencing confusion and chaos, you must find a place to be absolutely quiet, still, stimulus free. For this reason, you may need to live alone. When you achieve silence, the bones in your skull literally attune to the frequency that is most authentically "you"—the Word from which all manifestation emanates. That experience is more important and more healing than medicine, therapy, or physical exercise.

Jupiter in Silence

It is when you achieve absolute silence—when you still all the inner dia-logue and sit at peace—that the god of good fortune pats you on the back and says, "Job well done." These moments of silence and contemplation are essential for you, because without them you do not remember that you are well-loved, well-supported, and well-guided on your journey. More than most people, a practice of meditation or contemplation is an absolute life "must do."

Saturn in Silence

You have the ability to hear the "tone" of any form. You are especially good at it when you are in nature. You can stare at a tree or a rock or a lake, empty your mind, and hear the vibration of the form. And like a violin in the room with another violin, when that tone begins to penetrate your skull, you align with it. Your ability to commune with nature and its beautiful forms is astonishing. It may even be tempting to you to become a hermit and just live and vibe with nature. Of course, you can also do it with other forms—man-made forms—but that is harder because you have more levels of interference to move through. The realm of form, for you, holds the poten-tial of deeply connecting yourself to yourSelf.

Uranus in Silence

With Uranus in Silence, we know that you have those profound moments of self-realization when you are able to quiet your inner dia-logue and simply listen to the music of the spheres. When you are in a place in time-space-matter that allows absolute peace, the bones of your skull will buzz with the very tone that runs the universe. And in those moments, you remember your part of the Great Universal Plan. These moments are very precious and fairly rare for you, because the busy-ness of the mundane world invades so much of your consciousness. But you have them just often enough to keep moving toward your own awakening.

Neptune in Silence

Your birth group infused collective consciousness with the ability to be quiet and the memory of how to listen to the music of the spheres. While meditation has always been a part of human religions, your birth group re-introduced it as a tool that can be used for relieving stress, acquiring and maintaining health, as well as accessing the Divine. Your group came into life at a time when the species needed to remember the value of Silence, and part of your collective contribution to the realm of form is to practice Silence in your personal life.

Pluto in Silence

With Pluto in Silence, we know that your inner investigations—your underworld journeys—are about deep listening. When you feel pulled toward an internal inventory of emotions, you need time to be alone and very quiet. If that time and space is granted, your "depressions" do not last long. You simply listen deeply to the voice within, attune yourself to the sound of the cosmos, and move on. However, if that time and space is not afforded, the noise of the busy world begins to become deafening, and you lose perspective and sight of your path.

Mid-Heaven in Silence

The most direct path to the level of soul for you is through a true experience of Silence. That, of course, means that stilling the mind and halting the inner dialogue is a spiritual imperative for you. It does not, however, mean that the soul itself is quiet. You are connected through soul lines to a massive collective consciousness that, through sound, weaves the universe together. An understanding of the relationship among silence, sound, and form is one of the most paradoxical and sophisticated spiritual principles. Each time you truly touch the level of soul consciousness, you return to ordinary awareness with an expansion that is a gift to us all.

~ 27 Peace ~

Sun in Peace

If your Sun is in the principle of Peace, your main objective in life is to reach a state of consciousness that allows you to go beyond duality, polarity, and separation. You are constantly seeking a place in your mind/heart that allows respite. Your only goal—your only desire—is to be in full relationship with your soul. It may be hard for you to integrate this longing with the harshness and demands of mundanity. Whatever your challenges are in life, your biggest challenge is to allow the peace that passes understanding to flow in your body always.

Moon in Peace

Your mastery, then, is Peace. This means that you know how to maintain a perspective that allows you to go beyond the conflict and see the wholeness. Your ability to look at the "isness" of any situation gives you a vocabulary that is quite practical. Peace is a principle that is not very emotional. It is not woo-woo. It is not "love and light." It is, instead, real. It asks for the facts and just the facts. It then incorporates all the realities of a situation and synthesizes them. Peace is best represented by the High Priestess in the tarot deck. She holds the book of life—the truth—and operates from that perspective. Her gown, then, becomes the flowing river of all the rest of the deck!

Ascendant in Peace

When you make a decision about what to do (any doing decision), you always factor in the principle of Peace. That means that you are most interested in making everyone comfortable (so there will not be any fights). It means, instead, that you are very practical. You look at the facts, the "isness" of a situation, and make your decisions from a real grounded position. You use common sense as your basic motivation for action, and your ego development is thoroughly wrapped around taking care of yourself in the world. You do not make emotional decisions, and sometimes you may catch yourself being discounting or judgmental of people who do.

Mercury in Peace

Your mind is like a laser beam. When you want to focus on something, nothing else exists for you. You like facts. You like to see things in concrete terms. You prefer to study something mentally before you allow your emotions or your body to really experience it. You easily dump anything that does not prove to be true, even if you feel some sort of resonance with it. After you have thoroughly taken something apart and studied its pieces, the result is that you put it back together (mentally) in a way that allows you to see the wholeness and interconnectedness of the universe.

Venus in Peace

Venus in Peace tells us that your emotional body experiences energy as a call to deeper and deeper levels of peace. In other words, when you have an emotional experience, you do not stop with it until you return to a non-duality, a level of calm and deep understanding. Emotions may throw you a little, because they call you out of the calm and into the storm. However, when you return to the calm, you experience a renewal and a regeneration of peace that expands your wisdom.

Mars in Peace

Mars in Peace tells us that you live life more through your head than through your body. Your body is solid, strong, reliable, and sort of "above it all." You may be so used to depending on your body that you forget to pay enough attention to it and it has to break down to get your attention. The person contracted with Peace in Mars carries the challenge of learning that Wholeness makes itself known in form through apparent separation. In other words, your body may feel like a separate unit—relatively uninvolved with life, until you remember that your body is the vessel through which life expresses.

Jupiter in Peace

When you have an experience that takes out of the realm of duality, you are overcome with a sense of divine protection. This experience may come in the form of a disaster—after which everyone joins hands and works together to save lives and clear the debris—or it may come in the form of falling in love—or seeing something in nature that moves you. Whatever it is, when your consciousness overrides the belief is separation and division, and you see all things as deeply connected, you are blessed by the arm of Jupiter. The god of good fortune is never far away.

Saturn in Peace

You have a perspective of the realm of form that is highly unusual. You see balance rather than polarity. You understand that everything that reaches its maximum expression, everything that finds its ultimate form, immediately begins to decompose! As soon as the mountain is built, the river starts delivering it, grain by grain, back to the sea. It is something of a paradox, because form is not static to you—it is constantly in motion toward deconstruction and reconstruction. That motion ironically creates a sense of the principle of Peace.

Uranus in Peace

You have personal glimpses of your true self when something happens in your life that takes you outside the usual polarized view of right and wrong, black and white, good and bad. These experiences hit you like a lightening bolt. They come when you least expect them, and they are usually the result of either something someone says or something you hear through the media. That something suddenly jolts you out of your typical state of mind, and you are able to expand your vision of a situation. You see both ends of the spectrum of a situation, and you understand the interconnectedness of all things. In that moment, you remember who you are.

Neptune in Peace

Your birth group came in to hold the principle of Peace for the planet. In order to stabilize the species, a group of you infused the collective consciousness with a frequency that is beyond division, death, and war. Your job was to carry that principle into form as a reality on a level of consciousness that could see past the time of war even though Peace, as a spiritual principle, is not the "opposite" of war. It is a principle that is needed to anchor the collective consciousness in an understanding of "beyond war" so that we could make decisions to move toward the Age of Peace.

Pluto in Peace

With Pluto in the principle of Peace, we know that your underworld journeys are less like the depressions that many people feel and more like deep internal investigations that eventually bring a sense of calm and deep understanding to you. A true experience of Peace extends beyond understanding—"the peace that passeth understanding"—into a realm of deep knowing and wisdom. It is therefore important for you to have time, solitude, and freedom to take these interpersonal journeys often. You must allow yourself the luxury of simply stopping the world for a few days every once in a while in order to let these dark times enrich your life. In return, you will share that deepening through your actions toward others, and the whole world will be enriched.

Mid-Heaven in Peace

The principle that connects you directly with the level of consciousness known as soul is Peace. This means that you are most "at home" when you have moved beyond all the "isms"—racism, sexism, ageism, genderism—into a space of nonduality. Peace is your natural state of being. Though your life may be fraught with battles, you are so deeply rooted in the tranquil essence of your beingness that you rarely lose contact with the inner calm of your essential self. You know that a majority of your personal energy and attention resides outside the realms of polarized thinking, and you secretly long for the day when you will be free of the need to interface with duality and mundanity. Contemplate peace, and you are home.

~ 28 LOVE ~

Sun in Love

Your primary reason for taking this incarnation is to learn, understand, and practice the principle of Love. This is quite a challenge, because it essentially says that you are walking a relatively untrodden path. In our New Age, we are changing the old paradigms—one of which has been the path of violence, hatred, separation, and war. You are one of the beings who has pledged to face those aspects of yourself, transform them, and become a vessel through which Love can embody. You are a lover—in the most mystical sense of the word—and your only real quest in this entire incarnation is reuniting with the Beloved.

Moon in Love

You love like the angels love. Your mastery is unconditional love. This does not mean that you will or should have "perfect" relationships. Even with a mastery in Love, you will have to work through all the personality problems that everyone else has to conquer to create deep personal relationships. However, your ability to love mankind, to love life, and to love the gift of live exceeds most people's. You innately understand that love is the glue of the universe, and that it is not an "optional" experience, but one that is at the very core of physical existence. As you become more and more comfortable with your mastery, you will become a teacher of it.

Ascendant in Love

When you make a personal behavioral decision, the angels are guiding you. (Provided you have taught yourself how to listen to the angels.) This is a magnificent Placement of your behavioral body but also certainly a challenging one. On the one hand, your personality is made of the stuff that holds the universe together. On the other hand, you can lose yourself and become diffused because you are so BIG in that way. It is part of your life's mission to actually become unconditional love. This can lead to grandiosity or humility. You choose! (I know what you have chosen, my friend. Grandiosity would not have led your eyes to read this page.)

Mercury in Love

Mercury in the principle of Love means that your mind is one that craves the free flow of information. Your mind is able to take in information without the need to make judgments on it, without the need to categorize it, and without the tendency to say "been there, done that" before distilling the truth out of it. You have a mind that grants dignity and validity to all information. Yours is an inclusive mind, one that observes life the way the angels do—sort of hovering over life without the need to interfere yet being willing to give help wherever it is evoked.

Venus in Love

With your emotional body in the principle of Love, we know that communication—the free flow of information—is essential to your emotional health. As long as you know that communication is open, you are able to bring the vibration of love into any circumstance. In fact, as you mature, the most liberating aspects and experiences of your life will revolve around information flow. Venus is the goddess of Love but not exclusively of erotic love. That post was reserved for a male—Eros. Venus is the goddess of intelligent love—love based on the sharing of information. Your entire emotional being is sourced in intelligent, unconditional love.

Mars in Love

You may have set up a real challenge for yourself with Mars, your physical body, in the principle of Love. Love is so expansive, free flowing, and boundless that you may tend to forget the boundary and solidity of your body. You will most likely never be seriously injured because you have a flock of angels around you at all times. However, angels do not have the kinds of bodies we do; therefore, they also forget the limitations of solid form. However, as you have matured and learned to live—an angel in form—you have most likely learned exactly what you must do in order to regenerate, take care, and heal. Your physical contract is very profound. You are literally practicing being the truest level of shaman. You are spending a lifetime letting unconditional love infiltrate every cell of your being.

Jupiter in Love

You are absolutely surrounded by and sponsored by angelic beings. When you stop and truly feel the energy around you, you know that your incarnation is not only protected but strongly supported. No matter how tough things become in the external world, you have Jupiter's arm of good fortune around you—although circumstances may not always look like your lower personality's definition of "good fortune." You may relax into the deep knowing that you are loved and that you are Love.

Saturn in Love

With Saturn in this principle called Love, we know that the realm of form is not particularly "solid" for you. Some people really NEED form to hold its contract. (They need walls to be solid, trees to stay in the ground, water to be fluid.) You, on the other hand, see form as a spiritual configuration of energy, and it will not particularly bother you for it to change. Seeing through a wall might be curious to you but not overwhelmingly disturbing. You are more interested in the glue—the love—that holds the world in place.

Uranus in Love

You have moments of authentic self-knowing, ironically, when you completely forget about yourself and enter the collective space of uncon-ditional love. In those moments, you may literally see the lines of energy that connect all beings and all material objects with the spiritual and unseen forces in which they are sourced. You may see energy bodies or energy fields spontaneously, and in that moment, you have a memory of the truth behind all form. When you have the Uranian experience, it causes your priorities to shift slightly: Your life becomes smooth, your decisions include a wide range of people and dynamics, and your heart feels very open and inclusive.

Neptune in Love

Your birth group brought the gift of Love to the planet. This infusion was necessary in order for the species to prepare for what was to come in the rest of the century! An awareness of the unifying nature of Love is nec-essary for us to make a meaningful world. Quantum physicists are presently even saying that love is the glue of the atom, and therefore of the universe. It is out of Love that all things come into being. It is into Love that they even-tually disappear. You have a particularly intimate relationship with the power of Love, for it is the gift of your birth group!

Pluto in Love

Your underworld journeys have profound results for you because they provide a passage to the experience of unconditional Love. Most likely, you shut down and go into a deep self-investigation after a period of not lov-ing yourself. When you become too self-critical, you are called—impelled really—to go deeply into your own psyche, and there you find the power of Love. This deepening of your self-understanding may look and feel like depres-sion early in your life, but later, after you have learned to trust the journey, it becomes a cherished part of your life cycle.

Mid-Heaven in Love

One might think that Love is the principle that leads us all directly to the level of soul. And they will be right—ultimately. However, for you in particular, Love is the vibrational frequency that is necessary for you to remember who you are as a divine being. You must, of course, move through (though not exclude) all the social pictures of "what love looks like" and become a true lover in the way that the Sufis and the poems of Rumi demand. You must go mad with the desire to love and be loved by your own essential self and by God. Your soul principle is the glue in the universe—the force that holds atoms together. Becoming a true agent of love is your life task.

~ 29 MOVEMENT ~

Sun in Movement

With your Sun in the principle of Movement, we can definitely see that you came into this incarnation to do some powerful work on behalf of the human soul. Movement is the highest of the principles, the most galactic, the most subtle. You are here to bring the vibration or frequency of soul into form. You are a dancer of life, a choreographer of energy, a person who knows how to animate the densest of ideas/materials/systems. You work with the avatars—the ascended masters—or at least they work with and through you—to help you bring your gifts to the planet. With your Sun in the principle of Movement, enlightenment and awakening are entirely within your grasp.

Moon in Movement

Your Moon/mastery in Movement indicates that you know the principles of the vibration of energy on a very profound level. You cellularly know how to allow the evolutionary force to generate your life toward more complex and more efficient forms of expression. You have a talent for designing ceremonial space because you deeply understand the intent and purpose of ceremony. You know how to animate or inspire people and groups into action that reflects the light. You are also quite masterful at relationship, because movement is the glue (the vibrational frequency) that holds the universe together. You know how to bond, stay connected to others without becoming needy of them, and show them their own power.

Ascendant in Movement

With your behavioral body in the principle of Movement, we know that you are always looking for the most benevolent possible way to deliver your soul's gift to the planet. "Highest" could mean most efficient, or it could mean most evolved. Each time you make a decision, you take all kinds of things into consideration, including how this decision will affect all the dynamics—personal, family, social, the plants, the animals, the planet, the angels, all the way to God and back. You may not be fully aware of this need to "serve" all sentience, but it is certainly in the implicate order of your contract. It is a very strong ethical position and may sometimes feel like a burden if you do not fully understand the power behind your choices. Each choice you make DOES indeed affect the universe. Some part of you knows that.

Mercury in Movement

You have a very sophisticated and well-developed mind. You think with the avatars. Your thought processes include a wide spectrum of possibility and a deep consideration for all of Creation—not just yourself or your immediate surroundings. If you have also been successful in developing compassion in your personality, this means you are a profoundly generous thinker, and people will probably gravitate to you for advice, leadership; and spiritual—as well as professional—support.

Venus in Movement

With Venus in Movement, we can understand that your emotional body is quite powerful and a very important part of your incarnation. That sounds obvious to you, but you must remember that not all people have the same intensity of feeling that you do. When you have a strong emotional response, it reverberates through all your systems. Emotion changes your thinking, affects your body, and adjusts your ethic. Emotional energy is the primary frequency of your life. The Movement principle carries with it the ability to make even ideas a feelings seem solid—it gives them a level of reality for you that is not experienced in other people.

Mars in Movement

Mars in Movement tells us that your deepest source of spiritual information is your body. When the energy is moving well, you are very graceful and well-coordinated. You tend to be movement oriented. Too much sitting almost paralyzes you. You balance energies in your body as well as in your mind. You respond physically to your environment. It is therefore important for you to incorporate physical movement into your daily routine. Be careful, though, because you can exhaust yourself—never being quite willing to sit and regenerate until everything is in its place.

Jupiter in Movement

Your most poignant moments—the ones in which you realize that you are totally supported by the universe—come when you have been moving. This may involve dancing, hiking, Tai Chi, yoga, or a big move—like changing cities, jobs, and so forth. Or it may simply be an evolutionary shift that you make in one of your personal pillars. Whatever form the Movement takes, the result is the same. Jupiter puts his arm around you and says, "Well done, sweetheart." Your heart leaps with joy because you suddenly remember that you are absolutely a child of the divine marriage of spirit and matter—and that your spiritual parents will always provide everything you need to enjoy a rich life.

Saturn in Movement

With Saturn in Movement, we can say that you obey the laws of form but you do not "buy" them. You know on a very deep, perhaps even unconscious level, that form is an illusion and that any form that appears to be solid is really vibration. It may have been particularly hard for you as a child, because all those people who were initiating you into humanhood wanted you to see form differently. They wanted you to NOT see through walls and NOT put your hand through tables. Solid geometry had to be taught to you because it does not come naturally. Dancing is your meditative medium. You need to move. If you do not dance, life is too dense to bear. You need to allow the vibration of life to live in your body. Again, you may or may not have had encouragement to dance as a child. If not, it may have taken you years to understand your relationship to the realm of form.

Uranus in Movement

Uranus in Movement means that when you are in alignment with the property of light that vibrates—when your physical frequency matches your soul's vibration—then you receive this bolt of enlightenment. In those moments, you have to dance. They are highly ecstatic moments, reminiscent of many of the states of consciousness described in Rumi's poetry. They are mystical moments. They are moments of being infused with divine light. In those moments you have full memory of who you are, who you always have been, and who you always will be.

Neptune in Movement

Your birth group came in to "stir things up." Things were getting a little stagnant, and your birth group infused the entire planet with the courage and the will to make changes. Very few of you stayed at home after you grew up. You moved, you changed, you shifted your consciousness, and therefore participated in a cultural shift that was urgently needed.

Pluto in Movement

Your underworld journeys—your depressions or deep investigations—take you to very interesting, paradoxical places. It is in those times of life that most people call "depression" that you get most thoroughly aligned with the vibrational frequency of your soul. By moving deeply into yourself, you connect with the essential core of yourself. That is true of most people, of course. But for you, the Movement principle takes you into who you are—whereas for most people a depression or underworld journey takes them to who they are NOT so that they can release that "is-not-ness." Your underworld journeys are like the quantum physicist's journey into the nucleus of an atom—the further you go in, the more you discover that there is nothing there other than a vibrational tendency to BE. Wow.

Mid-Heaven in Movement

The principle that points you toward "home" is Movement. This means that when you experience the divine and subtle frequency that animates the cosmos, you have an experience of soul consciousness. It may happen for you when you dance, hike, ski, or it may happen when you are very still and you simply allow the fibers of your navel to extend into space. You need to experience this frequency periodically in order to stay in touch with the soul intent that brought you to form!

Appendix B

Chart of Principles

Principle	External Anchor Point	Internal Anchor Point
Placement	*Natural Micro Universes*	*Feet*
Innocence	*Archetypal Worlds*	*Heart*
Purity	*Devic Worlds*	*Liver*
Memory	*Stone Devas*	*Bones*
Beauty	*Stone Beings*	*Throat*
Extension	*Plant Devas*	*Hands*
Regeneration	*Plant Beings*	*Breasts*
Generosity	*Animal Devas*	*Below Heart*
Goodness	*Animal Beings*	*Kidneys*
Awareness	*Paradoxical Realms*	*Pancreas*
Reciprocity	*Inter Dimensions*	*Lungs*
Flowering	*Reptilian Memory*	*Thymus*
Creativity	*Astral Realms*	*Stomach*
Intelligence	*Human Micro Universes*	*Nervous System*
Ecstasy	*Body Wholeness*	*Adrenals*
Resistance	*Self-Consciousness*	*Muscles*
Unity	*Genetic Consciousness*	*Ribs*
Attraction	*Cross Cultural Consciousness*	*Intestines*
Focus	*Planetary Consciousness*	*Pineal Gland*
Service	*Soul Consciousness*	*Knees*

Gratitude	Consciousness of Sentience	Spleen
Harmony	Integrating Darkness	Colon
Dreaming	Hearing Info of the Void	Womb
Randomness	Bridging Dark and Light	Ovaries/Testicles
Humility	Integrating the Light	Skin
Desire	Hearing Info of the Light	Eyes
Silence	Bridging Higher Dimensions	Skull
Peace	Working in Higher Dimensions	Blood
Love	Angelic Realm	Brain Stem
Movement	Avatars	Navel

Works Cited

Attenborough, Richard, ed. *The Words of Gandhi*. New York: Newmarket Press, 1991.

Aurobindo, Sri. *Letters on Yoga III*. Pondicherry, India: Sri Aurobindo Ashram, 1971.

Bailey, Alice A. *Discipleship in the New Age I*. London: Lucis Press Ltd., 1944.

———. *Discipleship in the New Age II*. London: Lucis Press Ltd., 1955.

Berry, Thomas. *The Dream of the Earth*. San Francisco: Sierra Club, 1988.

———. *The Great Work: Our Way Into the Future*. New York: Bell Tower Press, 1999.

———. "Spirituality and Ecology." *The Catholic World*. July/August (1981): 159-162.

Black Elk, Nicholas. *Black Elk Speaks: Being the Life Story of a Holy Man of the Oglala Sioux As Told Through John G. Neihardt (Flaming Rainbow)*. New York: Simon and Schuster, 1959.

Bly, Robert, ed. *The Soul Is Here for Its Own Joy: Sacred Poems from Many Cultures*. Hopewell, NJ: The Ecco Press, 1999.

Capra, Fritjof. *The Tao of Physics*. New York: Bantam Books, 1975.

Coke, K.C. *The Universe and the Teacup: The Mathematics of Truth and Beauty*. New York: Harcourt Brace and Company, 1997.

Cooper, David A. *God Is a Verb: Kabbalah and the Practice of Mystical Judaism*. New York: Riverhead Books, 1998.

Craine, Renate. *Hildegard: Prophet of the Cosmic Christ*. New York: Crossroads Publishing Company, 1997.

Douglas-Klotz, Neil. *The Hidden Gospel: Decoding the Spiritual Message of the Aramaic Jesus*. Wheaton, Il:·Quest Books, 1999.

———. *Prayers of the Cosmos: Meditations on the Aramaic Words of Jesus*. San Francisco: Harper San Francisco, 1993.

Emerson, Ralph Waldo. *The Essays of Ralph Waldo Emerson*. Norwalk, CT: The Easton Press, 1979.

Fox, Matthew. *Breakthrough: Meister Eckhart's Creation Spirituality in New Translation*. New York: Image Books Doubleday, 1989.

———. *The Coming of the Cosmic Christ*. San Francisco: Harper and Row, 1988.

———. *Creation Spirituality: Liberating Gifts for the Peoples of the Earth*. San Francisco: Harper and Row, 1991.

———. , ed. *Hildegard of Bingen's Book of Divine Works*. Santa Fe, NM: Bear and Company, 1987.

———. *Illuminations of Hildegard of Bingen*. Santa Fe, NM: Bear and Company, 1985.

———. *Meditations with Meister Eckhart*. Santa Fe, NM: Bear and Company, 1983.

———. *One River, Many Wells: Wisdom Springing from Global Faiths*. New York: J.P. Tarcher/Putnam, 2000.

———. *Original Blessing*. Santa Fe, NM: Bear and Company, 1983.

———. *The Reinvention of Work: A New Vision of Livelihood for Our Time*. San Francisco: Harper Collins, 1994.

———. *Sins of the Spirit, Blessings of the Flesh: Lessons for Transforming Evil in Soul and Society*. New York: Harmony Books, 1999.

———. *A Spirituality Named Compassion*. San Francisco: Harper and Row, 1979.

Fox, Matthew and Rupert Sheldrake. *The Physics of Angels: Exploring the Realm Where Science and Spirit Meet*. San Francisco: Harper, 1996.

Freke, Timothy and Peter Gandy. *Jesus and the Lost Goddess: The Secret Teachings of the Original Christians*. New York: Harmony Books, 2001.

Gandhi, Mohandas K. *Gandhi on Non-Violence*, edited by Thomas Merton. New York: New Directions Publishing. 1965.

———. *Prayer*, edited by John Strohmeier. Berkeley, CA: Berkeley Hills Books, 2000.

Goethe, Johann Wolfgang von. *Theory of Colours*. London: The M.I.T. Press, 1840.

Harvey, Andrew. *The Direct Path: Creating a Journey to the Divine Using the World's Mystical Traditions*. New York: Broadway Books, 2000.

———. *Light Upon Light: Inspirations from Rumi*. Berkeley, CA: North Atlantic Books, 1996.

———. *Love's Fire: Recreations of Rumi*. Ithaca, NY: Meeramma, 1988.

———. *Love's Glory: Re-creations of Rumi*. Berkeley, CA: North Atlantic Books, 1996.

———. *The Return of the Mother*. Berkeley, CA: Frog, Ltd., 1995.

———. *Speaking Flame*. Ithaca, NY: Meeramma, 1989.

———. *Teachings of Rumi*. Boston: Shambhala, 1999.

———. *The Way of Passion: A Celebration of Rumi*. Berkeley, CA: Frog, Ltd., 1994.

Hawking, Steven. *A Brief History of Time: From the Big Bang to Black Holes*. New York: Bantam Doubleday Dell Books, 1998.

Hill, Julia Butterfly. *The Legacy of Luna: The Story of a Tree, a Woman, and the Struggle to Save the Redwoods*. San Francisco: HarperSanFrancisco, 2001.

Hillman, James. *The Soul's Code: In Search of Character and Calling*. New York: Random House, 1996.

Hirshfield, Jane, ed. *Women in Praise of the Sacred: 43 Centuries of Spiritual Poetry by Women*. New York: Harper Perennial, 1994.

Houston, Jean. *A Mythic Life*. San Francisco: Harper San Francisco, 1996.

Kaplan, Connie. *The Woman's Book of Dreams: Dreaming as a Spiritual Practice*. Portland: Beyond Words Publishing, Inc., 1999.

Keck, Robert. *Sacred Quest: The Evolution and Future of the Human Soul*. West Chester, Pennsylvania: Chrysalis Books, 2000.

Keyes, Ken, Jr. *The Hundredth Monkey*. Coos Bay, OR: Vision Books, 1983.

Liberman, Jacob. *Light Medicine of the Future*. Santa Fe, NM: Bear and Company Publishing, 1991.

Mello, Anthony de. *Wake Up to Life* (Audio Tape Series). We and God Spirituality Center: St. Louis. 1989.

Merton, Thomas. *Thomas Merton on Peace*. London: Mowbrays, 1976.

Mitchell, Stephen, trans. *Tao Te Ching*. New York: HarperCollins, 1988.

Payne, Katy. *Silent Thunder: In the Presence of Elephants*. New York: Penguin Books, 1999.

Pearce, Joseph Chilton. *Magical Child Matures*. New York: E.P. Dutton, Inc., 1985.

———. *The Biology of Transcendence: A Blueprint of the Human Spirit*. Rochester, VT: Park Street Press, 2002.

Rael, Joseph and Mary Elizabeth Marlow. *Being & Vibration*. Tulsa: Council Oak Books, 1993.

Ray, Paul H. and Sherry Ruth Anderson. *The Cultural Creatives: How 50 Million People are Changing the World*. New York: Harmony Books, 2000.

Richards, M.C. *Centering: In Pottery, Poetry, and the Person, 25th Anniversary Edition*. Middletown, CT: Wesleyan University Press, 1989.

Robinson, James M., ed. *The Nag Hammadi Library in English*. San Francisco: Harper San Francisco, 1978.

Rumi, Jalal Al-Din. *The Essential Rumi*. Translated by Coleman Barks with John Moyne. San Francisco: HarperCollins Publishers, 1995.

———. Translated by Robert Bly and Coleman Barks. *Poems of Rumi*. Minneapolis: Audio Literature, Inc., 1989.

Sheldrake, Rupert. *Dogs That Know When Their Owners Are Coming Home And Other Unexplained Powers of Animals*. New York: Crown Publishers, 1999.

———. *The Presence of the Past: Morphic Resonance & the Habits of Nature*. Rochester, VT: Park Street Press, 1988.

Some, Malidoma Patrice. *The Healing Wisdom of Africa: Finding Life Purpose Through Nature, Ritual, and Community*. New York: J.P. Tarcher, 1998.

Swimme, Brian. *The Hidden Heart of the Cosmos: Humanity and the New Story*. Maryknoll, New York: Orbis Books, 1996.

———. *The Universe Is a Green Dragon: A Cosmic Creation Story*. Santa Fe, NM: Bear and Company, 1984.

Swimme, Brian and Thomas Berry. *The Universe Story*. San Francisco: HarperCollins, 1994.

Tompkins, Peter. *The Secret Life of Nature: Living in Harmony with the Hidden World of Nature Spirits from Fairies to Quarks*. San Francisco: HarperCollins, 1997.

Vaughan-Lee, Llewellyn. *Catching the Thread: Sufism, Dreamwork & Jungian Psychology*. Inverness, California: The Golden Sufi Center, 1998.

Washington, James M., ed. *A Testament of Hope: The Essential Writings and Speeches of Martin Luther King, Jr*. San Francisco: Harper and Row, 1986.

Wolf, Fred Alan. *Star Wave: Mind, Consciousness, and Quantum Physics*. New York: McMillan Publishing Company, 1986.

About
the Author

D r. Connie Kaplan, who holds Master's degrees in Communications and Psychology and has a Doctorate of Ministry, is the author of *The Woman's Book of Dreams* (Beyond Words, 1999) and *Dreams are Letters from the Soul* (Random House/Harmony, 2002). Acclaimed as manifestos for dreamers, these books have made Kaplan instrumental in the rapidly growing international phenomenon, dream circles. Called the "red tents" of the twenty-first century, dream circles are intimate gatherings where dreamers come together, listen deeply to one another's dreams, and unveil the spiritual wisdom encoded therein.

For thirteen years, in talks and seminars across the country, Kaplan has revolutionized traditional views of dreaming by teaching that dreams are a hotline to deep spiritual connection. The ultimate dream guide, Kaplan has aided many in understanding these nocturnal messages from the soul.

Connie began her own dreamtime journey in 1986 when she was struck with a mysterious illness that sent her to bed for over 18 months, ending a successful career in television production. During the 15 hours a day she slept, dream teachers more fascinating than any Hollywood characters came to her and taught her the secrets of dreaming as a spiritual practice.

Kaplan is neither a guru nor a channel. She is simply a powerful and popular spiritual guide whose revolutionary information does not point toward the teacher but rather toward the unique and genuine wisdom of the student.

The dreamer's Website, www.turtledreamers.com, averages 75,000 hits per month and hosts a fascinating on-line international dream circle.

She lives in Santa Monica, California with her husband and children, and leads a waking life that is as ordinary as her sleeping life is extraordinary.

We hope this Jodere Group book has benefited you in your quest for personal, intellectual, and spiritual growth.

Jodere Group is passionate about bringing new and exciting books, such as *The Invisible Garment*, to readers worldwide. Our company was created as a unique publishing and multimedia avenue for individuals whose mission it is to impact the lives of others positively. We recognize the strength of an original thought, a kind word, and a selfless act— and the power of the individuals who possess them. We are committed to providing the support, passion, and creativity necessary for these individuals to achieve their goals and dreams.

Jodere Group is comprised of a dedicated and creative group of people who strive to provide the highest quality of books, audio programs, online services, and live events to people who pursue life-long learning. It is our personal and professional commitment to embrace our authors, speakers, and readers with helpfulness, respect, and enthusiasm.

For more information about our products, authors, or live events, please call (800) 569-1002 or visit us on the Web at www.jodere.com.

JODERE
GROUP   SAN DIEGO